Interactive Multimedia - Multimedia Production and Digital Storytelling

Edited by Dragan Cvetković

Published in London, United Kingdom

IntechOpen

Supporting open minds since 2005

Interactive Multimedia - Multimedia Production and Digital Storytelling
http://dx.doi.org/10.5772/intechopen.77566
Edited by Dragan Cvetković

Contributors
Laura Delgaty, Geoffrey Edwards, Jocelyne Kiss, Ernesto Morales, Coralee McLaren, Serge Lacasse, Juan Nino Falcon, Jonathan Proulx Guimond, Marie Louise Bourbeau, Charles Potter, Borka Jerman Blažič, Andrej Jerman Blažič, Rodrigo Fernandes, Toshimasa Yamanaka, Thiago Messias, Daniela Domingos, Heliana Soares, Luis Felipe Lima, José Feijó, Anthony Diniz, Consolato M. Sergi, Abdellah Ibrahim Mohammed Elfeky, Marwa Yasien Helmy Elbyaly, Nicholas A. Giudice, Jenna L. Gorlewicz, Jennifer L. Tennison, Hari P. Palani, Nadia Diyana Mohd Muhaiyuddin, Dayang Rohaya Awang Rambli, Dragan Mladen Cvetković

First published in London, United Kingdom, 2019 by IntechOpen
IntechOpen is the global imprint of INTECHOPEN LIMITED, registered in England and Wales, registration number: 11086078, The Shard, 25th floor, 32 London Bridge Street
London, SE19SG - United Kingdom
Printed in Croatia

British Library Cataloguing-in-Publication Data
A catalogue record for this book is available from the British Library

Additional hard and PDF copies can be obtained from orders@intechopen.com

Interactive Multimedia - Multimedia Production and Digital Storytelling
Edited by Dragan Cvetković
p. cm.
Print ISBN 978-1-78923-911-9
Online ISBN 978-1-78923-912-6
eBook (PDF) ISBN 978-1-78984-980-6

For EU product safety concerns:
IN TECH d.o.o., Prolaz Marije Krucifikse Kozulić 3, 51000 Rijeka, Croatia, info@intechopen.com or visit our website at intechopen.com.

Meet the editor

Dragan Cvetković graduated in Aeronautics from the Faculty of Mechanical Engineering, University of Belgrade, in 1988. In the Aeronautical Department he defended his doctoral dissertation in December 1997. So far, he has published 63 books, scripts, and practicums about computers and computer programs, aviation weapons, and flight mechanics. He has published a large number of scientific papers in the Republic of Serbia and abroad as well. Since March 20, 2007, he worked at the Singidunum University in Belgrade as an assistant professor. And from October 1, 2013, he has been working as the Dean of the Faculty of Informatics and Computing at the same university. He became a full professor in the field of informatics and computing in March 2014.

Contents

Preface

Multimedia is the common name for media that combine more than one type of individual medium to create a single unit. In everyday language, the term multimedia usually presents an interactive computing project that uses film, text, and sound, such as, for example, interactive encyclopedia, educational compact discs, or DVDs.

Interactive media are the means of communication in which the outputs depend on the inputs made by the user. It is obvious that the user is an active participant in this kind of communication. Media have the same purpose, but the input parameters made by the user add an interaction to this whole story and lead to interesting options when it comes to the output of a given system. Perhaps the most important characteristic of interactivity is the interaction between user and machine, where each of the "participants" intends to have an active role.

Interactive multimedia allows users to combine, control, and manipulate different types of media, such as text, graphics, audio and video materials, and animations. Interactive multimedia obtains the integration of computer, memory, storage, data, supporting devices, and other information technologies. The most common multimedia applications include interactive education and training programs, various games, and electronic encyclopedias. It should be noted that in recent years, multimedia has been increasingly used in education. The possibility of the unification of multiple components (five pillars of multimedia—audio and video, text, graphics, and animation) helps educators to transfer knowledge to students in a unique way. Students learn better and faster using these methods, and teaching material becomes more interesting and the whole process of learning more amusing.

Chapters are listed in a logical order, but they can be arranged differently, depending on the point of view.

The first chapter is an introductory chapter that presents the basic guidelines when it comes to multimedia and interactivity. Special attention is paid to models of interaction and to interactive design. One part of the introductory chapter is dedicated to the patterns of interactions that are defined by conditions and modes of interaction, while the other part is dedicated to the interactivity design and simplified view of the four major phases that define this discipline.

Other chapters can be classified in two sections: Interactive Multimedia and Education (Chapters 2, 3, 4, 5, and 6) and Interactive Multimedia and Medicine (Chapters 7, 8, 9, 10, and 11).

The second chapter deals with the importance of cloud storage in the area of pedagogy, where the collaborative task expresses the interaction between learners of individual differences who learn within collaborative purposes and skills to fulfill a specific purpose. The authors have shown how cloud storage allows information owners to host their information in the cloud and how data access control is an efficient way to ensure information security in the cloud.

The third chapter introduces two concepts that are currently present in the development of play tools for children: *interactive design*, represented by toys that can integrate interactive sensors and actuators to promote new play possibilities, and *design for interaction*, a new tendency focused on how children interact with each other, and how new designs can contribute to these interactions. The authors have obtained a series of studies of children's social interactions when under the influence of different game conditions.

The fourth chapter intends to present the use of gaming on touchscreen multimedia devices for the learning of digitals skills by the elderly. The usage of digital devices like cellphones can be difficult for older adults due to a lack of digital skills required in the use of multimedia devices. The case study was carried out with a group of older adults in four different European countries with multimedia tablets before they attended the training process for learning how to use cellphones.

The fifth chapter provides a critical look at the literature surrounding distance learning education and targets transactional distance theory. It examines in detail three components: structure, interaction (or dialog), and autonomy.

The sixth chapter discusses both the diverse challenges involved in creating an opera and the co-creation environment. The idea of the project was to design a short one-act interactive opera that could be managed within a modest budget. The authors have recycled the 3D virtual designs as the substratum for an online co-creation environment that could be used to elicit public participation in the future development of their operas.

Graphical access is one of the most pressing challenges for individuals who are blind or visually impaired. The seventh chapter discusses some of the factors underlying the graphics access challenge, reviews prior approaches to addressing this long-standing information access barrier, and describes some promising new solutions.

The eight chapter focuses on a reading, writing, and spelling program based on Luria's theories of automaticity, which uses repetitive paired reading and phonological referencing to develop fluency in reading, writing, and spelling. All materials used in program implementation are electronic and are currently delivered using email and cellphone technologies. The first half of the chapter describes the theoretical basis of the program, while the second half focuses on the modular training course and its aims.

The ninth chapter emphasizes the importance of using quantum computing protocols on encrypted data, which is crucial for the permanent implementation of virtual pathology in hospitals and universities. The encryption of digital images may be a requirement for the accreditation of laboratory services—quantum computing results in quantum-mechanical phenomena, such as superposition and entanglement. Digitalization of imaging in radiology is a reality in several healthcare institutions worldwide.

The tenth chapter deals with image-based virtual reality, which is a type of virtual reality but with limited interaction function. Despite this limitation, a realistic virtual environment in image-based virtual reality is expected to enhance users' spatial presence experience, which is supported by a spatial presence theoretical model. The most important part in this theoretical model are primary egocentric reference frames adapting calmness to produce a spatial presence experience.

The eleventh chapter is dedicated to the development of a mobile application called BloodHero. The lack of blood in hemocenters is an intermittent health problem in Brazil, since there are many difficulties in attracting blood donors. The number of regular donors in Brazil in recent years barely reaches 3% of the population. The proposed application works as a social network, with a game methodology known as gamification, with the theme of blood donation.

I would like to express my sincere gratitude to all the authors and coauthors for their contributions. The successful completion of the book *Interactive Multimedia - Multimedia Production and Digital Storytelling* has been the result of the cooperation of many people. I would especially like to thank the Author Service Manager Ms. Sandra Maljavac for her support during the publishing process.

Dragan Cvetković
Singidunum University,
Faculty of Informatics and Computing,
Belgrade, Republic of Serbia

Section 1

Introductory

Chapter 1

Introductory Chapter: Multimedia and Interaction

Dragan Cvetković

1. Introduction

Interactive media are means of communication in which the output values depend on inputs. This means that the user is actively involved in the communication. The media still has the same purpose, but entries or inputs made by user create the interaction and some interesting options when it comes to the output of the system. Interactive media is referred to conceptual design of interaction, new media, interactivity, interaction between people and computers, graphical user interface, digital culture, interactive design, and virtual reality. One of the most important characteristics of interactivity is the interaction between user and machine, where each of them has an active role.

Interactive multimedia allows the user to control, combine, and manipulate a variety of media types, such as text, computer graphics, audio and video materials, as well as animation. Interactive multimedia integrates computer, storage, data, phone, TV, and other information technologies. The most common interactive multimedia applications include education and training programs, video games, electronic encyclopedias, and travel guides. The user or participant in an interactive multimedia application changes their role—for the viewer becomes an active participant. It is expected that interactive multimedia systems become the next generation of electronic information systems. It should be mentioned that another name for interactive multimedia is hybrid technology, because it is able to combine the possibilities for storage capacities of computers and a digital database with an advanced tool for viewing and manipulating these materials.

Nowadays, the fastest-changing area is dedicated to the development of teaching materials based on usage of computers, particularly interactive multimedia programs that run on personal computers. These new computer and information technologies offer students and teachers access to materials like never before. Through the storage capacity of the computer, multimedia can "deliver" enormous amounts of data to users in more useful and accessible ways [1, 2].

2. Interaction models

The interaction itself involves at least two parties—the user and the system. The previously mentioned participants are complex and completely different in the way of communication and perception of task. The interface must be a link between them in order to have successful interaction. This transcription can fail in a great number of cases for several reasons. The usage of interaction models can help better understand what is happening in the interaction and to identify possible problems. Models allow, together with developing environment, to compare the different styles of interaction and to discuss issues of interaction as well [3].

2.1 Terms of interaction

Traditionally, the purpose of an interactive system is to assist the user in achieving the goals from the application domain. **Domain** defines the area of expertise and knowledge in real-world activities. The domain consists of concepts, which emphasize its important aspects. **Tasks** represent operations for manipulation of concepts within the domain. **Objective** is defined as desired output of the accomplished task, while the **intention** represents the specific action which is required for task accomplishment.

Task analysis includes the identification of problems in terms of domains, objectives, intentions, and tasks. It can use human knowledge about tasks and objectives, in order to assess an interactive system that is designed to support them. The terms (concepts) which are used in the design of a system and a customer description are separated, so that they can be treated as separate components—the system and the user, respectively [3–5].

2.2 Ergonomics

The term **ergonomics** or **human factors** is traditionally related to the study of interaction of physical characteristics—design of controls, physical environment in which the interaction takes place, arrangement, and the physical properties of display. The primary focus is on the user's performances and how interface affects them. In order to assess these aspects of interaction, ergonomics will certainly touch on human psychology and systems' limitations.

2.2.1 Display and control setup

Besides cognitive aspects of design, physical aspects are also important. Sets of controls and display components should be grouped logically, in order to allow faster access to the user. This is not so important when only one user is active. But, when we take controls in power plants, aircrafts, and air traffic into consideration, it becomes vital. In each of these cases, users are under pressure, and they are faced with a huge range of displays and controls, so their appropriate physical appearance is significant.

The importance of a logical grouping of controls has already been mentioned, as well as the fact that the controls should not be separated. The exact manner of organization (which will be presented) will depend on the domain of application itself. Possible ways of organizations can include the following things:

- **Functional controls and displays** are organized to place together the elements which are functionally linked.
- **Sequential controls and displays** are organized to reflect the order of their use in a typical interaction.
- **Frequent controls and displays** are organized according to the frequency of usage, but the most commonly used controls should be easily accessible.

Apart from setting up the controls and displays, the whole interface system should be properly distributed according to the position of the user himself. Thus, for example, a user should be able to reach all necessary controls and to see all the displays without excessive body movement. The most important displays should be at eye level, and controls should be adjusted for space maneuvering. Display reflections should be avoided as well [3, 6].

2.2.2 Interactions of the physical environment

Ergonomics deals with solving physical problems in the interface schedule and arrangement and takes into account the design of work environment as well. Where will the system be used? Who will use it? Will people sit, stand, or move around? Again, this will depend on the domain in a great extent, and it will be critical when it comes to specific controls and operational settings. However, the physical environment in which the system is used can affect the health and safety of its users. This should be taken into account in any design [2].

2.2.3 Health issues

Work on computer should not be considered as a dangerous activity, but one should bear in mind the possible implications of design on the health and safety of users. Factors in the physical environment directly affect the quality of interaction and user's performances:

- **Position of a user.** As previously mentioned, users should be able to fetch all of the controls comfortably and to see all the screens. Users should not stand for a long time, and if they are sitting, they should be provided with the rear seat backrest. If the user is ought to be in a certain position for a long time (e.g., when typing), one should be provided with a certain period of time to rest.

- **Temperature.** Most users certainly can adapt to small changes in temperature, with no adverse effect, but extreme temperatures (excessively warm or cold) will affect their performance and in excessive cases will affect their health. Experimental studies have shown that the performance deteriorates at high or low temperatures, and users are not able to concentrate.

- **Brightness.** The brightness level will, again, depend on the working environment. Adequate lighting should allow users to view the computer screen without discomfort or eyestrain. The light source should be positioned in such a way to avoid glare.

- **Noise.** Excessive noise can be harmful to health, causing user's pain, and, in acute cases, can lead to hearing loss. The noise level should be maintained at an appropriate level in the work environment. This does not necessarily mean that there is no noise at all. Noise can be an incentive for users and can provide the necessary confirmation of system activity.

- **Time.** The time users spend using the system should be controlled. As previously mentioned, it has been said that excessive use of CRT displays can be harmful to users, especially for pregnant women [4, 6].

2.3 Ways of interaction

The interaction can be observed as a dialog between the user and the computer. The choice of interface style can have a profound effect on the nature of a dialog. There is a great number of common interface styles including:

- Command line inside the interface

- Menus

- Natural language
- Dialogs with inquiries, questions, and answers
- WIMP (windows, icons, menus, pointers) interface
- 3D interfaces [1, 2]

3. Interaction design

Some of the interactions between humans and computers (or machines or technology) focus on understanding, which means that the attention is paid to the way how people interact with technology. However, a great deal of interaction between man and computer refers to how things work and how they are created. The credits for these features go to **design** [4].

In this part, attention will be paid to the **interaction design** or **design interactivity**. It should be borne in mind that it is not only thought about the design of interactive systems but about interaction design itself. Thus, interaction design is not just an artifact[1] that is produced, regardless of whether it is a physical device or a computer program. Apart from that fact, the artifacts do not give people only these devices and programs but also guides, tutorials, and online help systems. In some cases, it may be understood that no additional system is necessary for all elements, but it is probably easier to propose a different way of using existing tools [3, 5, 7].

3.1 About design in general

When someone is asked what design is, simple definition might be that the design is related to the achievement of objectives within the constraints. This definition does not say everything about the design, but it helps users to focus on the following elements:

- **Objectives**—What is the purpose and design of future product? For whom is it made? Why do they want it?
- **Limitations**—What materials should be used? What standards should be adopted? How much will it cost? How much time is needed to develop the product? Are there any health and safety issues?
- **Exchange (compromise)**—One should choose and define the objectives or restrictions which may be adopted in a milder form, and limits must be respected to the smallest detail.

It is impossible to accomplish all of the user's objectives within constraints, but in life, everything is a matter of compromise, even in such cases. The best designs are created in areas where the designer understands the compromises and the factors affecting them.

The most important part of interaction design or interactivity is user. It is necessary to set up a user in the first place and to keep the user in the central place [3, 6, 8].

[1] The artifact is every object that is made or revised and used by a man. The artifact may be a final product but can also be a by-product of the production process.

3.2 Briefly about design process

Here is a brief overview of the simplified view of the four major phases focused on interaction design and interactivity, as well as supporting iteration loop:

- **Requirements.** The first phase is based on definitions of needed requirements. Before phase one, it is necessary to know what is currently happening. For example, how do people watch movies? What kind of personnel is currently being used?

- **Analysis.** The results of observations and interviews should be delivered so that the key issues can be removed from them for the later stages of design. Usually, this is about the scenarios, the stories about the interaction, which may be combined with a task analysis or be independently recorded in order to create a colorful and real interaction.

- **Design.** There is a central phase when it starts from "what is desired" to "how to do it." There are a number of rules, guidelines, and principles of design, which can be used as an aid in order to obtain good results.

- **Repetitions (iterations) and prototyping.** People are complex and cannot be expected to reach the right design immediately. That is the reason why the design should be evaluated in order to be seen how it works and where it could be improved.

- **Implementation and deployment.** Finally, when it comes to the stage when the design is rated as well as done, then it should be created and applied. This includes the development of appropriate elements, writing documentation, and manuals.

One man cannot read and look at all the required techniques. Time is limited and there is no link between the period of design and quality of the final design. This means that a design should be accepted as final, even if it is not perfect; it is often better to have a product which is acceptable, is done on time, and costs less than to have one that has perfect interaction but was not done on time and was over a budget. For example, if a user encounters a system that appears to be perfect, one can be pretty sure that it is a poorly designed system; the system is poorly designed, not because the design is bad but because a lot of effort has been spent for the design process and designing [7, 8].

Author details

Dragan Cvetković
Faculty of Informatics and Computing, Singidunum University, Belgrade, Republic of Serbia

*Address all correspondence to: dcvetkovic@singidunum.ac.rs

References

[1] Dix A, Finlay J, Abowd GD, Beale R. Human-Computer Interaction. Third ed. Harlow, England: Pearson Education Limited; 2014

[2] MacKenzie S. Human-Computer Interaction—An Empirical Research Perspective. Waltham, USA: Morgan Kaufman is an imprint of Elsevier; 2013

[3] Schneiderman B, Plaisant C, Cohen M, Jacobs S, Elmqvist N, Diakopolous N. Designing the User Interface—Strategies for Effective Human-Computer Interaction. Sixth ed, Global Edition. Harlow, England: Pearson Education Limited; 2018

[4] Garrand T. Writing for Multimedia and the Web—A Practical Guide to Content Development for Interactive Media. Third ed. Waltham, USA: Focal Press; 2006

[5] Steane J, Yee J. Interaction Design—From Concept to Completion. New York, USA: Bloomsbury Visual Arts; 2018

[6] Vaughan T. Multimedia: Making it Work. Ninth ed. New York, USA: McGraw-Hill Education; 2014

[7] Costello V. Multimedia Foundations: Core Concepts for Digital Design. Second ed. Abingdon, England: Routledge; 2016

[8] Barfield L. Design for New Media—Interaction Design for Multimedia and the Web. First ed. Boston, USA: Addison-Wesley; 2004

Section 2

Interactive Multimedia and Education

Chapter 2

Multimedia: Different Processes

Abdellah Ibrahim Mohammed Elfeky
and Marwa Yasien Helmy Elbyaly

Abstract

The topic includes four main themes: (1) The Collaborative Work in Cloud Storage Services: The collaborative work is seen as a force for the individual and community. It, in the field of education, expresses the interaction among students of individual differences who work within collaborative aims and skills to achieve a specific aim. In addition, cloud storage predicts a tremendous change in the way information is stored and applications are run. That is, instead of storing information and running programs on PCs, everything will be hosted in a cloud that can be accessed anywhere and processed by addition or deletion collaboratively. (2) Computer- supported collaborative learning environment (CSCL): Collaborative learning is an umbrella term for a variety of educational approaches involving joint intellectual effort by students, or students and teachers together. It is based on the idea that learning is naturally a social act in which the participants talk among themselves. A group of students engaged in collaborative learning works together to achieve shared goals. (3) Mobile learning: Mobile learning is a term that has been used widely in different places all over the world. it has been encouraged to be used in higher education institutions because of a set of factors such as the availability of mobile phones, their ability to motivate students, and the freedom and privacy they provide to share information. Mobile learning is defined as E-learning that uses mobile devices or learning connected to a mobile device, Laouris & Eteokleous. (4) Open-Source Learning Management Systems: The integration of many Educational technologies in education have been widely promoted for their potential to enrich, enhance and extend student-learning experiences. Hence, pioneer educational establishments all over the world try to benefit of these technologies as much as possible to convey knowledge resources to both of the learner and teacher in least time, effort and cost. One of these educational technology tools which has been prominent in the field of education and technology integration is Learning Management Systems known as LMS.

Keywords: cloud storage, CSCL, mobile learning, learning management systems

1. The collaborative work in cloud storage services

The collaborative task is seen as a strength for the individual and community. The collaborative in the area of pedagogy, expresses the interaction between learners of individual differences who learn within collaborative purposes and skills to fulfill a specific purpose. Furthermore, cloud storage prophesy a massive change in the way data is stored and run of applications [57]. Thus, instead of storing data and running programs on personal computers, everything will be harbored in a cloud that can be accessed everywhere and processed by addendum or deletion collaboratively. Kamara & Lauter [1] Confirms that improvements in networking technology and the raise in the need for computing resources have induce many organizations to outsource their store and computing needs. Yang et al. [2] mention that cloud storage is an important employ of cloud computing. Kumar and Lu [3] add that the cloud heralds a new time of computing where application employs are provided through the Internet. Cloud storage allows information owners to host their information in the cloud and data access control is an efficient way to ensure information security in the cloud. Lin and Tzeng [4] also confirms that cloud provides long-term store services through the Internet. In addition, Bowers et al. [5] Confirms a family of increasingly public Internet services for archiving, backup, and even main storage of files.

In cloud computing, information owners host their information on cloud servers and employers who are information consumers can access the information from cloud servers, which allows information owners to move information from their local computing systems to the cloud ([6]: p. 1717). It lets information owners and employers to access all applications and files anywhere in the world. Cloud computing frees them from the limits of the desktop and makes it easier for group members in several locations to collaborate [7]. Using it, employers can remotely store their information and relish the on demand high feature applications and services from a shared gathering of configurable computing resources, without the burden of local information storage and maintenance [8]. In addition, it has been envisioned as the next-generation information technology architecture for projects, due to its long list of adorable advantages in the information technology history: location independent resource pooling, ubiquitous network access, on-demand self-service, fast resource elasticity, usage-based pricing and transference of hazard [8, 9].

Kamara & Lauter, [1] locate three kinds of services that Cloud storage includes:

1. Infrastructure as a favor, where a client makes use of a service provider's computing, storage or networking infrastructure.

2. Platform as a favor, where a client leverages the provider's resources to run custom applications.

3. Software as a favor, where clients use software that is run on the provider's infrastructure.

Virtual resources in the cloud are cheaper than dedicated material resources connected to a personal computer or network. Information stored in the cloud is safe from unwitting erasure or hardware crashes, for cloud is duplicated across multiple material machines. In addition, it continues to labor as normal even if one or more machines go offline since multiple copies of the information are kept constantly [7]. Teeny and medium-sized projects with restricted budgets can fulfill cost savings and productivity rises by using cloud-based services to manage enterprises and make collaborations [10]. On the other hand, Cloud storage providers can differentiate themselves by offering services above-and-beyond basic storage that include integration with other cloud computing produces [11].

Besides, collaboration is defined as the mutual work of more than one person where the task is undertaken with a feel of shared aim and attitude that is heedful and responsive to the environment, Montebello [12]. Collaborative working is came from the concept of virtual workspaces, and is related to the concept of e-task [13]. Arguably, it system is an organizational unit that protrudes anytime when collaboration takes place, whether it is informal or formal, unintentional or intentional [12]. Collaboration provides the traditional concept of the professional to contain any type of knowledge operator who intensively employs Information and Communications Technology environments and tools in their working practices [14]. Collaboration, in most organizations, happens naturally. Ill-defined task practices may make barriers to natural collaboration, while well-designed collaborative tasks systems not only conquer these natural barriers to communication, but also establish a cooperative task culture that becomes an integral part of the organization's framework [15].

2. Computer-supported collaborative learning environment (CSCL)

Collaborative learning is a global concept for a variety of pedagogical approaches involving joint intellectual effort by learners, or learners and teachers together [16]. Specifically, collaborative learning is based on the idea that education is surely a social act in which the learners talk among themselves [10]. A group of learners engaged in collaborative learning works together to fulfill shared aims ([9]: p. 365). Furthermore, collaborative learning is based on the model that information can be formed within a population where members actively react by sharing expertise and take on asymmetry roles ([17]: p. 330). In addition, it involves the reciprocal engagement of learners in a arranged effort to solve the problem together, and leads to critical thinking, shared understanding, deeper level learning, and long-term retention of the educated material ([18]: p. 337). Knowledge construction promotes in a collaborative learning environment where learners communicate by sharing data in groups for solving given works ([19]: p. 216). Lehtinen et al. [20] discusses that preparing students for participation in a networked, knowledge society in which information will be the generality critical resource for social and economic development is one of the basic requirements for learning in future. CSCL is one of the most favorable innovations to improve education and learning with the help of modern knowledge and communication technology. CSCL is an emerging branch of the education sciences concerned with studying how learners can learn jointly with the help of computers ([21]: p. 409). Thus, computer-supported collaborative learning enables all learners to express themselves and make considerable contributions to the final work ([22]: p. 356). Besides, CSCL is as a dynamic, international, and interdisciplinary field of research focused on how technology can ease the sharing and creation of information and expertise during peer interaction and group education processes ([23]: p. 67). Online collaborative learning permits discussion to happen at greater depth where information can be constructed remotely ([19]: p. 216).

The primary purpose of computer-supported collaborative learning is to supply non-task situations that allow social, off-task communication (e.g. casual communication) and that ease and increase the number of impromptu encounters in work and non-work contexts during the inclusion of persistent presence and consciousness over time and space of the other members of the distributed learning group ([18]: p. 349). Furthermore, the field of it is increasingly becoming a trans-disciplinary field of inquiry inclusive educational technology, educational psychology, cognitive science, computer science, communication, epistemology, augmented reality, and virtual reality ([23]: p. 67). Overall, this scope draws heavily on knowledge theories such as social cognitivist learning and constructivist theories. With respect to social interaction that is main to collaborative learning, collaborative learning builds onto the cultural theory and socio theory where a causal connection exists among social interaction and personal cognitive change ([24]: p. 193 and [19]: p. 217).

Furthermore, computer-supported collaborative learning environments contain synchronous and asynchronous software, communication tools, and shared workspaces ([25]: p. 111). CSCL also contains reactive group learning, social construction of knowledge, deep learning, sustained critical dialog, and competency-based education. More specifically, CSCL is known as education based on the acquisition of information, skills, and attitudes, as well as to the application in an ill-structured environment [71]. Besides, CSCL focuses on embracing group education, constructivist learning, critical thought, and competency-based learning and confirms social interaction [26, 27].

Shukor et al. [19] discusses that previous studies found that learners chose to share and compare the available data rather than progressing to construct new information through collaborative discussions. It shows that learners resort to interact at the level of rapid consensus, where learners resort to accept peers' opinions not necessarily, for they agree with each other, only merely to speed the discussion. Besides, CSCL environments promotes their potential to support current insights in instruction and learning that depend heavily on the social interaction between the group members [27]. In addition, CSCL is significant to confirm the fact that utilize of technology in educational environments should be based on the prevalent learning theories [28], which in turn applies to computer-supported collaborative learning environment as a form of technology employment in the learning process.

Education according to situated educational theory, for instance, is not merely an acquisition of information by students; only rather, it is primarily an operation of social participation [29]. The important implications of this theory with regard to computer-supported collaborative learning environment are summarized in the fact that it confirms the social context and participation in education. While education according to Sociocultural Theory happens at premier, in a social form during the interaction with the social environment more than its occurrence in an individual way [30]. Implications of such theory are summed up in what is so called social situation and participation computer-supported collaborative learning environment. Among the applications of this theory are social networking, forums, RSS [31]. The hypothesis of Dialog education can be summed up in "education is embedded in dialogue among different cognitive regimes" statement [32]. Reliance on communication and interaction is the most significant implication of this hypothesis. Communication between learners and collaborative task are the most significant applications of dialog education hypothesis [31].

Many of the researches conducted in this scope showed that utilize of computer-supported collaborative learning environment was emboldening and effective in developing students' achievement and skills. Baharudin and Harun [33] aimed to identify the better pattern of interaction that occurs in computer-supported collaborative learning environment that helps to maximize learners' critical thinking skills and achievement. Results showed that computer-supported collaborative learning environment improved learners' performance and their conception in the "Programming Language Concepts and Paradigms" course. CSCL also amended their level of critical thinking skills. Matthee et al. [58] confirmed also that computer-supported collaborative learning can be effectively performed in an IS learning environment and can be used to fulfill specific aims apart from simply promoting the learning process. CSCL could develop students' communication skills; prepare learners for task environment, enable higher education institutions to share certain workloads and work effective to utilize of their scarce resources. Dewiyanti et al. [34] purposed to earn response from distance learners on their experiences with collaborative learning in asynchronous CSCL environments. Results showed that the distance students appreciated the opportunities to task collaboratively. They presented positive practices and were quite contented with collaborative learning. Results as well proved that group show influences group operation regulation and group cohesion influences learners contentment with collaborative learning. Ada [35], confirmed that utilize of computer-supported collaborative learning environment created some good skills that supported learner-centered learning and prepared learners to be lifelong learners. Iinuma et al. [36] presented that administering computer-supported collaborative learning improved learners` awareness in collaborative practices such as interpersonal practices, inquiry practices and group management practices, as well as CSCL raised their dependability level of computer skills.

3. Mobile learning (M-learning)

M-learning is an expression that has been utilized widely in several places all over the world [72]. M-learning has been supported to be utilized in tertiary institutions because of a set of factors like the availability of mobile phones, their ability to motivate learners, and the freedom and privacy they supply to share data. It is defined as electronic learning that utilizes portable devices or learning connected to a portable device, Laouris & Eteokleous [28]. M-learning is fundamentally based on mobility of technology, mobility of students and mobility of education that augments the tertiary institutions [37]. Tertiary institutions are these days facing the reality of the speedy development and diffuse of mobile phones, which are considered one form of those mobile devices utilized for electronic learning all over the world. It is noteworthy that development has included a raise in both mobile phones speed and store capacity. On the other hand, the continuous decline in prices has resulted in the great diffuse of these mobile phones making them one major component of most students' daily lives. More specifically, mobile phones are not accessory anymore; they are incorporated like our wear [38]. Arguably, it is fact that mobile phones are fundamentally utilized for completely communication objectives. Besides, some lecturers have begun to consideration them as a core educational activity in tertiary institutions [37]. The number of those lecturers and learners who have begun to utilize them as an instruction or learning tool is growing extremely. Most learners have begun overcoming their difficulties related the place and time of sessions through the effective utilization of their mobile phones or what has been so called M-learning. Lecturers, on their turn have begun to consider seriously of providing their learners with the instruction materials and activities via their mobile phones. Thus, students have exceedingly accepted M-learning. Specifically, learning through M-learning is exceedingly accepted by the student community for its application in addition to its philosophy and standards [33, 39].

Furthermore, the instruction- learning materials should be re-prepared, developed, and carried out in a way that adapts this new type of education and makes it most effective. The improvement in technology utilized in today's mobile phones qualify them to be pedagogical as well as communicational tools. Besides to their major purpose, mobile phones, are these days utilized to send and receive pedagogical messages via text, voice or even forms [40]. In addition, mobile phones and consequently M-learning ease accessing various pedagogical resources on Internet and help developing and making interesting instruction content that can be utilized inside or outside schoolroom [41]. M-learning can deliver the right knowledge to the right learner at the right time better than any other learning/instruction technology yet designed [33]. In addition, learners' interest to utilize all available resources of M-learning via their mobile devices and Personal Digital Assistants (PDAs) to access data anytime and anywhere has as well played an important role in the success of M-learning prevalence [42]. In other words, M-learning not only fosters the way we access data, but also helps students be innovative and kindly problem-solvers [43].

3.1 M-learning and E-learning

M-learning is a massive method for engaging students on their own terms and promotes their broader education experience because of its mobility quality and supporting platform. Thus, M-learning is considered merely an extension of electronic learning joint to mobile computing. Learners of M-learning should be aware of mobile devices' utility and specific restrictions when delivering M-learning quality, ([44]: p. 65). The development of electronic learning, as a new type of distance learning whose nomenclature is close to those of traditional learning, has promoted the diverse applications of M-learning. However, M-learning is a distinguish technology and has its own nomenclature that adopts expressions such as spontaneous, informal, situated, intimate, connected, and lightweight, while electronic learning utilizes different expressions like hyperlinked, multimedia, interactive, and media-rich environment, ([45]: pp. 1926–7). Laouris and Eteokleous [28] have presented **Table 1** below to contrast among the nomenclature of both expressions.

3.2 Rationale of M-learning

It is noteworthy that technology utilize in pedagogical environments must be based on the predominant educational theories and approaches [46], which is thus applied to M-learning as one form of technology utilize in instruction. For example, education, any education, according to Behaviorism, takes place while a conditional correlation is established among a particular stimulus and a specific response [47]. In other words, M-learning, applications of Behaviorism are limited to its major precept, which is stimuli and responses. That is, learners through M-learning are provided by the education content, the stimuli in this situation, while the attached tasks, short exams, and feedback are the learners' responses that follow. On the other hand, cognitive Approach concentrates on enabling the student to reorganize his/her cognitive structures in a task that allows him to process and storage newly acquired data that will be saved and recalled in future [48]. Thus, students should be provided in advance with the education materials and new information. The

E-learning	M-learning
Computer	Mobile
Hyper learning	Constructivism, situations, collaborative
More formal	Informal
Media-rich	Lightweight
Hyperlinked	Connected
Collaborative	Networked
Interactive	Spontaneous
Distance learning	Situated learning
Multimedia	Objects
Simulated situation	Realistic situation
Bandwidth	GPRS, G3, Bluetooth

Table 1.
Terminology contrast between electronic and mobile learning [28].

availability of multimedia included in students' mobile devices will help them process, organize, storage, and recall the data they need anytime and anywhere. Situated Learning Theory hypothesizes that education is not merely a process of information acquisition yet firstly a social participation that seeks a resolution for a problem [29]. Therefore, an emphasis on making real social cases in which new information can be delivered to students provides them with a wealthy opportunity to simulate real life. Through the utilize of social communication and networking means available on mobile devices such as blogs, learning, groups, and discussions at task environment can promote and foster learning more than any other way.

Contextual Learning Theory blends modernistic developments of status-aware computing with instruction strategies that boosts situational and status-sensitive education [49]. Arguably, M-learning can make education contextual via specific practices based on mobile devices' technology that can bring real existence in front of students. A learner can administer the education context based education content, browse, and restore it whenever he wishes. Location-based learning theory aims to fulfill what is known as Just-in-Time Learning linked to the physical location in which the student lives. In other words, M-learning should account for the place of education where the student can be given a hand to acquire and study not any information but conceptual information [50]. According to the Cognitivist, education is an active, constructive, accumulative, and self-directed process that is dependent on the mental activities of the student [51]. Arguably, taking into regard all these points discussed previously, one can argue that M-learning, because of the sophisticated technology embedded inside, can provide such contextual, mental, social, and locative activities through micro learning all the day long and make the study process more self-directed and regulated (2011).

3.3 M-learning theoretical framework

Today's mobile devices are various those ones that were common 5 or 10 years ago. Arguably, mobile phones each month get smarter and smarter. Learners of all kinds and fundamentally university students keep pace with all technological developments Included in these devices. These learners are more skilful in utilizing them than parents or grandparents. Besides, users of mobile devices can be directed to utilize them for pedagogical, as well as, for communication aims in a way that makes their study easier and more interesting. Learners that have investigated how lecturers can do so are many. Besides, learners that have checked whether mobile devices make an effect in learners' academic achievement are many, too. For instance, Jabbour [52] showed that 3G technology based-mobile devices when utilized for educational aims affected learners' attitudes. Learners could enjoy themselves and attempt a positive learning experience. Their prospects of mobile devices' effectiveness had a positive effect on their learning outcomes. While Dos [38] revealed that university, learners heavily utilized mobile devices. Learners' metacognition awareness and academic achievement were developed and improved because of these devices sets usage. Wang et al. [53] also concluded that M-learning activities could engage learners in the learning process much better than traditional ones. Learners changed into active students. They were intellectually, behaviourally and emotionally involved in their education works. Bidaki et al. [54] on the other hand proved that utilize of M-learning process had quite significant effect on both learners' self-regulation learning and academic achievement.

Nevertheless, other researchers found that utilize of M-learning was not always effective. For example, [47] also concluded that unexpectedly control group learners' achievement was better than the achievement of learners in the experimental group who were learning through mobile devices. No variation among learners' extraneous cognitive load and germane cognitive load were found. While there was a variation among learners' mental load degree in favor of the experimental group. Kuznekoff and Titsworth [55] after examining the impact of utilizing mobile devices on learners' learning through video watching concluded that learners who were utilizing their mobile phones wrote down and recalled less information. The notes they took were few. Their achievement degree on the exam were lower than peers who did not utilize their mobile devices actively [73].

Thus, it is true that M-learning phones definitely influence learners' university life whether positively or negatively. Nevertheless, once they are utilized in the right way, they can influence interaction patterns of lecturers as well as learners. They can promote learning and teaching practice. Therefore, pedagogical, organizational and curricular factors affecting the adoption of M-learning in tertiary institutions should be accounted for as long as we wish to utilize them effectively. Students will be in danger and can be insecure to superficial learning if M-learning practice are not well designed. Besides, mobile phones might distract learners from learning and deteriorate the type of interaction among lecturers and learners, Handal et al. [56].

4. Learning management systems (LMS)

The incorporation of numerous Educational technologies in instruction have been widely confirmed for their potential to enrich, promote and extend learner-learning experiences, ([59]: p. 330). Therefore, pioneer tertiary institutions all over the world try to profit of these technologies as much as potential to convey information resources to both of the student and lecturer in least time, cost and effort, ([60]: p. 6). Nevertheless, without a favorable shift from the lecturer-centered education to student-centered education, this incorporation will remain worthless. That is, lecturer-centered education deals with technology as a complement to lectures to display the teaching content to the students while student-centered education believes in greater incorporation of technology into classroom and yields great gains in learners' achievement. Besides, the function of technology incorporation should modification the roles of both the lecturer and the student. It also should be utilized as experiential education activities such writing, study, analysis, and collaboration, ([61]: p. 14). One of these educational technology tools which has been eminent in the field of learning and technology incorporation is LMS. Iwasaki, et al. (2011:479) indicated that the issues, which pedagogues in general, have been facing for more than 15 years such the lowering academic and lowered motivation ability have led to the appearance and adoption of theses learning management systems to promote active learning not restricted to a specific time or classroom, communication among the lecturer and learners, and collaborative learning between learners.

A report by Durham College Leadership Team in 2015 has Confirmed that LMS refers to both software and web-based technologies that are utilized by lecturers and learners to access, plan, perform, complement, observe, and/or assess learning or to communicate about learning. Learning management systems are centralized, online platforms that commodity curriculum, and estimate delivery and reception, ([62]: p. 302). LMS is a highly developed style of distance learning because it provides a set of software tools that help to transfer and manage the education content [63]. Esther [64] emphasizes that learning management system as a teaching tool has been developed to control and regulate the administrative works of tertiary institutions and other organizations. Lecturers and instructors who utilize learning management system have the chance to share syllabus, course materials, notes, calendars, links, idea, and online assignments [65]. One of the most public LMS is Moodle, which favors collaborative education, enabling interactions with resources

DOI: http://dx.doi.org/10.5772/intechopen.81987

from different media and between all lecturers [66]. Much web-based learning which has the ability to address the needs of end employee and student is facilitated through learning management system like Moodle, Blackboard, and Sakai [67, 68]. Moodle for example, is equipped with all aspects of online learning like the ability to store the education resources, connection and activities that are based on certain education topics [69]. When utilizing Moodle, persons or institutions can download the system free of charge and the downloading comes with permit (William, 2006). Nordin [70] also concluded that the motivating features of Moodle contain downloading and sharing of files, developing content in HTML, discussions or forum, questionnaire, grading, journal writing and other features, which are seen as significant to the development of online learning. In addition, Moodle is characterized through its site administrator and management tools; a variety of utilize management choices, containing multiple authentication choices, online profile building. Role-based tasks and licenses; enrollment and registration tools and plug-ins; and course administrator and communications choices, containing chat, questionnaire builders, forums, wikis, are also within the difference features of Moodle, (Monarch Media, Inc., 2010).

Author details

Abdellah Ibrahim Mohammed Elfeky* and Marwa Yasien Helmy Elbyaly
Kafrelsheikh University, Egypt

*Address all correspondence to: marwa.mohamed1@spe.kfs.edu.eg

References

[1] Kamara S, Lauter K. Cryptographic cloud storage. In: Paper Presented at the International Conference on Financial Cryptography and Data Security, Financial Cryptography and Data Security. 2010. pp. 136-149 Available from: https://link.springer.com/chapter/10.1007/978-3-642-14992-4_13

[2] Yang K, Jia X, Ren K, Zhang B, Xie R. DAC-MACS: Effective data access control for multi-authority cloud storage systems security for cloud storage systems. IEEE Transactions on Information Forensics and Security. 2013;**8**(11):1790-1801

[3] Kumar K, Lu Y-H. Cloud computing for mobile users: Can offloading computation save energy? Computer. 2010;**43**(4):51-56

[4] Lin H-Y, Tzeng W-G. A secure erasure code-based cloud storage system with secure data forwarding. IEEE Transactions on Parallel and Distributed Systems. 2012;**23**(6):995-1003

[5] Bowers KD, Juels A, Oprea A. HAIL: A high-availability and integrity layer for cloud storage. In: Paper Presented at the Proceedings of the 16th ACM Conference on Computer and Communications Security. 2009. Available from: http://citeseerx.ist.psu.edu/viewdoc/download?doi=10.1.1.215.4730&rep=rep1&type=pdf

[6] Yang K, Jia X. An efficient and secure dynamic auditing protocol for data storage in cloud computing. IEEE Transactions on Parallel and Distributed Systems. 2013;**24**(9):1717-1726

[7] Wu J, Ping L, Ge X, Wang Y, Fu J. Cloud storage as the infrastructure of cloud computing. In: Paper Presented at the Intelligent Computing and Cognitive Informatics (ICICCI). 2010. DOI: 10.1109/ICICCI.2010.119

[8] Wang C, Chow SS, Wang Q, Ren K, Lou W. Privacy-preserving public auditing for secure cloud storage. IEEE Transactions on Computers. 2013;**62**(2):362-375

[9] Chiu M. Adapting teacher interventions to student needs during cooperative learning: How to improve student problem solving and time on-task. American Educational Research Journal. 2004;**41**(2):365-399

[10] Bosworth K, Hamilton SJ, editors. Collaborative Learning: Underlying Processes and Effective Techniques: New Directions for Teaching and Learning. Number 59. Vol. 73. Jossey-Bass; 1994

[11] Abu-Libdeh H, Princehouse L, Weatherspoon H. RACS: A case for cloud storage diversity. In: Paper Presented at the Proceedings of the 1st ACM Symposium on Cloud Computing. 2010. Available from: http://www.cs.cornell.edu/~hweather/publications/racs-socc2010.pdf

[12] Montebello A. Beyond Teams: Building the Collaborative Organization. OH USA: Personal Psychology; 2003

[13] Prinz W, Loh H, Pallot M, Schaffers H, Skarmeta A, Decker S. ECOSPACE--towards an integrated collaboration space for e professionals. In: Paper Presented at International Conference on the Collaborative Computing: Networking, Applications and Work Sharing. 2006. Available from: http://ieeexplore.ieee.org/document/4207540/?reload=true

[14] Carreras MM, Skarmeta AG. Towards interoperability in collaborative environments. In: Paper Presented at International Conference on the Collaborative Computing: Networking, Applications and Work

Sharing. 2006. Available from: http://ieeexplore.ieee.org/document/4207510/

[15] Neilson GL, Martin KL, Powers E. The secrets to successful strategy execution. Harvard Business Review. 2008;**86**(6):60

[16] Smith B, MacGregor J. What is collaborative learning?, collaborative learning: A sourcebook for higher education. In: National Center on Postsecondary Teaching, Learning, and Assessment at Pennsylvania State University. 1992 http://evergreen.edu/facultydevelopment/docs/WhatisCollaborativeLearning.pdf

[17] Mitnik R, Recabarren M, Nussbaum M, Soto A. Collaborative robotic instruction: A graph teaching experience. Computers & Education. 2009;**53**(2):330-342

[18] Kreijns K, Kirschner PA, Jochems W. Identifying the pitfalls for social interaction in computer supported collaborative learning environments: A review of the research. Computers in Human Behaviour. 2003;**19**(3):335-353

[19] Shukor NA, Tasir Z, Van der Meijden H, Harun J. Exploring students' knowledge construction strategies in computer-supported collaborative learning discussions using sequential analysis. Educational Technology & Society. 2014;**17**(4):216-228

[20] Lethinen E, Hakkarainen K, Lipponen L, Rahikainen M, Muukkonen H. Computer supported collaborative learning: A review. In: CL-Net Project. 1999 Available on http://nexus.hs-bremerhaven.de/library.nsf/bf25ab0f47ba5dd785256499006b15a4/30bb62d76118ded3c12578530056a136/$FILE/CollaborativeLearning.pdf date accessed 24/5/2016

[21] Stahl G, Koschmann T, Suthers D. Computer-supported collaborative learning: An historical perspective. In: Sawyer RK, editor. Cambridge Handbook of the Learning Sciences. Cambridge, UK: Cambridge University Press; 2006. pp. 409-426

[22] Rimor R, Rosen Y, Naser K. Complexity of social interactions in collaborative learning: The case of online database environment. Interdisciplinary Journal of E-Learning and Learning Objects. 2010;**6**(1):355-365

[23] Resta P, Laferrière T. Technology in Support of collaborative learning. Educational Psychology Review. 2007;**19**:65-83. DOI: 10.1007/s10648-007-9042-7

[24] Dillenbourg P, Baker M, Blaye A, O'malley C. The evolution of research on collaborative learning. In: Spada E, Reiman P, editors. Learning in Humans and Machine: Towards an Interdisciplinary Learning Science. 1996. pp. 189-211

[25] Dillenbourg P, Fischer F. Basics of computer-supported collaborative learning. Zeitschrift fur berufs-und Wirtschaftspadagogik. 2007;**21**:111-130

[26] Kirschner P, Vilsteren P, Hummel H, Wigman M. A study environment for acquiring academic and professional competence. Studies of Higher Education. 1997;**22**(2):151-171

[27] Kreijns K, Kirschner P, Jochems W. The sociability of computer-supported collaborative learning environments. Educational Technology & Society. 2002;**5**(1). Available from: http://www.ifets.info/journals/5_1/kreijns.html

[28] Laouris Y, Eteokleous. We need an educationally relevant definition of mobile learning. In: Proc. 4th World Conference on Mobile Learning, mLearn 2005, Oct 25-28, Cape Town, South Africa. 2005. Retrieved from:

http://www.mlearn.org.za/CD/papers/Laouris%20&%20Eteokleous.pdf

[29] Brown JS, Collins A, Duguid P. Situated cognition and the culture of learning. Educational Researcher. 1989a;**18**(1):32-42

[30] Vygotsky LS. Mind in Society: The Development of Higher Psychological Processes. Cambridge, MA: Harvard University Press; 1978

[31] Keskin NO, Metcalf D. The current perspectives, theories and practices of mobile learning. Turkish Online Journal of Educational Technology-TOJET. 2011;**10**(2):202-208

[32] Sharples M. Disruptive devices: Mobile technology for conversational learning. International Journal of Continuing Engineering Education and Life Long Learning. 2002;**12**(5/6):504-520

[33] Little B. Effective and efficient mobile learning: Issues and tips for developers. Industrial and Commercial Training. 2012;**44**(7):402-407. DOI: 10.1108/00197851211267983

[34] Dewiyanti S, Gruwel SB, Jochems W, Broers NJ. Students experiences with collaborative learning in asynchronous computer-supported collaborative learning environments. Computers in Human Behavior. 2007;**23**:496-514. DOI: 10.1016/j.chb.2004.10.021

[35] Ada M. A longitudinal study of the use of computer supported collaborative learning in promoting lifelong learning skills. In: Issues in Informing Science and Information Technology. 2009. p. 6. Retrieved from: http://www.ied.edu.hk/jol_e-mag/mag_upload/article/IISITv6p065-086MA565.pdf

[36] Iinuma M, Matsuhashi T, Nakamura T, Chiyokura H. Student awareness change in computer supported collaborative learning (CSCL) environment. International Journal of Information and Education Technology. 2016;**6**(6):448. DOI: 10.7763/IJIET.2016.V6.730

[37] El-Hussein MOM, Cronje JC. Defining mobile learning in the higher education landscape. Educational Technology & Society. 2010;**13**(3):12-21. Retrieved from http://www.ifets.info/journals/13_3/3.pdf

[38] Dos B. The relationship between mobile phone use, metacognitive awareness and academic achievement. European Journal of Educational research. 2014;**3**(4):192-200. Retrieved from: http://files.eric.ed.gov/fulltext/EJ1085990.pdf

[39] Lan YF, Huang S-M. Using mobile learning to improve the reflection: A case study of traffic violation. Educational Technology & Society. 2012;**15**(2):179-193. Retrieved from: http://www.ifets.info/journals/15_2/16.pdf

[40] Kim D, Rueckert D, Kim DJ, Seo D. Student' perceptions and experiences of mobile learning. Language Learning & Technology. 2013;**17**(3):52-73. Retrieved from: http://llt.msu.edu/issues/october2013/kimetal.pdf

[41] UNISCO. In: Kraut R, editor. Policy Guidelines for Mobile Learning. France: The United Nations Educational, Scientific and Cultural Organization (UNISCO); 2013. Retrieved from: http://unesdoc.unesco.org/images/0021/002196/219641e.pdf

[42] López GJL, Royo TM, Laborda JG, Calvo FG. Methods of adapting digital content for the learning process via mobile devices. Procedia Social and Behavioural Sciences. 2009;**1**(1):2673-2677. DOI: 10.1016/j.sbspro.2009.01.472

[43] West DM. Mobile Learning: Transforming Education, Engaging Students, and Improving Outcomes,

Centre for Technology Innovation at Brooking. 2013. Retrieved from: http://www.brookings.edu/~/media/research/files/papers/2013/09/17-mobile-learning-education-engaging-students-west/brookingsmobilelearning_final.pdf

[44] Behera SK. E- and M-learning: A comparative study. International Journal on New Trends in Education and Their Implications. 2013;**4**(3):65-78. Retrieved from: http://www.ijonte.org/FileUpload/ks63207/File/08.behera.pdf

[45] Korucu AT, Alkan A. Differences between M-Learning (mobile learning) and E-learning, basic terminology and usage of M-learning in education. Procedia Social and Behavioural Sciences. 2011;**19**:1925-1930. DOI: 10.1016/j.sbspro.2011.04.029

[46] Patten B, Arnedillo-Sanchez I, Tangney B. Designing collaborative, constructionist and contextual applications for handheld devices: Virtual learning. Computers and Education. 2006a;**46**(3):294-308

[47] Smith PL, Ragan TJ. Instructional Design. 3rd ed. Hoboken, NJ: Wiley; 2005

[48] Good TL, Brophy JE. Educational psychology: A realistic approach. In: White Plains. 4th ed. NY: Longman; 1990

[49] De Jong T, Specht M, Koper R. A reference model for mobile social software for learning. International Journal of Continuing Engineering and Lifelong Learning. 2008;**18**(1):118-138. DOI: 10.1504/IJCEELL.2008.016079

[50] Johnson DW. Reaching out: Interpersonal Effectiveness and Self-Actualization. 10th ed. Boston: Allyn & Bacon; 2009

[51] Shuell T. Cognitive conceptions of learning. Review of Educational Research. 1986;**56**:411-436. Retrieved from: http://rer.sagepub.com/content/56/4/411.short

[52] Jabbour KK. An analysis of the effect of mobile learning on Lebanese higher education. Bulgarian Journal of Science and Education Policy (BJSEP). 2013;**7**(2):280-301. Retrieved from: http://bjsep.org/getfile.php?id=145

[53] Wang M, Shen R, Novak D, Pan X. The impact of mobile learning on students' learning Behaviours and performance: Report from a large blended classroom. British Journal of Educational Technology (BJET). 2009;**40**(4):673-695. DOI: 10.1111/j.1467-8535.2008.00846.x

[54] Bidaki MZ, Naderi F, Ayati M. Effects of mobile learning on paramedical students' academic achievement and self-regulation. Future of Medical education Journal. 2013;**3**(3):24-28. Retrieved from: http://fmej.mums.ac.ir/article_1524_0.html

[55] Kuznekoff J, Titsworth S. The impact of mobile phone usage on student learning. Communication Education. 2013;**62**(3):223-252. DOI: 10.1080/03634523.2013.767917

[56] Handal B, MacNish J, Petocz P. Adopting mobile learning in tertiary environments: Instructional, curricular and organizational matters. Education in Science. 2013;**3**:359-374. DOI: 10.3390/educsci3040359

[57] Elfeky AIM. The effect of personal learning environments on participants' higher order thinking skills and satisfaction. Innovations in Education and Teaching International. 2018;1-12

[58] Matthee MC, De Villiers C, Roode JD. A South African case study: Using computer-supported co-operative mathematics learning in teacher education. In: Working Paper. University of Pretoria: Department of Informatics; 1998

[59] Masadeh TSY, Elfeky AIM. Efficacy of open-source learning management systems in developing the teaching skills of English language student teachers. American Journal of Educational Research. 2016;**4**(4):329-337

[60] UNESCO Institute for Information Technologies in Education. Internet in Education: Support Materials for Educators. Moscow, Russian Federation: UNESCO;2003. Retrieved from: http://unesdoc.unesco.org/images/0013/001330/133023e.pdf

[61] Anonymous. Professional Development for Technology Integration, Washington: Hanover Research; 2014. Retrieved from: https://ts.madison.k12.wi.us/files/techsvc/Professional%20Development%20for%20Technology%20Integration.pdf

[62] Park JY, Mills KA. Enhancing interdisciplinary learning with a learning management system. MERLOT Journal of Online Learning and Teaching. 2014;10(2):299-313. Retrieved from: http://jolt.merlot.org/vol10no2/park_0614.pdf

[63] Dede C, Ketelhut DJ, Whitehouse W, Breit B, McCloskey EM. A research agenda for online teacher professional development. Journal of Teacher Education. 2009;**60**(1). Retrieved from: http://jte.sagepub.com/content/60/1/8.full.pdf+html

[64] Esther S. One-stop shopping with learning management systems. THE Journal. 2008;**35**(6):18-20

[65] Papadakis S, Dovros N, Paschalis G, Rossioi E. Integrating LMSs in the educational process: Greek teachers' initial perceptions about LAMS. Turkish Online Journal of Distance Education (TOJDE). 2012;**13**(4). Retrieved from: http://files.eric.ed.gov/fulltext/EJ1000414.pdf

[66] Elfeky A. Social networks impact factor on students' achievements and attitudes towards the "computer in teaching" course at the college of education. International Journal on E-Learning. 2017;**16**(3):231-244

[67] Santos L, Inan F, Denton B. Examination of factors impacting student satisfaction with a new learning management system. Turkish Online Journal of Distance Education (TOJDE). 2012;**13**(3)

[68] Lewis BA, MacEntee VM. Learning management system comparison. In: Proceedings from the 2005 Informing Science and IT Education Joint Conference; June 16-19; Flagstaff, Arizona, USA. 2005. Retrieved from: http://www85.homepage.villanova.edu/timothy.ay/DIT2160/LMS/P03f55Lewis.pdf

[69] Williams BC. Moodle 1.4. 3 for teachers, trainers and administrators. 2005. Available in: http://download.moodle.org/docs/moodle_1,4

[70] Nordin N, Ibrahim S. Leveraging open source software in the education management and leadership training. Turkish Online Journal of Educational Technology-TOJET. 2012;**11**(3):215-221

[71] Elfeky AIM, Elbyaly MYH. The use of CSCL environment to promote students' achievement and skills in handmade embroidery. European Journal of Training and Development Studies. 2017;**4**(2):19-32

[72] Elfeky AIM, Masadeh TSY. The effect of mobile learning on students' achievement and conversational skills. International Journal of Higher Education. 2016;**5**(3):20-31

[73] Elfeky AIM, Elbyaly MYH. The impact of learning object repository (lor) in the development of pattern making skills of home economics students. British Journal of Education. 2016;**4**(2):87-99

Chapter 3

Interactive Design vs. Design for Interaction: Developing Interactive Play Tools that Promote Interactions between Children

Rodrigo Fernandes and Toshimasa Yamanaka

Abstract

How do children interact with each other and how can interactive technology contribute? In this chapter, we are going to introduce two concepts that are currently present in the development of play tools for children: (1) interactive design, represented by toys that can integrate interactive sensors and actuators to promote new play possibilities, and (2) design for interaction, a new tendency focused on how children interact with each other and how new designs can contribute to these interactions. Through this chapter, existing works will be utilized to exemplify these concepts illustrating differences and connection points in-between. These will be followed by a series of studies of children's social interactions when under the influence of different game conditions. By looking into the fundamental aspects of design and interaction, we will discuss how play can promote positive interactions and how interactive technology can contribute to those. We aim to contribute to the establishment of guidelines for the development of new designs for interactions.

Keywords: children, sociability, game elements, technology, toys

1. Introduction

Children have a universal need to play, and by playing, they can learn a series of skills vital for their social and cognitive development. Playing is a self-motivating and pleasurable activity, and through gamification (the application of game elements), different tasks can become more engaging. Maria Montessori defined play as the work of children and something that must be encouraged for a healthy childhood development. Disciplines such as social game studies consider the activity of play as an important way for children to understand their surroundings, communicate, and develop affection [1, 2].

Known as play tools, toys have an important role as facilitators of children's growth and learning [3]. A toy is a dedicate artifact for the act of playing. Humans are sensory animals and toys can allow more materialized, stimulating, and easily understood play experiences. The existence of toys can date as old as 3.000 BCE, but it was only through the rise of the industrial age that they became widely available for children at a global scale. Up until the 1980s, toys were mostly represented by a highly profitable plastic industry. However, since the 1990s, the rise of electronic technology together with the digital video game industry has reconfigured the general ideas of what a toy could be.

Nowadays, electronic games can be considered toys and the boundaries between the virtual and tangible elements are not so strict [4]. For example, the fast development of tablet computers has developed into one of the current most profitable play markets. Different tablet applications for children (be they games, dedicate programs, or play kits) gives an array of engaging and playful possibilities at little development cost. With tablets representing a big parcel of the play market, children today have become much more exposed to digital/screen media than previous generations. This extended exposure has been linked with different changes in children's behaviors. As examples, current studies are linking extended screen exposure to autistic-like symptoms, hyperactivity, and obesity rates [5–7]. The overall recommendation is that, specially at young ages, screen time should be minimized at the same pace that active play time should be encouraged. However, technology cannot be stopped and children's interest to interact with technology should not be discouraged, but rather utilized to support their development.

This context led to a series of new play tool proposal called "interactive" or "smart" toys. By combining the traditional play values with modern technologies, interactive toys can provide more direct feedback and narrative possibilities for the users. Interactive toys can also engage children through sensory stimuli such as LED lights, digital sounds, and haptic inputs for touch [8]. The "interaction" from interactive toys comes from these expanded possibilities between the user and the artifact facilitated by modern technology. In other words, the toy is interactive. Being that a new frontier, designers from all over the world are trying to develop new interactive toys that can bring unique experiences to the user.

The interaction between children with others is potentially more important to their social development than the interactions they can have with different toys. Considering that, a parallel view entitled "Design for Interaction" is rising by prioritizing children's social relationships. In the design for interaction principle, play artifacts assume a support role, mediating or facilitating social relationships between children and peers or caregivers. Moreover, technology is not the main factor in this view and interactions can arise from different play media, be they analogic, electronic, or virtual.

The present chapter discusses the definitions, differences, and similarities between the "interactive design" and the "design for interaction" views when applied for children's product. Each section will illustrate and exemplify these views with schematic and cases. We follow by comparing some performed studies where group games, mediated by different toys, were utilized to evaluate children's task impressions and group behavior. Considerations will be at the end of the chapter about how to develop interactive play tools that can better support children's social development.

2. Interactive design and interactive toys

According to the Merriam-Webster dictionary [9], the word "interactive" can mean: (1) mutually or reciprocally active or (2) involving the actions or input of a user. This definition is especially related to a two-way electronic communication system. Therefore, the word interactive design has an inherent focus on how the design interacts with the user, and how to consider these interactions. The same concept can be applied with the definition of interactive toys. Nowadays, toys and games are being constantly designed with the advancement of digital technology and the changes in consumer habits. These new toys are named "Interactive" or "smart" toys [10].

From a technology standpoint, an interactive toy differs from traditional ones by adding the interactive attractiveness of modern technologies to stimulate play. All toys can be considered interactive, but traditional toy interactions are mostly mechanical. In other words, when interacting with traditional toys, such as a football, the user receives an instant sensory feedback which might motivate them to keep playing. Emotional-level interactions and imaginary play are also possible with traditional toys, but the toy acts mainly as a physical medium for these play interactions (**Figure 1**).

The main difference between the definitions of a traditional and an interactive toy is the integration of technology to provide dynamic interactions [11, 12]. By using different sensors and actuators, interactive toys can receive children's inputs and generate different outputs to actively encourage their play. It can, for instance, identify children's play pattern through an artificial intelligence and use this information to provide direct motivating feedback such as increasing or decreasing the difficulty of game, or changing the balance of sensory stimuli such as the intensity of lights and sounds. This interaction can be seen in **Figure 2** below.

It is important to note that both traditional and interactive toys can provide the same amount of play interactions, but the interaction of smart toys can be detected or encouraged with the applied technology. The constant feedback generated by the artifact in the response of children's inputs is what would define its interactivity and where technology is more deeply inserted. The second point is that smart toys are expanded to new media and devices such as tablets, augmented-reality and virtual reality glasses, breaking the division between digital and analogic experiences.

Considering that wide range, there is no current fixed limitation in the interactive toys' category. Interactive toy can involve products such as interactive floors or walls with sensors that react when children touch them, or it could be individual portable products, such as shoes or balls with LED lights and sensors to motivate active play. It can even be an entire installation, with different products exchanging information on a network-connected server [8].

A promising subcategory of the interactive toys is the interactive playgrounds. Interactive playgrounds are integrating technology to promote more engaging ways for children to exercise and establish social relationships. Like interactive toys, the idea of an interactive playground is not limited to traditional buildings and could be either a small prop, which the user can carry with them, or a digital application that can integrate with the existing playground environment. Although it is a new concept, Sturm et al. defined the following guidelines which designers can take when designing interactive playgrounds. Interactive playgrounds should:

- focus on social interactions,
- keep the game rules and mechanics simple,
- offer challenges,
- have clear goals, and
- provide different feedbacks to the users.

By using sensory technology, children can receive different sorts of feedback such as visual lights, sounds, or haptic outputs. Many of these elements are proven to have a positive effect on children development, since it can better direct and immerse them in the activities. For example, Zhao et al. found that haptic inputs increased the immersion children had when reading and listening stories [13].

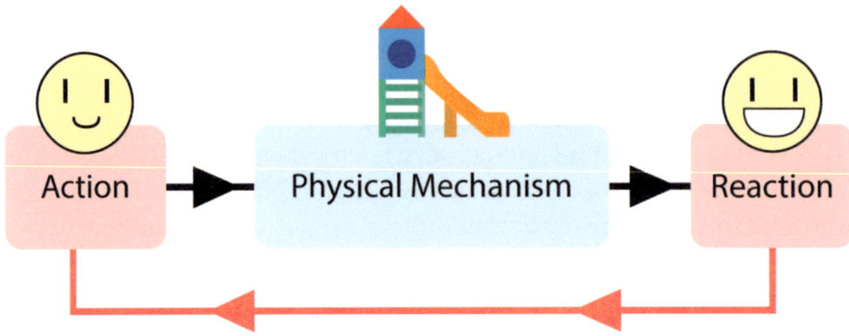

Figure 1.
Traditional toy play interaction flowchart. Users interact with the toy and the given mechanical feedback perpetuates different interactions.

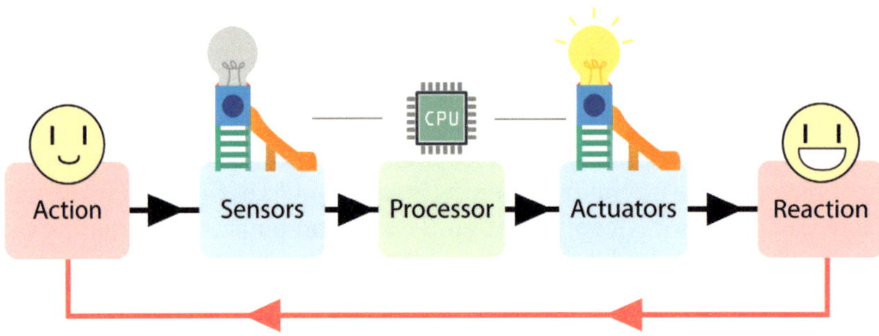

Figure 2.
Interactive toy play interaction flowchart. The user provides an interaction that is detected and processed by the toy, which then converts into a feedback through different actuators, perpetuating the interaction.

A point of caution is that a higher physiological arousal through interactive technology can also be associated with increases in user stress level [14]. With studies having yet to find the extension of these effects, this remains as an important step to responsibly design new interactive play tools. Moreover, the interaction with different technologies also affects children's social play interactions, which should be considered in the design of toy.

3. Design for interaction between children

Still according to the Merriam-Webster dictionary [15], the word "interaction" can mean: (1) the act of talking or doing things with other people; (2) the action or influence of things on one another, or; (3) mutual or reciprocal action or influence.

When comparing with the word "interactive," "interaction" carries a broader meaning involving different relationships between humans with living things and with artifacts. It is important to say that each interaction can generate different outcomes for the parties involved and that these outcomes can affect further interactions. This relationship can be seen in the scheme represented by **Figure 3**.

Likewise, the word "design for interaction" also has a more expanded meaning than the word "interactive design," involving not only the interactions between the user and the artifact but also the interactions that artifacts can foster between different people. In design for interaction, the artifact can act as a supporter for different social interactions. Considering that, this concept of an interactive toy is not only of one that provides engaging interactive feedback for children. Instead, interactive toys should facilitate relationship among children through play interactions. Under this view, exposure to different types of interactions among children is the most important aspect of their development. This can be observed in **Figure 4** below.

According to a study requested by the Kids Design Association (KDA), Japan [16], interactive products should encourage children to create relationships instead of being alone. Game experiences can help children realize their individual limitations and perceive playing together as a more fun activity. Considering that, the following guidelines where defined for designing artifacts for interactions among children. Designs for interaction could be:

- experiences that can only be felt when together with others,
- games that produce more significant results by joining force with others,
- artifacts to facilitate communication between children, or
- toys and games that can strengthen their affective bonds.

Under these guidelines, technology is not the main aspect of "interactive toys" and any toy or game that has been designed with social interaction in mind can be considered as "interactive" [17]. Playground environments provide an important role as "design for interactions," fostering social relationships through play activities.

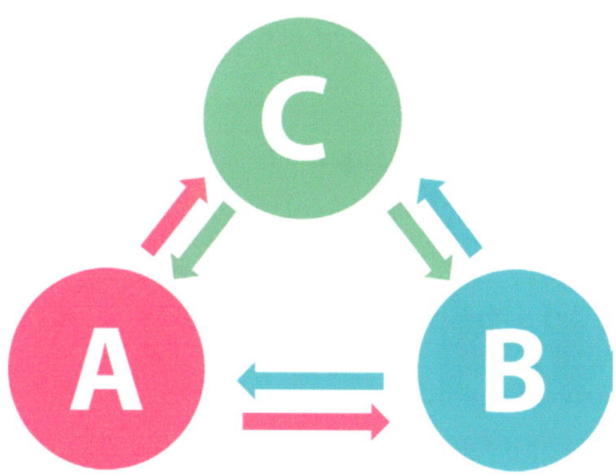

Figure 3.
Interaction scheme: the spheres influence each other, and each interaction generates different outcomes.

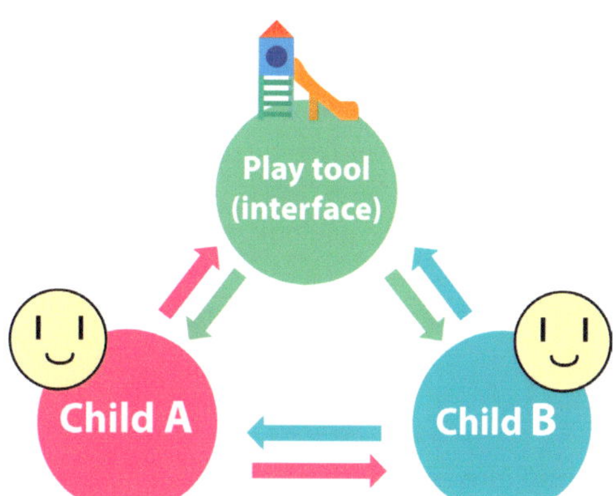

Figure 4.
Interactive play tools as mediating interfaces for different interactions among children through play activity.

Playgrounds are spaces where of different ages can get in contact with open nature, with each other and with their parents to, through dynamic play exploration, socialize, and develop different skills [18].

Considering children's sociability, a parallel field called "social game studies" seek to understand how different game elements can influence children's social development [19]. Through gamification, the application of game elements to other activities, educators can utilize the self-motivational aspects of games to encourage children's positive social behavior. This concept is widely used in "structured" or "ice-breaking" game scenarios, where the act of playing group games is linked with positive group behavior [20].

Working with social game concept, Hendrix et al. [17] developed a game to observe its impact on children's sociability. In this game, children would receive the role of architects to give instructions on how to build a structure for the other members in the group. The researchers noted that, during the game, children who often struggled with social interactions managed to more easily express their thoughts and intentions.

By looking at post effects of group games, Creighton and Szymkowiak [21] observed the classroom behavior of two groups of children after being submitted to different game conditions. While one group played games with a competitive focus for a week, the other group played cooperative games instead. Evaluating children's social behavior with an interaction frequency index, the authors observed that children who played the cooperative games displayed more positive interactions in the classroom than children who played the competitive games. These findings suggested that cooperative games may benefit the social interaction of pupils within the classroom.

Playing is an arousing activity that involves internal motivations and sensory stimuli [22]. With the body being the main channel for sensory interactions, Malinverni and Burguès [1] linked the usage of the full body during games to children's higher cooperative behavior. In their study, children played two different versions of a group game: (1) a digital version, where children interacted together through connected desktop computers, and (2) a physical version, where the game was projected in the wall and children could use their body to interact with together. Participants who played the full body game version achieved higher scores in the game, displayed better teamwork, and reported better impressions of their group members after the activity.

Considering social studies findings, we defined the following elements as possible contributors to children's social development, which should be aimed by interactive games:

- Existence of rules and attribution of specific roles
- Restriction of individual power and resources
- Challenging but achievable difficulty curve
- Excitement and novelty levels of game experience
- Rich sensory feedback
- Usage of natural body movement
- Focus on cooperativity rather than competitivity

When considering the effect of group game activities, or designing new interactive play tools, it would be of interest to further observe these elements as possible predictors of children's social behavior.

Note that technology is not directly mentioned as an important for social interactions, but that does not mean that it should be disregarded. Although society has been changing drastically, the basic structure of playgrounds has remained almost the same since 1920 [11], and traditional play tools today are not enticing the modern children as they used to. Children enjoy interacting with current technology and it would benefit their social interaction to utilize a medium which they can more easily engage. More importantly, modern technology provides an array of rich sensory feedback which can be utilized as elements to promote social interactions. As an example, Suzuki et al. [23] developed a musical device which converts each person's position into a single melodic note. When people gather to play together, the device can combine notes and create harmony, making the activity more meaningful and pleasurable. Another way of using technology to facilitate interactions would be by automatically altering the sensory stimuli or the difficulty level of a game according to the number of children or to their given feedback.

In this sense, this chapter definition of an interactive toy is of one who adopts different feedback technologies or devices to act as a mediating interface of real-time interactions between people. In this definition, while technology is still important, it is not the main factor, acting instead as a supporter of children's interactions. Considering the described elements of this section, it is important to investigate additional ways for technology and interactive toys to foster social interactions among children.

4. Case studies: how group games can promote interaction

During the years of 2017–2018, we conducted three different studies to investigate the relationship between children playing group games and their motivation to work together in a subsequent group task [24, 25]. Represented by **Figure 5**, throughout three studies, three different group games were utilized as "ice-breaking" activities: (1) an interactive building block game where the goal was to build electronic circuits, (2) a buildable tower block game, where the goal was to connect blocks together into a single standing tower, and (3) an interactive dance game, where the goal was to replicate the dance moves displayed in the game screen.

Different methods of evaluating children's impressions and cooperation were utilized between studies, limiting direct comparisons between the games' effects.

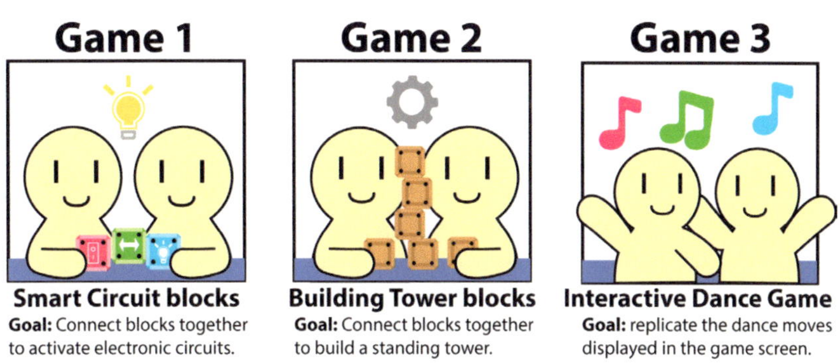

Figure 5.
Three group games utilized during different studies.

However, through observations of the three games' applications, reinforced by present guidelines in the literature, the research obtained indications on which aspects of the group games worked well and which needed further reconsiderations. Comparisons were established between these games.

The three studies worked with cooperative tasks and self-report scales where children could rate their feelings regarding the task and their group members. Overall, the main evaluations after playing or not variations of the group games were: (1) how difficult or pleasurable participants perceived the cooperative task to be; (2) how satisfied participants were with their group member and how mindful they were of each member feeling, and how well they executed the subsequent task at individual and group level (objective criteria were established). More information about the procedures and evaluations can be found in [24, 25].

It is important to mention that many unpredicted factors can happen when working with children in natural playful situations. Furthermore, the indications are about how the group sessions were administered and do not necessarily point out a certain toy or game task as more suitable to promote cooperation. A small description of each game session and the obtained results will be given.

4.1 Game session 1: smart circuit blocks

In game session 1, an interactive block toy set was selected as the game stimuli. The set was composed of circuit blocks that could be connected to activate different responses. For example, children could connect a switch to activate an electronic light, sound, or motor. Challenges were designed where 36 participants aged 6–16 divided into groups of four had to activate specific blocks in a 20 minutes time limit. Specific roles were also assigned for the challenge with one participant receiving the leader role, helping to manage their group members.

Three group conditions were formed: (1) easy game group, who played an easier version requiring simplified block combinations (e.g., activating a light block); (2) difficult game challenge, who played a version requiring more complex block activations (e.g., assembling a movable robot), and (3) no game group, who did not play the group game before performing the subsequent group task.

The subsequent group task of this study was a co-design challenge where had to design a new interactive toy together. Participants had 10 minutes to perform individual sketches and 10 minutes to perform group discussion. Video evaluation of the group discussion backed by the interaction rating scale [26] was performed to observe children social behavior. Developed sketches were collected for evaluation, and self-reports were applied after the task.

Results indicated no difference between participants who played the easy group challenge and participants who did not play the group game. This means that playing an easy game did not indicate to affect how easy or pleasurable participants perceived the group task to be, or how satisfied they were with their group members. Differences were observed, however, between the difficult game challenge and the two other group conditions. Participants in the difficult game condition also reported the design task to be more difficult, indicated to designed fewer elements in their toy sketches, and were less aware of their group members' feelings. In other words, the more difficult version of the game distressed participant's cooperation, affective impressions, and outcomes of the subsequent design task. We defined from these results that when administrating game as ice-breakers, the difficulty should not be excessively high. Games should instead seek to give a positive sense of achievement for the participants.

Other than difficulty, three aspects of the game may have influenced children's behavior: (1) the assigned roles, (2) the game complexity, and (3) time length.

Regarding the role assignment, it was noted that children who obtained the leadership role in the game task also tended to maintain the leadership position in the following design task. Through observation, it was noted that, depending on the age, this leadership position led to authoritarian behavior in the design task, with the leader not giving an equal voice for all group members.

While recommendations for group design tasks with children support the establishment of defined roles for better group work [21], this establishment indicated to be immature in the game sessions. The necessary leadership for completing a game challenge did not necessarily transpose into the necessary leadership skills for dialoguing in a group design task. Also, groups who established their roles without playing the game indicated better work dynamics. Unless due considerations are made, it is better to not establish roles during group games. Rather, group games can be good opportunities for children to explore different roles inside groups.

Regarding the complexity and time, another observation is that the interactive blocks were of high complexity and required children's extended attention. A fatigue effect might have happened from the game, reducing children's focus on the design task. Reconsiderations regarding the time length and the complexity of the game task were made to ensure children would be in good conditions for performing the following design task.

4.2 Game session 2: building tower blocks

Considering previous results, the game challenge was simplified for the game session 2. Instead of working with interactive toys and of creating two game conditions, this study investigated how playing a building block tower game could affect children's impressions and motivations for a subsequent task. About 21 participants aged 6–11 y/o were divided into groups of four. Roles were not assigned in this game session and each child had on average 20 connecting pieces to build into a single tower in under 10 minutes.

For the group challenge, participants had to design an invention to facilitate communicate among children. This context took opportunity of an existing children's design competition of the Interaction Design with Children 2018 (IDC2018) conference [27]. Participants had 10 minutes to sketch initial ideas and would then have a one-week deadline to submit their designs to the competition. Submission was voluntary.

Although no differences were observed on cooperation among group conditions, results indicated that participants who played the group game reported higher confidence with their designs and were significantly more likely to submit them to the competition. Results of this study mostly indicated that children who played the game were more motivated with the design task, associating an energizing effect of group games on subsequent activities. Compared with the previous session, game session 2 was shorter, the intention of the game was easier to understand, and children had the same initial conditions to participate.

4.3 Game session 3: interactive dance game

A third game challenge was designed to specifically observe its effect on children's group behavior. This session utilized the electronic game Just Dance 2018^{tm} as a simple interactive game. About 36 participants aged 6–14 y/o joined this study. The choice of this game was further backed by different studies which pointed positive effects of physical and energetic games on children's cooperation [1, 28]. Three group conditions were established: (1) a relaxing dance group, where participants would dance easier choreography songs with less movement, (2) an energetic dance group, where they would dance more energetic songs with a more demanding choreography, and (3) group conversation condition, where children did not play any game.

The cooperative task of this study was simplified and focused on children's social behavior. After performing one of the three game conditions, participants were submitted to a Reward Sharing Game. Based on the prisoner's dilemma [28], participants had to decide between sharing and keeping their reward with the group. The study evaluated how willing participants were to share their rewards according to their group conditions and how much they would trust the group to share the reward.

Results indicated that participants in both game groups displayed higher trust in their group members and were more willing to share their reward than participants who did not play the game. This indicated that the physical dancing game was a successful motivator for bonding participants. However, differences between game conditions were not found at significant level. In both game conditions, there were participants who displayed high and participants who displayed lower engagement with the task. Participants who displayed higher engagement were more likely to trust the group and share the reward.

This indicates that, instead of the energy level that the game is requiring from the player, the level of involvement they will have with the task is the main factor. Additionally, there were more incidences of participants not managing to follow the choreography due to higher movement demands in the energetic game condition. This might also have prejudiced their engagement.

These observations suggest that, among two physical game sessions, having an easier difficulty entry could be safer for more participants to join and engage with the group game task. However, a different observation in the test runs of the dance game sessions was that participant who could not select which song to play displayed less engagement with the task. Considering that, we believe that giving the choice to the players to select between a more relaxed or energetic session could also be positive for their engagement. When we consider the interactivity of games, it is important to allow some flexibility to attend to different children's preferences.

4.4 Relationship and considerations between game sessions

Considering all the game sessions, three main differences were observed between game sessions:

- Game session 3 worked with physical tasks involving body movement coordination, while sessions 1 and 2 focused on constructive building and coordination skills.

- Game sessions 1 and 3 worked with interactive games, while session 2 worked with a more traditional building block.

- Game session 1 indicated negative subsequent effects of the game stimuli on children's task impressions and performance, while game sessions 2 and 3 indicated positive effects.

Game session 2 observed group game effects on children's task engagement, while game session 3 focused on children's cooperative behavior. While existing literature reinforce that physical games are more successful for positively coordinating group behavior [1, 29], the present studies cannot reach a definite conclusion about physical dancing games being more suitable for motivating cooperation than constructive block games.

Although the smart blocks of game session 1 indicated negative effects for task impressions, these effects were not noted on the block games of session 2. We must then initially assume that block games would have a similar effect than the dancing game on children's group behavior.

When comparing with game session 1, both sessions 2 and 3 presented modifications which indicated to positively affect group behavior and task engagement. Acting as indications, these game elements can be observed in **Table 1** below:

Considering **Table 1**, we assume that the interactive dance game is possibly the best task motivator among the utilized games. The main considerations which led to this assumption were the game simplicity and the displayed engagement during game sessions. Although physically demanding, dancing is a simple group activity which does not require children to overthink situations and which can help with their movement synchronization. By leveling toward low difficulty dance, or by allowing groups to select more difficult songs according to their desires, the games can reduce children's frustrations and ensure that more group members will engage with the play activity.

Game simplicity, flexibility, and high engagement rate indicated to be the main contributive aspects of games to children's posterior impressions and behavior in the group tasks. We must also point that, if children are going to perform a group task after playing a game, they would need to be equally engaging. Therefore, if group games are meant to be utilized as ice-breakers, a balance must be established regarding the time and engagement of the session: either the game needs to be short and simple enough to ensure a smooth transition for the cooperative task, or a good rest time must be ensured with the group. Carefully considering these matters will help to ensure that group game sessions are successful in building group trust with children while motivating them for the following tasks.

It is important to mention that the presented studies only observed immediate to short-term effects of games as ice-breakers to influence children's task impression and group behavior. That said, different study designs and purposes could point

Game element	Interactive blocks	Tower blocks	Dance game	References
Rules and goals	Complex	Simple	Simple	[11]
Difficulty level	Easy/Hard	Easy	Easy/Medium	[11]
Time length	20 minutes	5–10 minutes	5–10 minutes	Study observation
Assigned roles	Different	Same	Same	[17]
Flexibility of game task	No	No	Yes	Study observation
Encourage physical movements	No	No	Yes	[23, 29]
Cooperative or competitive focus	Cooperative			[21]
Individual or group evaluation	Group			[16, 17]

Table 1.
Observations between the three administered game sessions.

to different effects of the mentioned game elements. If, for example, we consider a more longitudinal relationship of group games in children's behavior, some of the elements considered negative for ice-breaking challenges, such as conflicts and frustrations with the difficulty, can be considered as natural important elements which should not be strictly avoided.

According to LaFreniere [30] and Piaget [31], dealing with these matters during natural free-play situations can help children to develop perspective taking and learn how to control their displayed emotions, better preparing them for possible conflicts in the future. Therefore, we also consider that, regardless of its design, group games can have positive effects on children's continuous cooperation development.

5. Conclusions: what does "Design for Interaction" mean for the future of interactive play tools

This chapter discussed differences and similarities between the "Interactive Design" and the "Design for Interactions" principles when applied to the development of new interactive/smart play tools for children. In short, "Interactive Design" has a focus on the facilitated interactions between the toy and the child facilitated with the adoption of modern feedback technology. "Design for Interactions," however, focuses on the social interactions a child can have with others when facilitated by different toys or artifacts. Although the application of modern technology is not mandatory for the design of interactive toys, this does not mean it should be neglected.

Modern day technology possesses a wide range of smart detectors and sensory feedback devices that can still be better explored in new toy designs. However, under the "design for interaction" principle, technology should not be the main attraction of a toy but should rather assume a supporting role for encouraging children's social relationships. When giving the focus to social relationships, we can go beyond isolated experiences between the child and the play artifact, helping them establish meaningful bonds that can support the development of different social skills, such as cooperation.

We proceeded by introducing selected case studies which were designed to observe children's group behavior and task engagement after playing different ice-breaking group games. The games were mediated in different moments by technological and traditional toys, but technology integration did not indicate to be the main influencing factor of children's group interactions. Instead, some identified social game elements indicated to have stronger effects. Among them are the complexity of the game rules, the game difficulty, the time length, and the attribution of group roles during play activity.

While these game elements were directly manipulated by the authors of this research, they also represent possible technology integration points. Current technology can allow the adjustment of game elements (e.g., difficulty, goals, or time length) and of sensory feedback (e.g., light intensity and color, sounds, or vibrations). For promoting different interactions, modern play tools could then automatically manipulate some of these elements, recommending flexible choices for children to play according to their different inputs and group formations.

The design for interaction guidelines together with the results found in the presented studies reinforces how games should be carefully designed with social interactions in mind. Further studies are necessary to investigate both immediate and longitudinal effects of specific game elements on children's social development. With traditional playground environments serving as examples, a well-established toy or game that can promote different interactions among children is more likely to have a longer life-spam and more thoroughly aid on their personal growth.

Therefore, the main challenge for designing interactive play tools lies in researchers successfully identifying children's dynamic interaction patterns together with designers and engineers successfully developing new technologies and artifacts to support these interactions. These open paths not only for new research lines but also for the development of ideal play tools to support childhood.

Author details

Rodrigo Fernandes* and Toshimasa Yamanaka
University of Tsukuba, Tsukuba, Japan

*Address all correspondence to: rqk.fernandes@gmail.com

References

[1] Malinverni L, Burguès NP. The medium matters: The impact of full-body interaction on the socio-affective aspects of collaboration. In: Proceedings of the 14th International Conference on Interaction Design and Children. ACM; 2015

[2] Santer J, Griffiths C. Free play in early childhood: A literature review. National Children's Bureau; 2007

[3] Y-h L, Ma M-y, W-c L. The study on playability of toys for children based on different temperaments. In: KEER2014 Proceedings of the 5th Kanesi Engineering and Emotion Research; International Conference. Linköping; Sweden: Linköping University Electronic Press; 2014

[4] Hiniker A, Lee B, Kientz JA, Radesky JS. Let's play: Digital and analog play between preschoolers and parents. In: Proceedings of the 2018 CHI Conference on Human Factors in Computing Systems. ACM; 2018

[5] Hermawati D, Rahmadi FA, Sumekar TA, Winarni TI. Early electronic screen exposure and autistic-like symptoms. Intractable & Rare Diseases Research. 2018;7(1):69-71. DOI: 10.5582/irdr.2018.01007

[6] Robinson TN, Banda JA, Hale L, Lu AS, Fleming-Milici F, Calvert SL, et al. Screen media exposure and obesity in children and adolescents. Pediatrics. 2017;**140**(Supplement 2):S97-S101

[7] Canadian Paediatric Society, Digital Health Task Force. Screen time and young children: Promoting health and development in a digital world. Paediatrics & Child Health. 2017;**23**(1):83. DOI: 10.1093/pch/pxx197

[8] van Delden R. Towards a socially adaptive digital playground. In: Proceedings of the 11th International Conference on Interaction Design and Children. ACM; 2012

[9] Merriam-webster, Definition of Interactive [Internet]. 2018. Available from: https://www.merriam-webster.com/dictionary/interactive [Accessed: 01-01-2019]

[10] Cagiltay K, Kara N, Aydin CC. Smart toy based learning. In: Handbook of Research on Educational Communications and Technology. New York: Springer-Verlag; 2014. pp. 703-711. Available from: https://www.springer.com/jp/book/9781461431848

[11] Sturm J, Bekker T, Groenendaal B, Wesselink R, Eggen B. Key issues for the successful design of an intelligent, interactive playground. In: Proceedings of the 7th International Conference on Interaction Design and Children. ACM; 2008

[12] Soler-Adillon J, Ferrer J, Parés N. A novel approach to interactive playgrounds: The interactive slide project. In: Proceedings of the 8th international Conference on interaction Design and Children. ACM; 2009

[13] Zhao S, Lehman J, Israr A, Klatzky R. Using haptic inputs to enrich story listening for young children. In: Proceedings of the 14th International Conference on Interaction Design and Children. ACM; 2015

[14] Corbett BA, Muscatello RA, Blain SD. Impact of sensory sensitivity on physiological stress response and novel peer interaction in children with and without autism spectrum disorder. Frontiers in Neuroscience. 2016;**10**:278

[15] Merriam-webster, Definition of Interactive [Internet]. 2018. Available from: https://www.merriam-webster.com/dictionary/interaction [Accessed: 01-01-2019]

[16] Takashi, M. Design for Children's Creativity Development: the seven perspectives (Japanese). Kids Design Association [Internet]. 2016. Available from: http://www.kidsdesign.jp/cat31/vol14/index.html [Accessed: 01-01-2019]

[17] Hendrix K, van Herk R, Verhaegh J, Markopoulos P. Increasing children's social competence through games, an exploratory study. In: Proceedings of the 8th International Conference on Interaction Design and Children. ACM; 2009

[18] Duerr Evaluation Resources. Research paper: The Benefits of Playgrounds for Children aged 0-5 [internet]. 2xxx. Available from: http://www.imaginationplayground.com/images/content/2/9/2999/the-benefits-of-playgrounds-for-children-aged-0-5.pdf [Accessed: 01-01-2019]

[19] Goh DH, Ang RP, Tan HC. Strategies for designing effective psychotherapeutic gaming interventions for children and adolescents. Computers in Human Behavior. 2008;**24**(5):2217-2235

[20] Nottingham Trent University. Icebreakers Guide (Internet). 2017. Available from: https://www4.ntu.ac.uk/adq/document_uploads/running_a_course/187450.pdf [Accessed: 01-01-2019]

[21] Creighton S, Szymkowiak A. The effects of cooperative and competitive games on classroom interaction frequencies. Procedia-Social and Behavioral Sciences. 2014;**140**:155-163

[22] Pellegrini AD. The Role of Play in Human Development. USA: Oxford University Press; 2009

[23] Suzuki K, Kyoya M, Kamatani T, Uchiyama T. beacon: Embodied sound media environment for socio-musical interaction. In: NIME. 2008

[24] Fernandes R, Koyama S, Kawaguchi I, Yamanaka T. Interactive games effects on children's affective cooperation: Evaluating cooperation through kansei-based play and design sections. In: International Conference on Kansei Engineering & Emotion Research. Springer; 2018

[25] Fernandes R, Yamanaka T: The effect of group games on children's subsequent impressions of sketch tasks and on their design outcomes. International Journal of Affective Engineering. Special Issue on KEER 2018; 2019;**18**(2):49-58. DOI: 10.5057/ijae.IJAE-D-18-00011

[26] Anme T, Sugisawa Y, Shinohara R, Matsumoto M, Watanabe T, Tokutake K, et al. Validity and reliability of the interaction rating scale between children (IRSC) by using motion capture analysis of head movement. Public Health Research. 2012;**2**(6):208-212

[27] Interaction Design and Children Design Competition [internet]. 2017. Available from: http://idc-2018.org/research-design-competition/ [Accessed: 01-01-2019]

[28] Lergetporer P, Angerer S, Glätzle-Rützler D, Sutter M. Third-party punishment increases cooperation in children through (misaligned) expectations and conditional cooperation. Proceedings of the National Academy of Sciences of the United States of America. 2014;**111**(19):6916-6921

[29] White R. The Power of Play: A Research Summary on Play and Learning. St. Paul, Minnesota Children's Museum; 2012. https://www.childrensmuseums.org/images/MCMResearchSummary.pdf

[30] LaFreniere P. Children's play as a context for managing physiological arousal and learning emotion regulation. Psychological Topics. 2013;**22**(2):183-204

[31] Piaget J. The Moral Judgment of the Child. London: Kegan Paul, Trench, Trubner and Co.; 1932. ISBN 0-02-92-52-40-7

Chapter 4

Interactive Multimedia Touch Screen Tablets and Gaming as a Vehicle That Fosters Learning Digital Skills

Borka Jerman Blažič and Andrej Jerman Blažič

Abstract

As digital multimedia devices further pervade the lives of everybody including the older adults, the need for relevant training for these age groups of people grows. Older adults, not due to their frailty or age, but because accessing and using digital devices like smart phones can be difficult for them due to a lack of digital skills required in use of multimedia devices, do experience the digital divide sharply. This paper intends to present the use of gaming on touch screen multimedia devices in learning digital skills for the elderly. The case study was carried out with a group of older adults in four European countries with multimedia tablets before they attended the training process for learning how to use smartphones. A parallel group was not exposed to the same devices and the tablet game playing. The comparative results from both groups have shown that gaming on multimedia devices improves the skills necessary for active use of digital skills in everyday life and foster their adoption.

Keywords: gaming, older adults, education, training, digital skills

1. Introduction

As nowadays digitalization is permeating all sectors and everyday life, citizens require more digital skills to participate in modern society, manage their lives and advance their professional careers. According to the factsheet of EU-based facts presented at the Digital Summit in 2017, 44% of the European population lacks even basic digital skills, although in the near future 9 out of 10 jobs will require digital competence. It is moreover predicted that in 2020 the Information and Communication Technology sector in Europe will face a lack of 500,000 experts. Despite the improvements in data and the clear commitment on the political side, Europe still lacks the digitally-skilled citizens needed to fill the gaps. In addition, the problem with the older adult population seems to be even more crucial as only 55% of individuals aged 65 or older use the Internet, according to investigations reporting on the developments in some European countries [1], while around 80% of the entire European population uses the Internet [2]. The importance of digital skills among older adults rose in parallel with the new Internet-based services, such as e-health and others, with the purpose of extending their stay at home before they need to move to retirement homes. The problem of missing digital skills among older adults is related to the fact that older adults have no experience in using digital devices where the communication with the user most frequently uses an interface based on touchscreen technology. Among these devices, of major importance for older adults is the use of smartphones for social communication but also for the tasks of their everyday life. It is a well-known fact that social inclusion with the help of modern communication technology strengthens social contacts and reduces loneliness [3]. The problem of learning digital skills among older adults come from the way they have learned in their youth and from the feeling that they are outsiders to the digital culture. Older European adult citizens may either be retired or middle-aged, and they often lack the skills required to use the services accessible with modern smartphones or similar devices with touchscreen interfaces. Digital skills are increasingly required for performing instrumental tasks such as searching for contacts, medical help, measuring medical indicators in e-health services or paying bills, and taking part in democratic processes. To use them, older adults often visit public day centers where they can find assistance to perform even simple tasks. In EU 63% of the population is accessing internet via mobile phones and as a part of the access is the use of Digital Public services that are becoming important source of data, support and help. Measured by dimension indicators they show growth in 2017 in most of the EU countries, where Austria is among the leading, followed by Slovenia and UK [4].

In Europe, several initiatives were undertaken for overcoming this problem. Among them is the European Cooperation for innovation and the exchange of good practices dedicated to establishing cooperation between educations to exchange skill practices. The recently launched action known as Skill Agenda contains several initiatives that seek to improve the digital skills at all levels and among all citizens, with specific focus on older adults. One of the active projects that address the education for learning digital skills is the project GIRDA Gameplay foR Inspiring Digital Adoption from the ERASMUS+ program.

The work presented in this paper is aimed to provide another aspect and approach of learning digital skills by older adults by focusing on older adults with no prior experience with digital technology. These were offered game-playing on large tablets with touchscreen interfaces offering multi-media experience and touch screen use. The gaming was applied as an entertaining lessons prior the course for learning how to use smartphone.

This chapter provides an overview of the results and findings from the exploratory study carried out by the GIRDA partners. The focus of the study was on the use of an alternative learning approach expecting this to facilitate the adoption of digital literacy by older adults. At the same time, the study tried to find the underlying reasons for the older people's low pace in the adoption of the necessary digital skills and to prepare some guidelines for the mentors or instructors helping the learners in their effort to learn. The learning games offered to the groups of older adults were selected based on the different skills needed in game-playing. The study was carried out in four European countries, the UK, Austria, Slovenia and Macedonia, and the results were collected from 107 adults aged between 57 and 84, later elaborated, studied and compared. The country selection was based on the percentage of aged population in particular country and the portion of aged that used internet. UK and Austria have relatively high portion population with digital skills above basic e.g. 42% in UK and 35% in Austria. Slovenia portion of population is 27% and in Macedonia the number is even smaller (13%) [4]. The percentage of population of adults over 65 years in the EU population is between 16 and 18% in most of the EU countries, but the portion of this population that uses internet differ very much among the selected countries, from 63% in AT and UK, 43% in Slovenia and 21% in Macedonia.

The chapter briefly introduces the theoretical background of the research, the research setting, and the presentation of the findings accompanied by discussion and conclusion.

2. Theoretical background

A literature review on gaming by Connolly and co-workers [5] shows that different academic papers deal with the benefits of playing digital games, and that game-based learning "is used across many curricular areas, most notably in health, business, and social issues". It was found as well that the interest in games within a learning context is based on motivational reasons. Games seem to be "motivating and enjoyable" for the players. On the other hand, playing games can coincide with learning. This is true especially if the learnability property of the game is high [6]. Studies have found that cognitive abilities (knowledge creation, organization, and application) are mainly related to games that present solvable problems and challenges when used for obtaining a specific learning outcome. They are usually designed to be adaptable to the skills and the level of the learner's knowledge. The game-learning components associated with technical or motor skills are related to the game's attributes, known as the learner's participation and interaction, learner engagement, control and navigation [7]. Motivation has positive relations concerning the game's attributes that specify the goals and rules of the game, its fantasy component and the provision of specific feedback to the learner. Given the positive effects of gaming, older adults are considered a "great potential to accept" digital game-based learning [8].

Kaufmann also describes the motivational aspects and other additional benefits for older adults who play digital games, including the "mental experience", "dealing with loneliness or depression" or "developing confidence" [5]. Since playing digital games "does not require specific skills" [9], learners can start playing at a low competence level and can "gradually accumulate other types of skills while improving their gaming skills. However, the reported studies did not examine the effects of digital games on acquiring digital skills beyond the self-reporting of participants. The study presented below explored the effects of playing games on touchscreen tablets on the performance in using a smartphone after completing a training workshop, compared to another group of older adults without game experience in gaming on a touchscreen device.

Rather than testing existing assumptions about the behavior of older adults when facing digital technology, the decision was made to apply the Grounded theory as the theoretical background. According to several authors this theory is ideal for exploring integral social relationships and the behavior of a group of people where little exploration of the contextual factors that affect individual's lives are known. The Grounded Theory [10, 11] developed by Martin and Glaser in late 1970s enables exploratory studies to resolve different research questions, but equally importantly it allows to generate issues and questions during the ongoing investigation that may be answered after the experiment. The approach enables the simultaneous collection and analysis of data, the creation of analytic codes and categories developed from data without pre-existing conceptualizations. The theoretical sensitivity of the methods enables discovery of the basic social processes within the data, theoretical sampling to refine categories and writing analytical memos as the stage between coding and writing the integration of categories into a theoretical framework. The initial approach of the study was to look at categories related to the behavior of older adults toward digital technology, for example the emotions expressed by the participants during and after the gaming experiment. The type of the positive emotions that was supposed to formulate the categories was the pleasure when playing the game, increase in satisfaction and social interactions as the game-playing was conducted in pairs of older adults and among of a group from the same environment. The developed positive emotions were also expected to reduce the fear of older adults toward digital technology. It was planned data to be generated by coding the videotapes, by analyzing the post-experiment surveys, the processing of the questionnaire and by use of the data collected through the interviews carried out after the gaming sessions. The main research questions to be answered were:

a. Are there any issues or difficulties in learning and training digital skills for older adults when exposed to multimedia touch screen device that are specific for that group of learners?

b. Will older adults show positive emotions toward gaming?

c. Does population of older adults display any difference toward the adoption of digital technology depending on the local environment and the country where they live?

d. Do the skills acquired during gaming foster the adoption of digital skills required for access to digital services by smartphone devices or have other effects?

e. Is the training in smartphone use and the effectiveness in task performance influenced by the skills acquired by playing games on a touchscreen tablet?

f. Will older adults change their resistance toward digital technology?

National survey data from EU member states shows [12] that older non-users are not willing to explain their behavior and lack of interest in modern digital technology. This position is not necessarily straightforward as the lack of interest may obscure some other underlying lack. That was the reason why the approach of the Grounded theory was used to collect data from the interviews, and the questionnaire was expected to provide some insight into this issue.

The most commonly used methods recommended by the authors and practitioners of this theory are interviews based on open-ended questions that can be modified during the ongoing research. The second method is an observation of the focus group by deriving the coding and identifying the issues. Then an analytical method is used to analyze the collected data from the open coding analysis and the interviews with participants [11].

3. The study design

3.1 The experiment setting

The study design was based on two study phases: experiments with focus groups of older adults who played games, and the training courses for smartphone device use that followed after the playing sessions. In the second experiment, the participants were divided in two groups, a group that played games for 45 minutes before the course started compared to the second group that took the same training course but did not play games before the training course. Several games were used as a learning tool for developing and practicing skills critical for using touchscreen technology, for example, to tap, drag, rotate objects on the screen and moving objects. Besides the game properties known to enable the development of cognitive and motor skills along with participation and interaction, some additional criteria were considered when selecting the games, such as the familiarity from the 'real world' (card games, crossword puzzles and jigsaw puzzles, chess, and backgammon). Regarding the previous knowledge of the participants, the study team decided to select participants without any skills in playing games on touchscreen devices and with no knowledge or practice in using computers.

The study was designed as two-player games on a touch-table device (basically giant tablets, e.g. the Lenovo table, see **Figure 1**). The introduction to touchscreen functionality for older adult learners was made in an immersive low-pressure environment within a group from the same environment where the fact that participants were learning was actually 'hidden'. Older adults were invited to an "entertainment session". The Lenovo touch table used in the study offered a selection of pre-installed games that can support up from one to four people playing simultaneously. However, it was decided that the games would be played by pairs of older adults of the same gender or mixed genders and, if possible, from the same environment. Exploring the diverse range of game categories available on a Windows touchscreen device presented certain challenges to the study group as the wrong selection could be off-putting for new users trying to find their way in using the screen functionality. Another important criterion in game selection was the game to create [13] a non-stressful, enjoyable path to learning cognitive and acquiring motor skills. This implied game types that do not present a too heavy cognitive burden for the learner, as this usually distracts from the skill-learning process. The same applies to games with a complex set of rules that may burden the player's working memory. Popular games on the market were found to be overly sophisticated; 'educational' games are aimed at pre-school and primary school age children, while 'adult games' were found to be inappropriate for this type of experiment. More useful were the genres which included puzzles, board games, and casual games.

The decision was made that the first game to be introduced to the participants should use a basic drag action as an introductory lesson for using a touchscreen device. The drawing game was selected first as the most appropriate for users who had no experience with touchscreen technology or any other type of computer games before. The simple drawing tool in the game repertoire was selected as an introductory element so that the participants could have a first experience of just touching the tablet and getting an immediate visual result – be it a fingerprint-sized dot, a line, a house or a ship. The drawing game allows users to change the color using the tablet keys. The second game introduced the rotate action and the moving of objects on the screen; this was a puzzle game that requires from the players to complete the image. Puzzles are popular entertaining games, and the idea was that

Figure 1.
The puzzle game.

not much explanation would be needed for playing a simple puzzle game. However, this game enabled learning other skills, moving, rotating in dragging objects to come into the right position to assemble the image. The third game was selected from the list of games with in-situ judgment, such as the very popular heavy-traffic road crossing game known as Crossy Road. Another game selected was the Candy Crush game. In Crossy Road the player is moving an object across very busy roads, while trying to prevent the object from being crushed under fast-moving vehicles. If the crash happens before the object can reach the other side of the last road, the game closes and starts again. This game focuses on coordination of the vision/ recognition and motor activity of the player fingers. The Candy Crush game involves very short distance drag actions similar to the Crossy Road game. The actions often cause rapid system responses that are out of proportion with the input actions. This rapidity undermines the second participant's ability to observe and take in the active user's behavior. The pace of action is similar to the Crossy Road game. The selected games proved to be useful in identifying the key variations and their pros and cons of learning how to act on a tablet's touchscreen. The second phase of the experiment focused on the two groups of older adults who have enrolled in a training course for learning how to use a smartphone. The experiment was carried out in cooperation with Simbioza Genesis institution which maintains an inter-generation center in Ljubljana. Over the course of 5 years, they have connected more than 15,000 older adults and 9000 young people from all over Slovenia in a pan-Slovenian campaign of computer and Internet literacy [14]. In the last 2 years, Simbioza has developed a model for teaching older adults how to use a smartphone. Other countries participating in the experiment have set up similar cooperation with institution working with elderly e.g. in UK that was the Good Things Foundation which is responsible for managing the UK Online Centers Network for older adults with over 5000 community centers and a learning platform known under the name My Way, which supports over 2 million people. In Austria that was the Association for Older Adults in Upper Austria, in Slovenia and Macedonia cooperation was set up retirement homes. One half of the smartphone course participants were offered to play the same games as in the first experiment for 45 minutes on the Lenovo big tablet each day before they started the lessons that were spread over 1 month twice a week. At the end of the course each attendee was asked to answer the questionnaire which included the same questions as for groups of older adults in the first phase of the experiment; then they were asked to perform five different tasks specified by the mentors on the smartphone. The tasks are presented below. The same tasks were given to both participating groups - the group that had no experience in playing games on tablets and the second group that played games before the lessons in smartphone use.

The tasks were as follows

1. We would like you to apply for financial social assistance to the on-line Social Service. You do not know how to do it, so you need first to contact the Social Work Center. Find the appropriate public service to find a contact through the web.

2. The course mentor sent you as enroller a reminder about the terms of the course. You have found out that you will not be able to come at some of the course specified terms. Write an SMS as an apology to the mentor.

3. You have many interesting pictures in your phone's gallery. We would like you to send some of them as Multimedia Messages e.g. videos or photos of your close relatives. Open the gallery or photo/video application and select file you prefer to be sent and send it to the specified telephone number.

4. You would like to borrow a book from a nearby library. You need to know the address of the library so that you know how to go and reach the library. Find the address of the library closest unit in your area of living.

5. Today is Wednesday, and on Friday you would like to go on a trip to the neighboring hills or touristic spot. It worries you that the weather will be bad. Find a forecast for Friday by using the application on your smartphone.

3.2 The demography

The age of the participants ranged from 57 to 87. Most of them had no previous experiences with digital technology, as for the experiment novices were requested to form the groups. The level of participant's education ranged from high school up to the master's degree. Some of the participants had weaknesses in some of their motor abilities, and this governed the way data were collected after each of the completed sessions. The learners played the game in pairs. They were expected to collaborate in helping each other – a socializing effect enriched by the other members of the particular group present during the experiment. The presence of witnesses, i.e. friends interested in the gaming, is usually considered a key dynamic of co-learning. Participants take clues from watching the partner interact with the system and the consequent system response. One of the study tasks was to observe how people interacted with each other as well as with the technology, and how the choice of game or activity influenced the changes in these interactions.

In the UK, the participants were selected with assistance with Good Things Foundation. The emphasis for the UK team was to involve in the experiment older people close to retirement, or post-retirement, from socially deprived areas. Most of the UK participants (40 persons) were from the west of England, Stockport, while the other selected group came from the London area with the help from a local group supporting isolated women (20 persons). The participants in the Slovenian part of the study were recruited from three retirement homes in Ljubljana, Slovenia (Bokalce, DEOS Črnuče and Kolezija (30 persons)) and from two other retirement homes in the Velenje region in the north-eastern part of Slovenia, also retired people (30 persons). The Austrian participants were selected with assistance from the Association for Older Adults in Upper Austria (26 persons). The Macedonian and Slovenian team approached retirement homes that involved group of 60 persons in each of the countries that took part in the experiments. The groups of older adults who attended the smartphone training course consisted of 30 people aged from 55 to 75 years. Both genders were present, 18 men and 12 women; both groups had little or no prior experience with touchscreens. The first group was asked to play games on the giant touchscreen tablets with the same selection of games as in the first experiment, for 45 minutes before the training course started; the second group entered directly to the training lessons in smartphone use without contact with the gaming tablet.

4. Data collection and analysis

4.1 First part of the experiment

Video recording was made of each session for each group in the four European countries. The videos were analyzed with an aim to examine the problems encountered by older adults in maneuvering on the touchscreen and the cases of required help and support from the facilitators. After each session, the participants in each of the groups that took part in the experiment were asked one by one to take part in an interview with the facilitators and the members of the study group. They were also asked to complete the questionnaire with the same number of questions. The questions were developed according to guidelines for qualitative research in psychology.

The analysis that followed was based on the coding generated from the videos focused on finding answers and information about potential obstacles for building digital skills. Identification of the specific needs of older adults in learning and adopting digital technology was one of the objectives of the carried analysis. In addition, an input in developing mentor guidelines to support the learning of older adults was sought. Examples that illustrate this approach can be summarized as: do the participants experienced any difficulties in applying the motoric skills necessary to act on the touch screen, how strong was the players' immersion in the games (obtained from the facilitator's observation), was collaboration among the pairs present and was it seen as a support in solving the game. The analysis of the video data presented in Appendix A with one coding example from the experiment carried out in Slovenia showed that the learning hindrances experienced by the participants could be summarized as three types of actions required by the participants:

- Request for support from the mentor in cases when the game appeared to be locked,
- Support/help provided by the mentor in cases the touch screen did not reacted to the participant move, and
- A request for help from the gaming partner.

These actions usually followed a failure of motor control over the tablet and in cases of errors, such as the change of color, fixing the tablet in the expected position or re-activating the game in case of failure. In the case of Candy Crush and Crossy Road errors, the request for support most frequently happened when the participant misunderstood the rules of the game. However, in playing the whole set of games, supportive activities among the pairs and the witnessing members of the group were noticed as well as several examples of progress acknowledged by the accompanying persons. Both independent and cooperative activities were noticed as well as enjoyment and engagement in the game playing. The qualitative uses of the post-test interviews were meant to provide information about the emotions the participants felt [15]. The data collected from the conversation with each participant indicate that most of them (82%) described the action as pleasant and full of fun. However 18% found the gaming somehow tiresome. The most enjoyed game was the puzzle, followed by the drawing game. Crossy Road was somehow tiresome for some of them and maybe demanding due to the required speed of action and coordination of vision, cognition of the scene and the motor skills required for successful playing. Most of them (75%) said that they do not find the use of the touchscreen difficult; the other part (25%) declared that they had encountered some difficulties especially in the Crossy Road and Candy Crush games due to the speed required in moving the object. An important finding was that most of them (95%) did not experience any physical discomfort in using their fingers to play the games. The same results were obtained from the assessment of the feelings experienced and developed toward the novelty of the technology used and the attraction of playing games on a touchscreen table. Most of the participants did not find that playing games was difficult (80%) and the attractiveness of the approach was also assessed as high (90% of the participants agreed that the gaming was attractive).

The participants declared that they would describe this experience to others as fun and good entertainment. The collaboration – playing as a pair and with group support was also accepted positively by most of the participants.

The collected data from the post-test questionnaire was analyzed further with the similar aim as with the interviews: to reveal how older adults react and accept the new digital touchscreen technology, do they accept gaming as a way for learning and if is a fear from technology still present when they are faced with the use of digital devices after the experiment with the touchscreen gaming. Selections of processed data from all involved countries are presented in Appendix B and the sample of the coding of videos on Appendix A. The answers to the fifth question that asked if the participants had any fear in facing the touchscreen are not presented as the participants reported that no fear was felt at all. In general, the entire experiment was assessed by the participants as a very positive experience. Some participants asked will there be a second session with the same technology and the same facilitators. One of the main finding from the study was that the older adults from different countries regarding the level of digital technology use by elderly expressed very common attitudes e.g. No fear and readiness to learn through gaming and having fun was declared by the participants. The answers about the enjoyment they experienced when playing games were distributed between „strongly agree "and „agree "with the fun provided with the gaming. The Macedonian group responded with only „strongly agree "answer to this question. The same observation was found for the second answer from the questionnaire „ I have learned something about using a touch screen" which confirmed by majority of the participants. The statement "I would be interested in playing more games" got the highest positive answers in the UK and Macedonia (only "strongly agree" and "agree"). The answers from participants in Austria and Slovenia were more dispersed, however highest number of positive answers were still given to "strongly agree" and "agree." The statement „I now feel more positive about using digital systems after this "was approved in all four countries with the answers "strongly agree" and "agree." The chart from these data is presented in Appendix B. As a summary of the collected and analyzed data, it can be stated that older adults have developed positive emotions toward playing computer games on a large touch screen tablet.

4.2 The second part of the experiment

The data collected by measuring the timing and the success in performing each of the five tasks (specified in Section 3.1.) The members of the two groups of older adults who attended the one-month training course showed remarkable differences in the performance of the specified tasks. Both groups were smaller as there were 16 learners; each group consisted of 8 learners. The members of the first group played the same games on the same tablets as the learners in the first part of the experiment. The playing was arranged before the lessons for use of smartphone. This group displayed much more performance and skill in completing the complex tasks specified in Section 3.1 after the course was finished. The tasks were completed correctly by the group one learners, the required results/information specified in the tasks were obtained, and the timing for completing the task was much shorter compared to the timing required for tasks competition in the other group that did not played games. The first and the fifth tasks were simple and the differences in the efficiency of performing the tasks by the particular learner from both groups did not differ very much. The average timing for the members of both groups was close to 1 minute (0.58) for the first task and 0.3 minutes (0.23) for the fifth one. However, the differences among the timings of the more complex tasks, e.g. the task no. 2, 3 and 4 were remarkable. The average timing for task 2 was

1.196 minutes for the group that practiced gaming and 3.471 for the other group that did not payed games, task 3 required for successful task completion by the gaming group 1.178 minutes and in 2.272 minutes by the group without gaming experience, and task 4 required 0.492 minute for the gaming group and 1.16 minute for the control group. This gaming group performed the task no. 2 three times faster, the task no. 3 twice faster, and the task no. 4 1.4-times faster. This gaming group was interviewed as well and asked to answer the same questions in the questionnaire as the older adults participating in the first experiment. The collected data give additional positive insights about the role of game playing on touchscreen tablets for the adoption of digital skills by older adults.

5. Discussion

In most cases, the foundations of being a good user, meaning to develop trust, self-efficacy and perceived value, is growing slowly and steadily without anyone giving the matter much thought, often well before someone, for example a child, starts learning in a particular case. By the time the person is 17, s/he can easily understand the benefit of learning to drive as this helps the mobility. The person is also well aware of the risks of driving but also knows how they can be mitigated.

However, these learning foundations are often absent when it comes to non-users of digital technology, as several studies [3] proved that is very hard to teach them using the general 'show and tell' system. The first step – going from being a complete non-user to an engaged newbie – is the steepest process in the new digital area according to Häikiö [15], The challenge for digital inclusion practitioners is to ensure that the training for new users is fun, social and risk-free, while still building vital interface skills and encouraging experimentation and self-guided learning by the learner. Research shows that these factors are especially important for older learners, for whom the opportunity to play with digital technology helps to capture interest and build confidence [16]. These findings were confirmed in the presented study as well. However, some specific issues were noticed too.

In the studied sessions and the observation found in the described experiments show that almost all participants adopted the touch interaction method easily regardless of their motor skills. Evidence from the experiments presented above suggests also that the 'right' game depends on a number of factors, and that perhaps in this type of learning the mentors or facilitators would benefit from a diagnostic tool that will provide guidance in selecting games based on players' attitudes, skill levels and relationships with their partners. Most of the participants in the above studies understood the games easily, and some outperformed the others especially in playing the second game – the Koala puzzle. All of them were capable of drawing a figure on the tablet and changing colors; however, several trials were necessary to touch the right place on the screen and perform the right move. The differences in the flow observed among the participants might be attributed to the fact that the players with some motor weaknesses seemed to encounter more problems when interacting with the Crossy Road game (see **Figure 2**), as the game requires fast reactions with the finger. Immersion in the game was present as well. Collaboration among the players, coming both from the partner in the pair or from the group that gave loud advice how to act on the tablet, was very noticeable and in general it was supportive. Some of the participants were first watching before they actively entered the game. Observations during the sessions suggested that the cognitive load of managing the session sometimes required more than one facilitator. Altogether these findings came from the participants' observations, but also from the data collected from the interviews and the closed questionnaire. Despite the age-related cognitive and physical changes, all participants were able to play and to understand the questions in the questionnaire. More research regarding the test criteria, such as the reliability and internal consistency of the study, seems to be necessary especially when further learning is in place, like for example in the second part of the experiment with smartphone use courses.

The coding of the video clips from the playing sessions revealed the problems older adults face when they try to use the digital touchscreen technology for the first time. The facilitator and partners usually provided support after a learner sought help. Depending on the problem, they usually decided to use explanation, demonstration or instruction as support methods. Questioning as a method for helping people to continue the task was used also several times by the facilitator. The analysis of the video tapes has shown that the given support was not always correct, and this points to the need for experienced facilitators and good guidelines or a specially developed manual. However, overall supportive activities in most cases were appropriate, and the participants were usually able to continue the task successfully. The same problem re-occurred quite often after the facilitator's support and help was sought again, but the majority of the participants did not give up the gaming and they continued to play.

The analysis of these situations identified the following issues that need consideration:

- Failure in motor control
- Expected encouragement from the facilitator – the need for support
- Co-learning by the playing partners was expected but not always requested

These issues point out clearly that for older adults to adopt digital technology, but it is obvious that more attention should be provided by the facilitators who are supporting the learning or training of older adults. These people also need more information about the needs of older adults and instructions about how to solve problems that appear from the low motor skills and sometimes with the lower cognition capability or vision capacity of the learners. Their support should be given in the form of explaining, demonstrating, and instructing. Cooperation and social interaction by friends or family were found to be equally important [17]. These findings provide answers to the first research question. Yes, older adults need additional attention in preparing the environment and in terms of support during educational sessions dedicated to the adoption of digital skills.

Figure 2.
The Crossy Road game.

The interviews with the participants in both parts of the experiment have shown that acceptance of new digital systems is not a problematic issue for older adults. However, there were obstacles when an explanation how to handle some game hint was not immediately provided to the players by the support team. The coding of video tapes has revealed the problem. Some participants were afraid to make mistakes or to fail when using the devices and hesitated to act when the other person in the plying pair faced a problem. Social influence was welcomed, but it expected to be positive and helpful in the training. The accomplishment of the game also appeared to be more important for older people than a low effort as was found also by AlMahmud et al. [18] . These findings give a positive answer to the second research question: In our experiments, older adults have shown positive emotions toward gaming.

The answers to the questions in the questionnaire further confirmed the findings from the video tape analysis. Selections of the processed data from all countries involved in the experiment are presented in Appendix B. In general, the entire experiment was assessed by the participants as a very positive experience. Some participants asked will there be a second session with the same technology and the same facilitators. The charts in Appendix B show that the older adults from the countries studied have very common and similar attitudes toward new challenges and the possibility to learn through gaming and having fun as no big differences were found. The results from the second experiment served to find the answers to the research questions (d) and (e). The more efficient performance of the tasks displayed by the members of the gaming group clearly has shown that playing games could be a very useful tool in facilitating the training of digital skills for older adults for using of smartphones. Fun experiences during game-playing clearly help in faster and more successful learning to use a digital device which leads to faster adoption as well. The reported fun older adults had when playing games contributes to the development of positive emotions toward digital technology as this approach helps in removing fear from not being able to participate in modern society.

6. Concluding remarks

It is well known that to become a proficient user of anything, some absolute essentials are needed. Each person needs easy and regular access to the thing/device to be used, as s/he needs to develop the skills required for the effective use of it. But having that access and learning those skills are not of much use if there is no trust in the items that are used, and if the user does not have faith in his/her abilities to use them, or simply does not see the point. Just like any other skill, these internal conditions are not innate, and there are many factors that influence the degree to which someone possesses them and likes them, as they can be nurtured and grown with the right kind of support. The big difference from the classical teaching of digital inclusion is that games on touchscreen tablets can be very appealing, entertaining and incredibly easy to learn. In the case of the training of older adults, they need to be accommodated in order to for answer to the elderly specific needs. In fact, the easier and more familiar they are, the better for the elderly learner, at least to begin with. The rules for learning this type of games are not the rules of the game itself or for winning the game, but the rules of how to interact with a digital device. However, we can state here that the value of the approach in learning digital skills for older adults was confirmed by the presented experiment where gaming was used as a pre-learning activity in the smartphone use course for older adults. The group that played games before the course has shown a remarkably better efficiency in performing the more complex tasks required for interacting with digital services with use of a smartphone. This additionally implies that the gaming approach for older adults by means of touchscreen tablets needs to be further developed with approaches that accommodate the learning to the elderly specific needs. This applies especially for the process when mentors, facilitators or other persons involved select the most appropriate game that enables to equally practice both motor and cognitive skills. Playing and learning as a social activity is another dimension that should be further supported in learning digital skills by elderly, as the presented experiments have shown. A clear notice about the progress in learning digital skills by applying playing games as entertaining activity appeared to be an important property of the strategy applied in enhancing the learning of digital skills for older adults.

The study presented has some limitations and the source of this is the selection and the number of participants. It was envisaged that the number of participants from each country should be 60, which would make a total sum of 240 people. However, the final number was lower due to the difficulties in attracting relevant participants by the focus group that carried the experiments. So the total number was lower. Another limitation was the social status of the participant and the level of education that was not questioned. The only request followed was the lack of any experience in work with computers or similar technology. Further studies similar to the one presented in this paper are needed for more evidence to be collected for provision of e more complete answers to the research questions addressing the inclusion of elderly in the digital society and the erasing the digital divide between the young and the old.

It can be claimed that the study carried out in the context of the Gameplay for Inspiring Digital Adoption (GIRDA) project has considered most of the aspects of modern learning of digital technology by elderly. Older adults need to know how to use modern devices such as smartphones, to stay socialized and to enjoy the advantages of modern technology specially designed to help them when aging or to enable stay and live at home as long as possible. Many e-health applications nowadays are developed for older adults but their use and the benefits they bring depend on the users' digital skills and the understanding of the service offered. Playing games on a touchscreen table is obviously one of the methods to help them to acquire these skills more easily and in a friendly manner. Learning without knowing that the person learns is simply more acceptable as it is an easy way to adopt what is needed in the present and future digital world. However, further studies can contribute more the digital divide to become more noticeable. The future rounds of data collection by additional experiments and analysis should be aimed on the understanding of the optimum setup for this kind of r learning, and to the selection of games that will yield the best results. We hope that in future there will be opportunities to use this evidence to create tailor-made games that can develop the touch screen interface skills and help older learners to overcome the lack of confidence and a feeling that using touchscreen computers is risky and complicated.

However, the presented study provided some implication for the practice that can be summarized in the following recommendations:

- Teaching practices examples from the study about how to respond appropriately to older adult computer issues.
- Putting time and effort into selecting the best facilitators is vital to building good working relationships between older adults, facilitators, and staff.
- Reassuring older adults that they are progressing with often complex computer software applications is a vital strategy in encouraging them to persist with learning and training the digital skills.

A. Coding sample from the drawing game video tape

Issue/problems	Frequency	Description
Methods of motor control	2	Most of the learners used the index finger of the right hand for drawing and tapping.
		Learner switches between the index finger of the right hand and the thumb of the left hand (06_720,00:06:48)
Failure of motor control	3	Problems appeared in color changes as the learners did not use the exact button on the Lenovo tablet. Swiping the toolbar not possible.
		Learner tries to swipe but cannot activate the button (12_710, 00:03:02) (10_720, 00:05:01),
		• Tapping not exact enough.
		Learner wants to choose a color but does not tap exactly enough so it does not work (10_700, 00:05:11)
		Learner uses the fingernail for drawing; no results were produced (10_710, 00:03:16)
Errors	2	This issue is triggered by different reasons which are all related to the usage of the tablet:

B. Data from the post-experiment questionnaire

B.1 Austria data

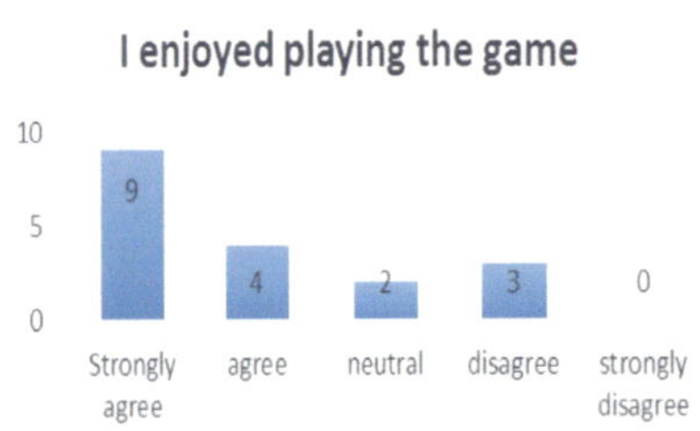

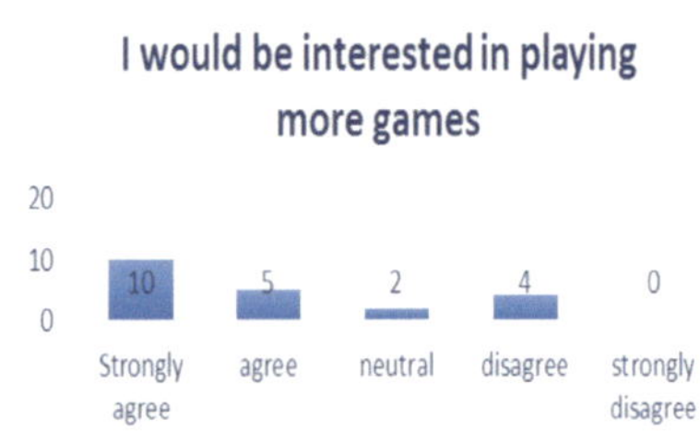

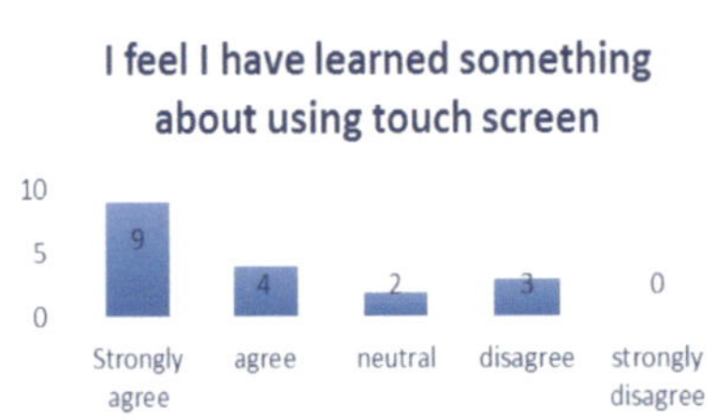

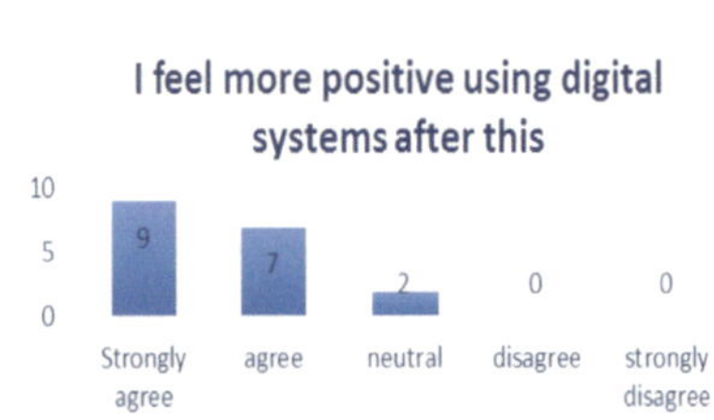

B.2 United Kingdom data

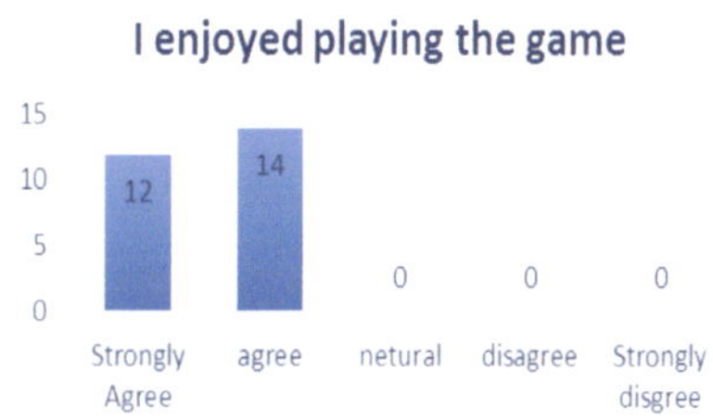

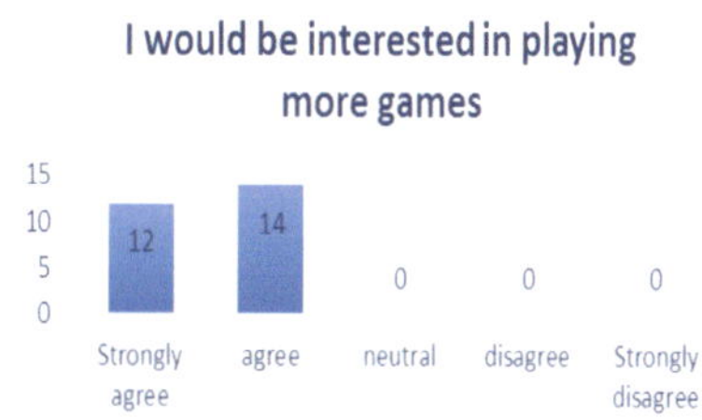

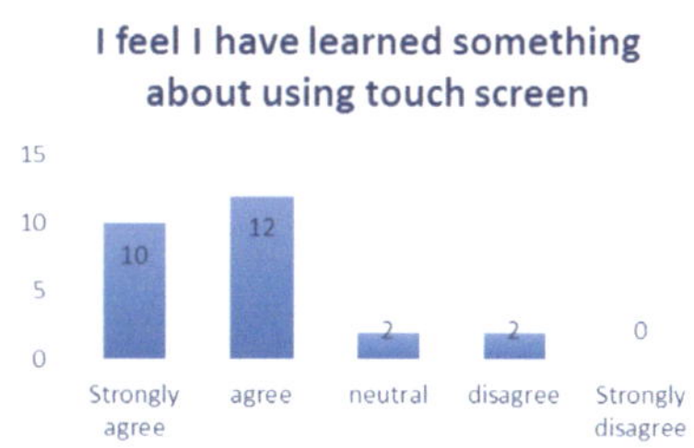

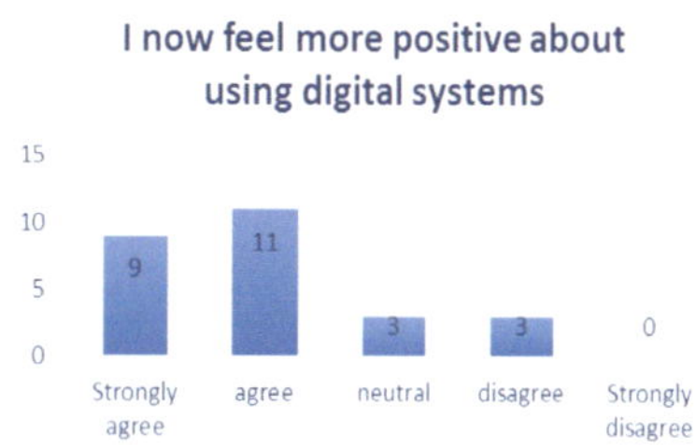

B.3 FYR Macedonia data

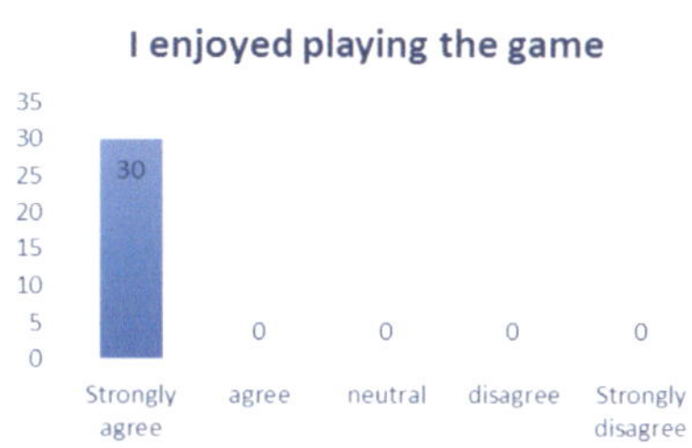

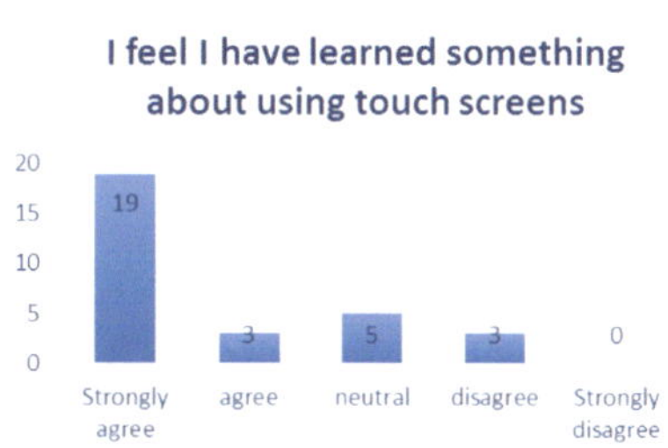

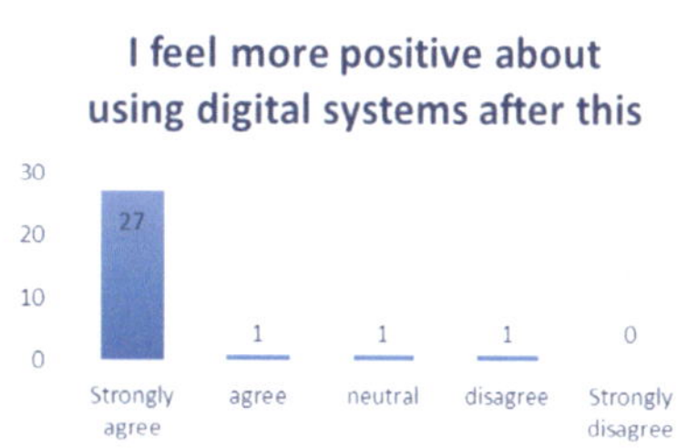

B.4 Slovenia data

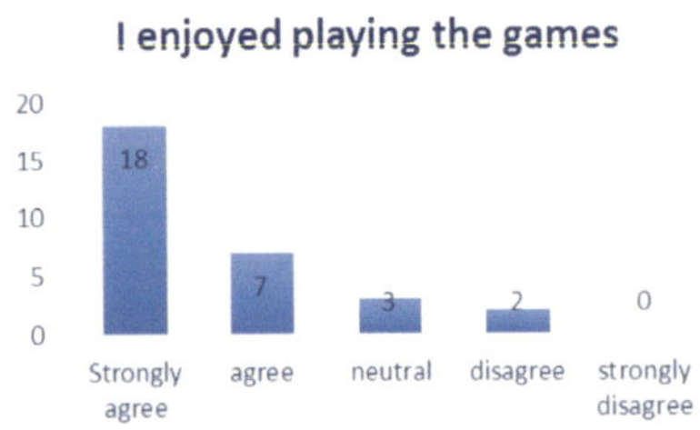

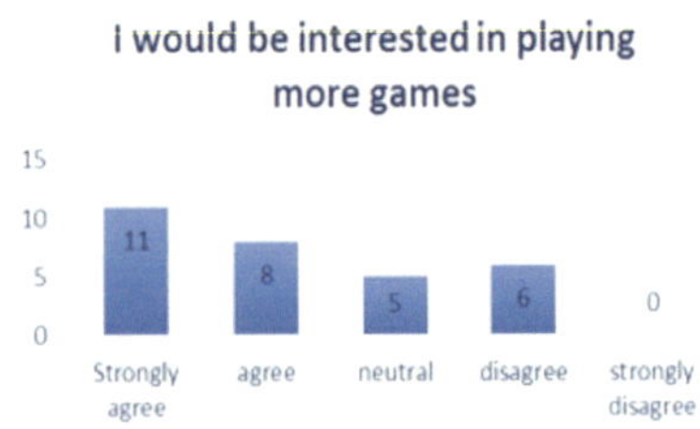

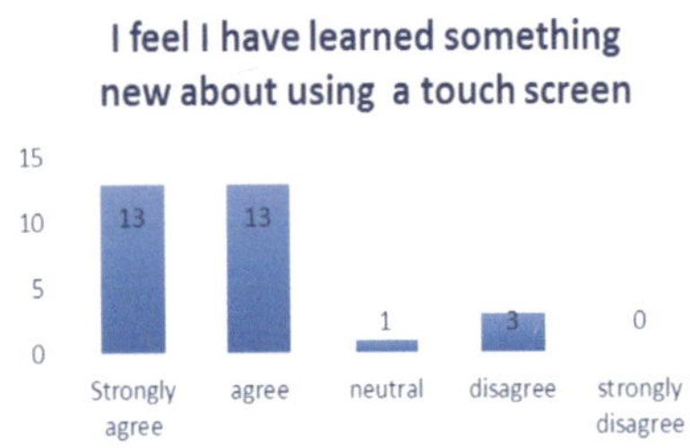

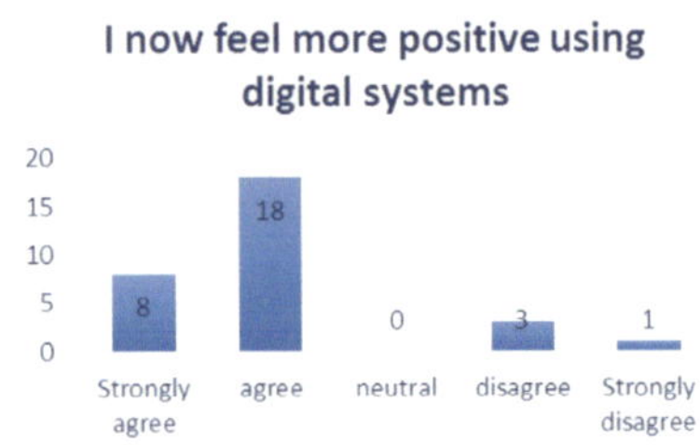

Author details

Borka Jerman Blažič* and Andrej Jerman Blažič
International Postgraduate School, Jožef Stefan Institute, Ljubljana, Slovenia

*Address all correspondence to: borka@e5.ijs.si

References

[1] Eurostat 2016 A. Digital economy and society statistics—Households and individuals. https://ec.europa.eu/eurostat/statisticsexplained/index.php/Digital_economy_and_society_statistics_households_and_individuals [Accessed: 5.8.2018]

[2] Eurostat 2016 B. A look at the life of the elderly in the EU today. https://ec.europa.eu/eurostat/cache/infographs/elderly/index.htm 2016 [Accessed: 5.8.2018]

[3] Damodaran L, Sandhu J. The role of a social context for ICT learning and support in reducing digital inequalities for older ICT users. International Journal of Learning Technology. 2016; **11**(2):156-175. http://irep.ntu.ac.uk/27281/1/4898_Sandhu.pdf

[4] EuDiPro. https://ec.europa.eu/eurostat/statistics-explained/index.php?title=Population_and_social_conditions. 2017 [Accessed: 11.11.2018]

[5] Connolly TM, Boyle EA, MacArthur E, Hainey T, Boyle JM. A systematic literature review of empirical evidence on computer games and serious games. Computers & Education. 2012;**59**: 661-686. DOI: 10.1016/j.compedu.2012.03.004

[6] Jerman-Blažič A, Jerman-Blažič B. Exploring and upgrading the educational business-game taxonomy. Journal of Educational Computing Research. 2015, 2015;**52**(3):303-340. DOI: 10.1177/0735633115572959 [Accessed: 4.11.2016]

[7] Biagi F, Loi M. Measuring ICT use and learning outcomes: Evidence from recent econometric studies. European Journal of Education. 2013;**48**(1):28-42. DOI: 10.1111/ejed.12016

[8] Wilson K, Bedwell W, Lazzara E, Salas E, Burke C, Estock J, et al. Relationships between game attributes and learning outcomes. Simulation & Gaming. 2008;**40**(2):229-243. https://dl.acm.org/citation.cfm?id=1517828, accessed 18.10.2018

[9] Wang F, Lockee BB, Burton JK. Computer game-based learning: Perceptions and experiences of senior Chinese adults. Journal of Educational Technology Systems. 2011;**40**:45-58. DOI: 10.2190/ET.40.1.e

[10] Martin P, Turner B. Grounded theory and organizational research. The Journal of Applied Behavioral Science. 1986;**22**(2):141

[11] Glaser BG, Strauss AL. The Discovery of Grounded Theory. Chicago, USA: Aldine Publishing; 1967. p. 215

[12] Eurostat 2016 C. https://ec.europa.eu/eurostat/statistics-explained/index.php/Eurostat_regional_yearbook [Accessed: 28.10.2018]

[13] Gerling K, Schulte F, Masuch M. Designing and evaluating digital games for frail elderly persons. In: ACM Conference proceeding ACE. Lisbon: ACM Conference proceeding ACE. 2011. pp. 119-127. http://hci.usask.ca/uploads/235-a62-gerling.pdf, [Accessed: 28.10.2012]

[14] Simbioza G. 2018. http://www.simbioza.eu/sl/2017/predstavitev [Accessed: 7.5.2018]

[15] Häikiö J, Wallin A, Isomursu M, Ailisto H, Matinmikko T, Huomo T. Touch-based user interface for elderly users. In: Proceedings of the 9th International Conference on Human Computer Interaction with Mobile Devices and Services—MobileHCI '07. 2007. pp. 289-296. https://dl.acm.org/citation.cfm?id=1378021 [Accessed: 2.9.2018]

[16] Gamberini L, Alcaniz M, Barresi G, Fabregat M, Prontu L, Seraglia B. Playing for real bonus: Videogames to empower elderly people. Journal of Cybertherapy and Rehabilitation. 2008; (1):37-48

[17] https://www.lemosandcrane.co.uk/dev/resources/Journal%20of%20CyberTherapy%20and%20Rehabilitation%20-%20Playing%20for%20a%20real%20bonus%20-%20videogames%20to%20empower%20elderly%20people.pdf [Accessed: 28.10.2018]

[18] Al Mahmud A, Mubin O, Shahid S, Martens J. Designing and evaluating the tabletop game experience for senior citizens. In: Proceedings of the 5th Nordic conference on Human-computer interaction building bridges - NordiCHI '08. 2008. pp. 215-222. https://pure.uvt.nl/ws/files/1049756/p403-al_mahmud2.pdf

Chapter 5

Transactional Distance Theory: A Critical View of the Theoretical and Pedagogical Underpinnings of E-Learning

Laura Delgaty

Abstract

This chapter provides a critical look at the literature surrounding Distance Education and targets Transactional Distance Theory. It will examine in detail the three components: structure, interaction (or dialogue) and autonomy. The structure necessary for successful distance learning starts the chapter. Next, interaction (or dialogue) is introduced and the complexity of this in relation to the student experience is discussed. Finally, autonomy is explored in detail. This overview will relate specifically to the student perspective. Alternative approaches, links to seminal authors and a critical viewpoint is taken throughout.

Keywords: transactional distance theory, autonomy, structure, interaction

> *'Theories Such as Transactional Distance Theory Are Invaluable in Guiding the Complex Practice of a Rational Process Such as Teaching and Learning at a Distance'* ([1], p. 3).

1. Introduction

Within this chapter, the objective is:

To review literature on the theoretical and pedagogical underpinnings of distance education, specifically transactional distance theory and the concepts of structure, interaction and autonomy.

1.1 Search strategies

Data bases were searched including: Scopus, Psychinfo, Web of Knowledge, Medline ERIC and CINAHL to identify potentially relevant material using the following terms:

(Effective or successful or valuable or useful) and (DL or distance learning or computer assisted learning or e-learning or elearning or online learning or online education or distance education or technology enhanced learning or computer mediated learning or computer based learning or ICT).

In Scopus alone, this wielded over 9000 results consisting of:

- work on effective DL investigating specific media or resources;
- undergraduate education;
- editorial and opinion papers;
- comparative studies (i.e. to traditional face to face teaching);
- systematic reviews (few);
- K-12 education;
- an abundance of 'how-to' books;
- reams of advocacy papers and success stories; and
- anecdotal and promotional articles.

The choice of databases reflected the heterogeneous nature of the research in the area of technology, education, and social sciences. Unless reviewing theoretical literature (learning or organisational theories), only technological literature published in the last 10 years was reviewed. Striving to strike a balance between comprehensiveness (or sensitivity) and precision this date restriction was chosen which is common practice in literature reviews. This time frame appears to be congruent with other literature reviews in this area including: 9 years [2] and 8 years [3]. The focus was specifically on higher education and online courses if possible (for example, excluded blended learning). Both synchronous and asynchronous delivery, were included. Abstracts of all identified papers were read and full copies of articles that appeared relevant were saved as electronic files in endnote. Duplicates were deleted. E-books, books and photocopied chapters of traditional books were used and organised manually by topics. Citation searches were done on all articles that related directly to transactional distance theory or reviews of DL. Searches were limited to English language books and journals.

1.2 Overview

Distance education was first introduced into mainstream lexicon in the 1970s [4]. There were early attempts to define it, and controversies around what it actually was. One of the barriers (and 40 years on, the most revolutionary argument for me) was basically this: Is distance education a geographic separation of learners and teachers, or a pedagogical concept? Moore suggested the latter. He developed Transactional Distance Theory (TDT) in an attempt to demonstrate and explain that distance education was more concerned with pedagogy than geography [4, 5].

1.3 Results

In 1973, Moore initially defined TDT as a psychological and communications gap that was a function of the interplay of *structure,* and *dialogue.* It was the cognitive space between teachers and students that must be crossed yet was a place of potential misunderstanding between the teacher and the learner. This space was continuous, relative and never exactly the same. Ideally, this distance or space needed to be minimised or shortened. Even in traditional education there was transactional distance and therefore the actual theory was a subset, albeit specialised, of conventional teaching and learning, [6]. However, in DL, due to the unique environment teachers and learners experienced more of a distance due to the physical distance (and if asynchronous, time) that separated these two groups. Therefore, transactional distance theory, more specifically, the transactional distance between teacher and learner was potentially more problematic at a distance and may have contributed to students' feelings of isolation, reduced motivation and engagement and eventually attrition in early DL [5]. Moore originally suggested that developers of DL must consider two variables that affect transactional distance: structure and dialogue [4]. Structure was the rigidity or flexibility of the instructional methods and strategies whilst dialogue referred to the interaction between the instructor and learner during a DL experience. Transactional distance was a function of dialogue and structure. With less dialogue and more structure, the transactional distance was higher (**Figure 1**).

In a course with little transactional distance, learners have guidance through ongoing dialogue [7]. This would be more appropriate, or attractive to learners who were less secure in managing their own learning. Moore later recognised with minimal dialogue, students were forced to make their own decisions for themselves and generally exercise autonomy [5]. Working with Kearsley, he later identified three interactive components or constructs [8] that needed to be considered to shorten the transactional distance and provide a meaningful learning experience for students. These included the original two:

- structure of the instructional programs;
- dialogue or interaction between learners and teachers and the new addition; and
- autonomy or the nature and degree of self-directedness of the learner.

This third hypothesised factor, autonomy, interacted with both structure and dialogue and the three together formed a model or theory [9] for understanding online learning [8] (**Figure 2**).

Structure was determined by the actual design of the activity, how the instruction was organised and the use of different media communications [8]. Dialogue could be synchronous, asynchronous and dialogue that was internalised within the student. Learner autonomy related to the individual learner's self-directedness or sense of personal responsibility. There appeared to be a relationship between structure, dialogue and autonomy. The greater the autonomy, the less teacher control

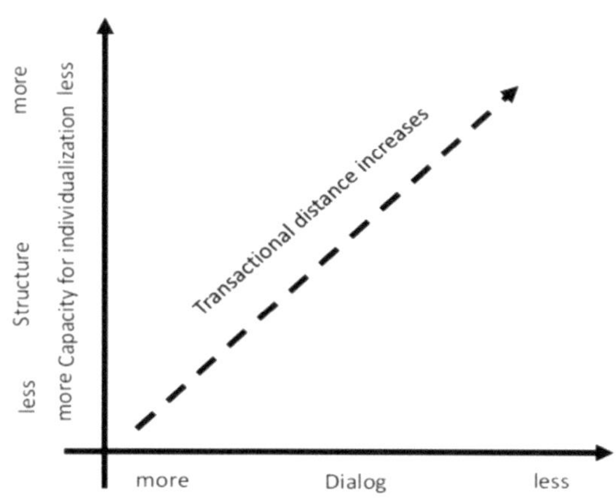

Figure 1.
Relationship of structure and dialogue to transactional distance [4].

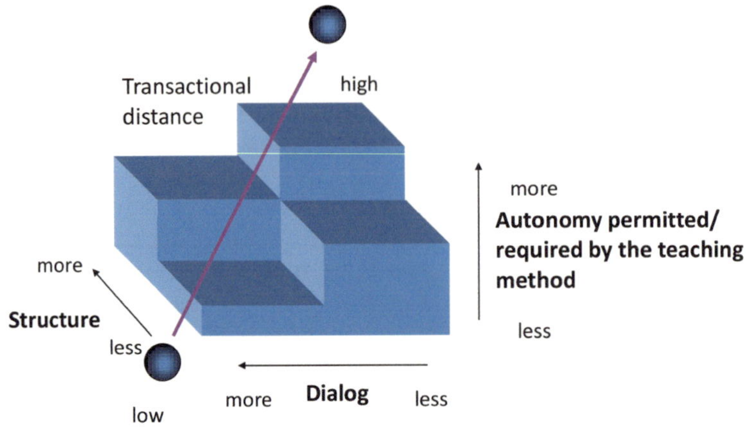

Figure 2.
Overview of transactional distance theory (3D model).

there needed to be to decrease the transactional distance and have a successful distance module. Conversely, with less dialogue and more structure, the likelihood of an increased transactional distance, which in turn led to less successful online programmes, was greater [10]. Successful distance environments depended on the teacher providing opportunities for dialogue and 'appropriately' [10] structured learning materials. This became extremely complex. Identifying the level of structure required, facilitating dialogue and encouraging individual learner autonomy was demanding and multifaceted as the greater the structure and the lower the dialogue, the more autonomy the student must demonstrate.

1.3.1 Deweyian link

These three complex factors relate to Dewey's seminal work. He suggested the educational process is a collaborative reconstruction of experience and has two sides: one psychological (cognitive) and one sociological. He warned that neither could be subordinated to the other or neglected without consequence.

Dialogue or interaction between learners and teachers: Dialogue, and engaging in interaction forces individuals to construct ideas in a deep learning sense [7]. Dewey [11] supported this constructivist approach to learning. He discussed the need to support learners' in their construction of meaning and argued only through social interaction and interaction with the environment could the learner construct conceptualisations and find solutions. He reasoned that through interpersonal, instructional dialogue the learner gains advantages in the pursuit of knowledge and understanding.

Structure of the instructional programs: Dewey described the function of education as improving the reasoning process [12]. Based on active experience, the role of the educator was to shape experience and structure the environment to promote experiences leading to growth. This role was one of a guide, or facilitator encouraging creative interaction and emphasising the development of solving problems and discovering knowledge. These higher order activities are encompassed in Dewey's practical inquiry model which includes four phases: triggering event, exploration, integration and resolution.

Autonomy or the nature and degree of self-directedness of the learner: Autonomy, the third factor in TDT is reflected in constructivist views encouraging active, collaborative and responsible learners [13]. The genesis of self-directed learning can be attributed to Dewey [7] who suggested that autonomy helped create the conditions that encourage individuals to exercise initiative, reflection and choice [11].

1.4 A critical view of transactional distance theory

Many researchers [1, 14–16] identified transactional distance as important and viewed TDT and as a basic analytical framework for understanding distance education systems.

'Transactional distance theory provides a useful conceptual framework for defining and understanding distance education in general and as a source of research hypotheses more specifically' ([14], p. 527).

Despite considerable time span over which this theory has evolved, there are critics and little empirical research has been carried out to test the validity and relationships of the constructs [16, 17].

TDT has been investigated from different perspectives. Two studies were found using questionnaires as data collection tools [18, 19]. Bischoff *et al.* were interested in student perceptions of transactional distance, structure and dialogue [18]. Transactional distance, dialogue and structure were all related to certain 'items' (in reality questions). Each variable was then measured using data generated from fixed questionnaire. Transactional distance was measured by two items, dialogue by one item and structure by three. The results supported Moore's theory showing dialogue and transactional distances were inversely proportional. However, dialogue (a complex variable) was measured by only one item, there was no discussion of quality of dialogue (only quantity) and the actual items being measured were not clearly defined.

In an attempt to investigate TDT further and create a clear connection between dialogue, structure and autonomy as they related to learning outcomes, 121 learners were part of a study in a DL environment [19]. Operational definitions were given and they looked at dialogue in terms of frequency and occurrence, structure in terms of delivery and implementation and autonomy in terms of personal ratings of independence. These variables were compared to student's self-assessment. The results found only two variables had significant effects on perceived learning outcomes: the greater the perceived transactional distance, the lower the perceived outcomes and the greater the frequency of discussion, the higher the perceived achievement of learning outcomes. The results support Moore's theory, although as in [18] a simple questionnaire was used, data was collected only once and dialogue was measured only by frequency.

Two articles were found addressing TDT that measured observable behaviour as opposed to student perceptions [20, 21]. Data was collected on 30 interactions between instructors and learners and measured behaviours using the 'systems dynamic model' [21]. Verbal behaviour was measured using a discourse analysis and, combined this with a measure of 'structure' of the programme then identified the variance. By measuring the rate of instructor and learner control, this variance (the ratio between amount of dialogue and extent of structure) was the transactional distance. The results demonstrated that transactional distance varied with dialogue and structure. As dialogue increased, distance decreased; as structure increased, transactional distance increased. This model produced values for transactional distance consistent with Moore's theory and suggested that transactional distance was directly proportional to dialogue and inversely proportional to structure. Although this supported Moore, the quantification of dialogue and structure of a programme was problematic to me. They looked only at one-to-one synchronous communications between learner and teacher. Therefore, the generality of the study is limited and it is hardly representative of the majority of DL trends. The effects of change in structure on dialogue was investigated during an audio-conferenced course [20]. Only structure and dialogue were compared. Over 100 students participated and dialogue was measured in frequency and duration whilst structure was defined by one aspect of instructional design (question asking behaviour of instructor). In support of TDT, different types of interactions and questions appeared to determine learner participation. According to the authors, of the four experimental procedures one was cancelled and one was biased. The instrument for measuring interaction was not shown to be reliable, the samples were not clearly described and the grouping unclear. Again, dialogue was measured in terms of frequency and duration. However, the results suggested that certain types of question-asking behaviour by the instructor could predict dialogue in the student [20]. The authors claimed that both structure and dialogue were important to success and by increasing dialogue and structure, one could increase student participation and decrease transactional distance.

Two articles were found [22, 23], from very different perspectives, using questionnaires to explore influences of variables in DL and presenting conflicting results. The effects of course format, satisfaction and perceived knowledge gained were examined during an online programme. Satisfaction was broken down into different aspects to relate to the constructs set out by Moore in TDT. A questionnaire was used and the instrument was described. A very low response rate (17%) was not explained, however, there did appear to be a relationship between course design and satisfaction. The more satisfied the learners were with the structure and with interaction, the more satisfied they were with their perceived knowledge gained. This supported Moore's assertion that structure needed to be appropriate for the learner and that low structure and high dialogue could lessen transactional distance. An interesting article, publishing negative findings investigated the impact of individual and instructional variables on 71 (87% return rate) learner's perceived transactional distance [22]. Once again, questionnaires were used to measure student perceptions (on a 23 item sliding scale) and results analysed against four variables. The results did show a high ratio of certain variables to perceived transactional distance. Although peripheral, their findings also included that neither face to face interaction during an online course or previous experience changed transactional distance. Interestingly, some of the results suggested a negative effect between transactional distance and 'online tutoring' or interaction although 'online tutoring' was not clearly described. Content validity of the survey was addressed in that 'experts' and 'educationalists' reviewed the tool and there was a high response rate. The conclusions were that alternative measures of transactional distance (qualitative, observation, interviews) would help understand these phenomena. Predominantly published literature was biased towards positive results [24], so this article was a valuable alternative perspective.

In 2009, a review classifying 695 articles on DL was carried out. The focus was to identify gaps and priority areas in DL research. A consensus of 25 experts reviewed research published between 2000 and 2008 [3]. The method and results were clearly described and this was one of the only DL reviews found that included non-English journals. (One of the criticisms of distance education reviews is the focus on 'peer reviewed' English language journals [2]). Fifteen main research areas and strong imbalances were described. They found research 'dreadfully neglected' on organisational change and development, costs and faculty support. These are all addressed in this submission and in my own review. However, closely related to TDT, they identified an imbalance with over 50% of all articles focusing on:

- instructional design;
- interaction and communication in learner communities; and
- learner characteristics (including motivation and autonomy).

Although not highlighted by the authors of this review, these corresponded directly with Moore's three components of TDT. Admittedly, TDT appears to be a descriptive, rather that predictive theory, but there is a clear collaboration with outcome variables [9]. Furthermore, Moore's concept of transactional distance was a significant paradigm shift for educationalists as it grounded the concept of distance in distance education in a social science framework and not in its usual physical science interpretations [7]. Whether there are strong empirical studies supporting Moore's theory or not, it is evident his three components continue to be a priority in research [2, 3, 16].

1.5 Summary of research on TDT

- TDT had roots in humanistic and behavioural ideologies.
- Structure and dialogue were the initial factors in Moore's [4] TDT theory and a third factor, autonomy was later added [8].
- Structure, dialogue and autonomy were related, dynamic and necessary, in successful distance education [8].
- Moore did not define any of the constructs operationally [17], which has led to lack of clarity in follow up research.
- Studies investigating the complex constructs of autonomy and self-directedness using closed questionnaires and scales were common.
- The majority of published work investigating TDT has been approached from a positivist paradigm looking for correlation and statistically significant relationships between complex concepts (for example, autonomy and perceived learning outcomes).
- None of the studies found supported or totally negated the proposition of transactional distance.
- All of the studies reviewed suggested that future research into this area should include interview or observational data [18–22, 25].

2. Student experience: structure or design

'*Educators must recognise that poorly designed educational programs...are not improved by being presented on a Web page*' ([26], p. s87).

2.1 Introduction

This section of the literature review addresses the three component parts of TDT separately.

2.2 Results

Formal 'instructional design' (ID) models, a systematic approach for developing educational products, used liberally when designing web-based courses at the University level [16, 27] all contained a number of key elements or components and have been widely adapted in e-learning [28]. The four core components of ID as they related to educational programmes are found in **Table 1** [29]:

Various models have adapted ID, but they are based on the desire to provide guidance to designers as they aim to develop effective and consistent educational solutions on a reliable basis [27, 28]. One of the most popular [30] and best documented models [31] was ADDIE, comprised of five stages of instructional design: analysis, design, development, implementation and evaluation. The ADDIE model specifically [31–33] and ID in general [27, 29, 30, 34, 35] have been researched intensely relating education to technology. This systematic approach to ID provides an empirical and replicable process when developing learning materials [31, 33].

2.2.1 A critical view of instructional design

Although there was a plethora of research suggesting these models were the clear way to structure DL, there were critics as well. Much of what is termed 'e-learning' was still based on the recursive decomposition of knowledge and skill principles of ID [28]. The supporters of rigid ID tended to be training organisations with a training philosophy whose intellectual base consisted of principles derived from behaviourism and associationism [28]. A well-known and published author in the field of ID in America, looked critically at four different 'tools' based on ID, including the ADDIE model. He critiqued all four for their expertise required, lack of collaborative learning, lack of authenticity and linear nature [32].

2.2.2 Structure or instructional design and transactional distance theory

Instructional design seemed uniquely poised to bridge the knowledge gap in the provision of DL by identifying what historically had been done in education and describing new directions in course design and structure [7]. This gap in knowledge relative to course design was especially applicable in the area of medical and allied health education [27]. Forty years ago, Moore prophetically discussed design or structure as being imperative in successful DL environments [4]. In 2010, design was addressed again and it was suggested it was an ideal term to use as it bridged both theory and practice [36]. Using surveys only, the structural factors affecting DL were investigated focusing on satisfaction, assessment of learning outcomes and perceived achievement of learning outcomes [37, 38]. 38,000 students taking 264 online courses in New York, were studied, analysing course documents and student questionnaires (38% return rate) [37]. In another study, 21 online courses were investigated using expert reviews of learning designs and student perception surveys [38] . Both studies demonstrated a correlation between greater structural consistency within the course, student satisfaction and perceived learning, used at least two methods of data collection and multiple raters for analysis of the data. However, the persistent attempt to quantify and measure people's perceptions of satisfaction and perceived learning is questionable given the complex nature of these constructs.

Components of instructional design
• Analysing the problem
• Designing a solution
• Implementing the solution
• Evaluating the degree of success of the solution

Table 1.
Core components of instructional design relating to educational programmes.

Regardless, students were more satisfied with courses that had defined structure and they felt they had learned more than totally open and flexible courses.

In a study using closed question surveys followed by interviews, data was collected data from 76 students who were asked to identify either challenges or useful components to their online experience [39]. The students were all undertaking a full degree using different technologies and structures, *yet all* from a distance. The closed response questions were followed by nine semi-structured interviews. Two researchers conducted the interviews and data was thematically analysed and used to substantiate and extend earlier results from the questionnaire. The results suggested (89%) that the design of the course was the most important component of a successful e-learning experience [39] which supported the necessity and importance of instructional design, regardless of the mode of delivery. The sample size was small; the response rate of the survey was not given, nor was the relationship of the interviewees to the students. However, this is one of the few studies using mixed methods that have approached instructional design and student learning or satisfaction from a less positivist approach. Multiple sources of data collection were used which may have allowed researchers to validate and crosscheck findings [40].

Two studies both investigated structure in relationship to student satisfaction and perceived learning [23, 41]. One surveyed 6088 (31% return rate) DL students in New York and compared levels of structure and instructional design to student satisfaction [41]. The other surveyed 201 (17% response rate) learners in a Midwestern American University comparing levels of satisfaction with structure and design, satisfaction and perceived knowledge gained [23]. Both of these studies used closed questions and rating scales, the questions were not clear to the reader and the response rates were low. However, in both studies, the central role of structure and student satisfaction or perceived knowledge gained was supported.

In one of the few studies specifically addressing context, Benson and Samarawickrema [42] compared six case studies of 'successful' DL initiatives in Australia. Definitions and programmes were clarified and their focus was to illustrate how e-learning designs (specifically those using Web 2.0 technologies) were instrumental in increasing success and decreasing transactional distance. With a practical focus and rich contextual description, these cases suggested that by carefully structuring and designing a course, transactional distance can be decreased. They also highlighted that design must be variable and provide a clear strategy for an analytic approach that is responsive to both the learners and the context of their learning.

2.3 Summary of research on instructional design or structure

Formal instructional design, in its prescriptive and inflexible sense was the basis for most early DL initiatives. Although when subscribing to a learner centred perspective this seems problematic, more progressive models have been developed incorporating constructivist and interactive approaches to planning DL. The amount and type of structure necessary appears to be inconsistent. However, there does appear to be a relationship between the level of structure and student satisfaction and an increase in perceived learning.

Originally, ID was developed to emphasise 'learning by doing' with immediate feedback on success, careful analysis and atomisation of learning outcomes and above all aligning these learning outcomes with instructional strategies and methods to assess the learning outcomes.

The ID approach to e-learning has become widely, yet perhaps unfairly discredited [28]. This may be due to the fact that a number of terms and expressions are used synonymously with ID and although the basis is behaviourism, or a teacher centred model, this is often an unfair association [43].

Many models that are labelled as 'constructivist' are indistinguishable from those derived from the associationist perspective [28].

Recently ID and general DL structure has moved towards creativity and interaction and away from low-level immediate responses [34].

Empirical and case study literature has repeatedly explored the relationship between (a) structure or design and (b) student satisfaction, transactional distance and learning.

There appears to be a close relationship between (a) structure and (b) transactional distance, student satisfaction and increase in perceived learning.

3. Student experience: interaction and communication

Learners interact with their environment ([7], p. 15).

3.1 Introduction

The published research on DL is abundant, however, the actual student experiences have gone relatively undocumented [44, 45] and are not fully understood [46]. The challenge was to understand, students' use of technology to support higher-order learning, interaction and dialogue [7]. The second factor contributing to an understanding of TDT was interaction, communication or dialogue and is the focus of this section.

3.2 Results

Communication, interaction and support from faculty and peers is consistently rated as having a major influence on DL [16, 39, 47–53]. However, our understanding of its use is seriously limited [7] by empirical research which has used rating scales and closed questionnaires to explore perceived support and perceived learning. With the exception of two papers, the papers above investigated student satisfaction and barriers or facilitators to DL [51, 52]. They were not directly focused on interaction or dialogue; they were exploring experiences generically. One paper specifically nurses' experiences. The findings supported the other studies; the interaction between the instructor and student, or student to student, was highlighted as integral to a positive learning experience or improved outcome [53].

A highly respected and well published five stage model illustrating online interaction or engagement (**Figure 3**) is found below [54].

This model is used as the basis for analysing and describing how the teacher or 'e-moderator' could support student learning. Other models and conversational frameworks of analysing online discourse [55–57] followed a relatively similar pattern of generating ideas, increasing interaction and information exchange followed by divergent thinking and development. These models have been criticised as being artificial, prescriptive and based on personal experience, not empirical research [9]. Salmon's work specifically has been criticised for its focus on the advancement of individual practitioners and the lack of attention paid to leadership and the institution as a whole. Successful initiatives must be scaffolded by dialogue and promote interaction and participation [54].

As discussed, the majority of the literature included interaction as one of the several factors affecting success in DL. A small amount of literature was found that addressed interaction, dialogue or engagement specifically.

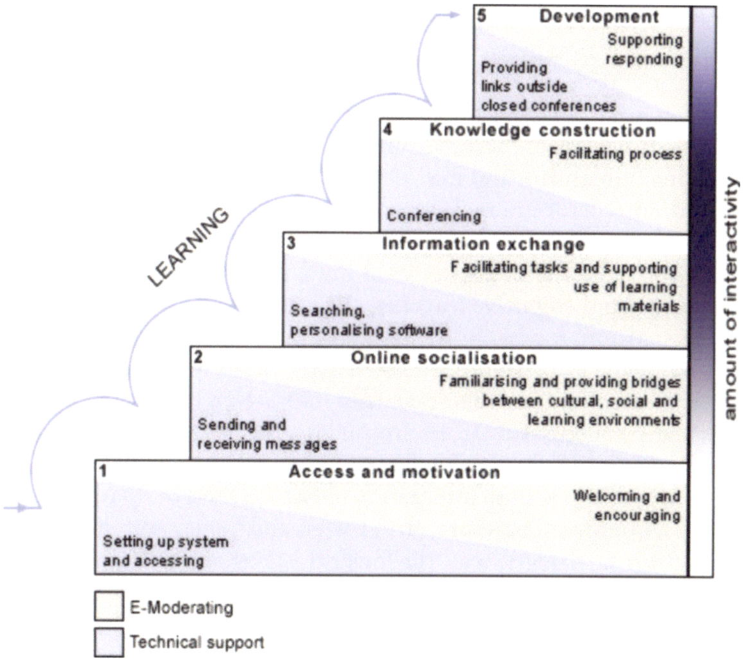

Figure 3.
Salmon's [54] five stage model of online learning and teaching (p. 29).

3.2.1 Learner-learner and instructor-learner dialogue

Learner-learner and instructor-learner dialogue was the focus in a study of 38,000 students taking 264 online courses in New York [37]. Course documents and student questionnaires (38% return rate) were analysed. Student perceptions were explored based on learning, interaction with instructor and classmates, and personal level of activity. She found significant correlations with student satisfaction and interaction with the instructor ($r = 0.761$, $p = 0.01$) and perceived learning ($r = 0.707$, $p = 0.01$). There were also significant correlations between interactions with other students and course satisfaction ($r = 0.440$, $p = 0.01$) and perceived learning learned ($r = 0.437$, $p = 0.01$). Her findings appeared consistent with the literature in that interaction with instructor and amongst peers was consistently associated with the success of online courses [37]. Although this study was supported by research in a similar vein [7], there were some fundamental issues that were problematic. The survey consisted of multiple-choice and forced-answer questions investigating the 'dimensions' of satisfaction and perceived learning with no explanation as to how these questions were developed. There was no explanation for this quantitative attempt to measure the complex nature of satisfaction and learning.

3.2.2 Instructor-learner dialogue

Instructor-learner dialogue, specifically, examining the relationships between verbal immediacy and affective and cognitive learning in DL was explored. 145 post-graduate students involved in an asynchronous online course were surveyed using a questionnaire based on several verbal immediacy scales (described in detail) and both cognitive and affective learning scales [58]. The verbal immediacy scale consisted of 20 statements concerning instructor behaviour, the affective learning scale six dimensions and the cognitive learning scale was designed to produce a measure of learning loss. The hypothesis of correlation between instructor immediacy and affective learning was supported ($r = 0.73$, $p < 0.01$). The hypothesis of positive correlation between instructor immediacy and cognitive learning was supported ($r = .054$, $p < 0.01$). The verbal immediacy scale was based on other scales developed in a traditional face to face environment, yet the use of them in a non –traditional asynchronous environment was not justified. These students were all studying humanities and may not represent other post graduates as their requirement for instructor interaction may be unique. Regardless, the conclusion included a positive relationship between instructor immediacy and affective learning. Students who rated their instructors as more verbally immediate expressed improved affective and cognitive learning. Although immediacy of feedback was part of the original aim, it was not the focus for review. The majority of the literature found investigated the value and necessity of speed in asynchronous interactions. Learner-learner and instructor-learner interaction has been shown to be effective in creating successful DL environments, but what has become key is timely interactions [7]. Timely interaction related to Moore's [4] concept of TDT. This psychological separation was an interaction between levels of dialogue and levels of structure or autonomy. Therefore, the greater, and faster, and more involved the level of interaction or dialogue was, the lower the level of psychological feeling of separation there would be [7]. Timeliness of interactions, frequency, occurrence, type of interaction and immediacy are all areas that need to be examined more in distance education research [7].

3.2.3 Learner-learner dialogue

Learner-learner interaction is essential [10]. Two recent studies were found specifically addressing collaboration and peer interaction on performance in DL. One investigated social performance in computer supported collaborative learning [51], while another [52] analysed participants' experiences thematically in web conferences. In the first study, 39 undergraduate students were assigned to groups with either specialised collaborative activities and structure or none [51]. Data was collected on group performance using self and peer assessments and a rating scale for both behaviour and performance. These terms were all defined, although the rating scales were not validated or transparent. The group exposed to the specialised collaborative activities demonstrated a perceived increase in team development, ability to deal with team conflict and a more positive attitude towards collaborative problem solving [51]. The second study explored dialogue relating to learning in participants undertaking web conferences on leadership. Using data from two series of online seminars lasting over a year, the authors analysed all recorded 'text chat' data using thematic analysis. Validity was addressed by making the analysis process transparent, the analysis itself was done by three researchers and the final data was compared to the literature. Themes identified relating to learning were: social interaction, information giving, internalisation, co-construction of knowledge and multi-process learning. The results of both of these studies suggest that online activities that promote learner-learner interaction are important for effective team performance and collaborative learning [51, 52].

3.3 Alternative approaches

Adults, as learners, need to see relevance or usefulness in their learning activities [59]. Therefore, these learners needed to see how interacting with their peers would benefit them and have relevance to their learning. Two slightly eclectic studies were found that addressed this from alternative viewpoints. One of the few longitudinal studies within this entire review followed groups of adult learners over 15 years [60]. This three-stage ethnographic-action research study tracked learners and their learning community at a virtual university in Australia as they undertook a Masters of Arts degree. The cycles, agents of change and staged findings were well explained. Conclusions suggested peer dialogue provided the mechanism for deep learning experiences and a sense of community. They related their findings to Bandura [61] suggesting that a community of learning requires:

- relevance-social and situational;
- involvement-reflective action and interpretive practice;
- technology-enabling and self-efficacy with ICT; and
- acceptance-recognition by peers.

The aim of this interpretive study was to explore how post-graduates could be guided to create conditions for effective peer discourse. In order to understand this, a study using traditional scientific methods would be inappropriate. Of the four concepts listed as necessary, the social relevance or usefulness appeared to play the biggest role to students. This study was not addressing whether group interaction was valuable but what conditions were necessary for it to occur and be valuable for students. Supporting these findings, but from an alternative angle, a case study was presented in which the interaction between learners was a failure [62]. This empirical positivist study used a questionnaire survey and statistical analysis addressing several hypotheses of why students did not participate in an online discussion forum at a University in West London. Hypotheses included low level of usage was due to either: attitudes of the student, low perceived usefulness of discussion board or technological complexity. The results from the 24 questions showed statistically significant results in that low perceived usefulness of the discussion board was the primary cause for its failure. The questionnaire consisted of scaled questions only and the development of the tool itself was not discussed. Although not made explicit, it appears that only 10% of the potential students completed the questionnaire. However, the conclusions support another study [60] that usefulness or relevance is necessary for successful learner-learner interactions. The approach to present findings of an unsuccessful initiative was unique. One of the general biases with published materials is the possibility of publication bias where negative studies are unpublished [24].

3.4 Summary of research on dialogue and interaction

- Interaction or dialogue was clearly related to student satisfaction and perceived learning whilst relevance, usefulness and immediacy of interactions appeared to be the most integral issues in decreasing TD and contributing to successful DL environments.
- Interaction/dialogue/engagement were terms used simultaneously in the literature and there were three different divisions: instructor-learner, learner-learner and learner-content.

- Literature overwhelmingly suggested that learner-instructor and learner-learner interaction was important to student satisfaction and the facilitation of learning [16, 39, 47–53].
- Online 'community' or collaboration was an important variable in online classes. Without this online discourse online courses became a mere transmission of information.
- Several frameworks for designing and analysing interaction in DL were found all aimed at student's progression into higher levels of thinking [54–57].
- E-moderators took on multiple roles: they moderated or facilitated discussion, answered emails and managed the flow of content or responses. Their presence and immediacy impacted on student satisfaction.
- Students required usefulness, value or relevance in online interaction or discussion for it to be adopted successfully.
- The roles that interaction and dialogue play in DL is not well understood Moore (1973) warned this area should not be underestimated and argued no other area of study will have a greater impact on the future of distance education.

4. Student experience: autonomy

4.1 Introduction

A hallmark of DL has been its reliance on learner autonomy [63] which was the third hypothesised element of TDT [8] and the focus of this section.

4.2 Results

Literature addressing autonomy in DL, unlike structure or dialogue which was relatively straightforward, was complex and multi-faceted [1]. Major reviews were found discussing autonomy in learning [64] and specifically autonomy in DL [4, 10]. In a review of autonomy and learning, literature was investigated over the last two decades, describing various definitions, and highlighting inconsistencies in the literature [64]. The review was divided into topics; however, there was no explanation as to search criteria or strategies. Autonomy was defined in terms of a redistribution of power concerning the construction of knowledge and the roles of participants. Although, DL was not addressed explicitly, the paper claimed autonomy was '*...a departure from education as a social process*' (p. 116). Over 2000 pieces of literature concerning autonomy were reviewed [4]. This visionary work (pre-internet!) explained '*The autonomous learner is not to be thought of as an intellectual Robinson Crusoe, castaway and shut-off in self sufficiency*' ([4], p. 669).

In a later review, research on autonomous learning was reviewed [7] and further, explained that there were two dimensions of autonomy in DL: self-management of pedagogy and self-monitoring of cognition, or metacognition. Both cognitive autonomy and taking responsibility for one's learning were essential. Focusing on the meta-cognitive aspects of learner autonomy, strategies were compared in classroom vs. DL [65]. Using questionnaires followed by verbal reports, the relationship was explored between autonomy and the instructional context of distance learners (n = 274) or classroom learners (n = 143) in a language programme. Variant analysis was applied to the questionnaire data to determine the relationship between learning strategies and context. The results showed that mode of study (distance vs. traditional) was the principal influence of the relationship between students and autonomy (more so than age, level etc.). Distance learners made greater use of metacognitive strategies than classroom learners, especially relating to self-management. A further analysis was done using verbal reports (n = 37) and the data was classified from the transcripts by the researcher and an independent rater. A total of 836 instances of strategies relating to autonomous work were identified. The average instance of strategy use from distance learners was 26.6 whilst a traditional student was 10.2. Instances of using metacognitive strategies in classroom learners was on average four, whilst distance learners reported an average of 15. The results suggested distance learners used more metacognitive strategies than classroom learners [65]. Critically, the numbers in the two groups were uneven and the development of the questions was not well described. However, the dual nature of the study, independent raters, transparency of inter-rater reliability and clear analysis suggested rigour. This study suggested that learners either approach DL with, or develop very quickly, metacognitive and self-management skills.

In a later study, metacognitive knowledge was investigated and experiences in distance education [66]. Thirty one students were interviewed focusing on a model of metacognitive knowledge comprising self, task, strategy and goals. Content analysis was used to identify categories of metacognitive experiences. There was an average of 19.7 instances of metacognitive knowledge per student and in descending order, the four dimensions of metacognition were: self-knowledge, strategy knowledge, task knowledge and knowledge of goals. Each student was able to recount at least one instance of a metacognitive experience. Conclusions included: students appeared to have experienced some, often extremely memorable, metacognitive experiences and metacognitive knowledge of distance students appeared to be primarily about self and strategy and less about tasks and goals. However, these dimensions were highly interactive and not distinct. The quantification of a complex concept such as metacognition, and the suggestion that students can identify a 'metacognitive experience' suggested a positivist approach to a subject containing multiple realties. However, the author attempted rigour in that the methods were clearly explained, two raters were used, and transcripts were revisited for further analysis with discussion to resolve differences. Overall, the metacognitive aspect of autonomy seemed to be occurring and seemed to be important in these student's DL experiences [66]. Knowledge about oneself and strategies were more important for successful learning than knowledge about tasks and goals. This perhaps, suggested that self-monitoring is one of the keys to autonomy in DL.

Another study investigated how DL students conceptualised the three elements in TDT: structure, dialogue and autonomy [67]. Using a pre-tested and piloted questionnaire, 169 distance education students (72% response rate) were surveyed. Learner autonomy was measured by students indicating which of 11 statements described themselves (i.e. able to learn without lots of guidance, able to develop a personal plan, able to find resources, self-directed, prefer learning in a group, need collaborative learning). The results were analysed using factor analysis and suggested a two-factor solution: independence and interdependence. Independence accounted for 29% of the total variance with a Cronbach's alpha of 0.82. Interdependence (interpersonal, interactive aspects) accounted for 26% of total variance with a Cronbach's alpha of 0.77. The results suggested that the concepts of dialogue, structure and autonomy were complex and that students tended to describe themselves as both independent and interdependent. The lack of correlation also suggested these features of autonomy were essential, but separate and distinct attributes. Although the attempt to quantify with statistical analysis something as complex as autonomy was fundamentally flawed, this study provided a particularly interesting idea: an individual's autonomy as a distance learner should be understood as including their abilities to work with others, or be interdependent. Autonomy is multi-faceted and interdependence appeared to be essential. These results suggested that there may be an attempt to move beyond the focus of independence in this environment and move towards 'interdependence'. Other) earlier findings support this 'personal control' [68]. It is suggested successful adult learners demonstrated appropriate dependency needs when participating in DL including: help, approval and support, leadership of others and sharing efforts and responsibility.

4.3 Summary of research on autonomy

- Autonomy or self-directedness has been a core feature of adult learning for years and closely relates to TDT. DL, when considered as a social process relates to this complex construct. Autonomy has been described as both self-management of pedagogy and metacognition. Furthermore, to 'traditional' autonomy, has been added 'interdependence' in group activities in DL.

- Moore and Kearsley (1997) suggested autonomy, a third factor in TDT, influenced and interacted with dialogue and structure in transactional distance.

- Self-directed learning/autonomy/independent learning were all used with a considerable degree of equivalence in the literature and became popularised in the 1970s.

- Literature appeared to focus on measuring autonomy and relationships of factors within TDT, attempting to quantify and compare a complex subject using statistical analysis and were often lacking a theoretical framework.

- There appeared to be varying perspectives concerning autonomy and independence vs. interdependence. I disagreed with Thanasoulas [64] that autonomy was a departure from education as a social process. I supported Moore [4], Garland [68] and Chen and Willits [67]. An individual's ability to work online in groups was essential.

- Individual autonomy has been classified as self-management of pedagogy and metacognition. Both of these appeared to be important and occurring in DL. Studies exploring these involved constructs have attempted to quantify these complex subjects.

- Studies that have compared the different dimensions of autonomy suggested knowledge about oneself and self-strategies were more important than knowledge about tasks and goals, yet students must manage both 'academic' learning and the process of learning.

Author details

Laura Delgaty
Medical Education, Newcastle University, England

*Address all correspondence to: l.e.delgaty@ncl.ac.uk

References

[1] Garrison R. Theoretical challenges for distance education in the 21st century: A shift from structural to transactional issues. The International Review of Research in Open and Distance Learning. 2000;**1**(1):1492-3831

[2] Berge ZL, Mrozowski S. Review of research in distance education, 1990 to 1999. American Journal of Distance Education. 2001;**15**(3):5-19

[3] Zawacki-Richter O. Research areas in distance education: A Delphi study. The International Review of Research in Open and Distance Learning. 2009;**10**(3):1-17

[4] Moore M. Towards a theroy of independent learning and teaching. Journal of Higher Education Policy and Management. 1973;**44**(9):661-679

[5] Moore M. Distance education theory. The American Journal of Distance Education. 1991;**5**(3):1-8

[6] Lowe W. Transactional distance theory as a foundation for developing innovative and reactive instruction. Educational Technology and Society. 2000;**3**(1):1-3

[7] Moore MG, Anderson WG. Handbook of Distance Education. 2nd ed. Mahwah, New Jersey: Lawrence Erlbaum; 2007

[8] Moore MG, Kearsley G. Distance Education: A Systems View of Online Learning. 3rd ed. Belmont, California: Library of Congress; 2012

[9] Wallace RM. Online learning in higher education: A review of research on interactions among teachers and students. Education, Communication and Information. 2003;**3**(2):241-280

[10] Moore MG. Theory of transactional distance. In: Keegan D, editor. Theoretical Principles of Distance Education. London: Routledge; 1997. pp. 22-38

[11] Dewey J. Democracy and Education. Middlesex: Echo Library; 2007

[12] Dewey J. The essential Dewey volume 1. In: Hickman LA, Alexander TM, editors. Pragmatism, Education, Democracy. Bloomington: Indiana University Press; 1998

[13] Tam M. Constructivism, instructional design, and technology: Implications for transforming distance learning. Educational Technology and Society. 2000;**3**(2):50-60

[14] Jung I. Building a theoretical framework of web-based instruction in the context of distance education. British Journal of Educational Technology. 2001;**32**(5):525-534

[15] Collins MP, Murphy KL. Development of communication conventions in instructional electronic chats. Journal of Distance Education. 1997;**12**(1):177-200

[16] Goel L, Zhang P, Templeton M. Transactional distance revisited: Bridging face and empirical validity. Computers in Human Behavior. 2012;**28**(4):1122-1129

[17] Gorsky P, Caspi A. A critical analysis of transactional distance theory. The Quarterly Review of Distance Education. 2005;**6**(1):1-11

[18] Bischoff WR et al. Transactional distance and interactive television in the distance education of health professionals. American Journal of Distance Education. 1996;**10**(3):4-19

[19] Chen YJ, Willits FK. A path analysis of the concepts in Moore's theory of transactional distance in a videoconferencing environment.

Journal of Distance Education. 1998;**13**(2):51-65

[20] Bunker E et al. A study of transactional distance in an international audioconferencing course. Proceedings of Seventh International Conference of the Society for Information Technology and Teacher Education Phoenix. 1996. pp. 40-44

[21] Saba F, Shearer RL. Verifying key theoretical concepts in a dynamic model of distance education. American Journal of Distance Education. 1994;**8**(1):36-59

[22] Chen YJ. Transactional distance in World Wide Web learning environments. Innovations in Education and Teaching International. 2001;**38**(4):327-338

[23] Stein DS et al. Bridging the transactional distance gap in online learning environments. American Journal of Distance Education. 2005;**19**(2):105-118

[24] Cook DA et al. Internet-based learning in the health professions. The Journal of the American Medical Association. 2008;**300**(10):1181-1196

[25] Kanuka H, Collett D, Caswell C. University instructor perceptions of the use of asynchronous text-based discussion in distance courses. American Journal of Distance Education. 2002;**16**(3):151-167

[26] Chumley-Jones HS, Dobbie A, Alford CL. Web-based learning: Sound educational method or hype? A review of the evaluation literature. Academic Medicine. 2002;**77**(10):s86-s93

[27] Joiner RC, Adkins MAC, McLenighan HX. Social Support Tools in Allied Health Online Instruction, in School of Education. Ann Arbor, Michigan: Capella University; 2008

[28] Beetham H, Sharpe R. Rethinking Pedagogy for a Digital Age. London: Routledge; 2010

[29] Smith P, Ragan T. Instructional Design. 3rd ed. New York: Wiley Publishing; 2005

[30] Ipek I, Izciler M, Baturay MH. New Trends and Approaches in Instructional Design and Technology: From Schools to Industry, in International Educational Technology Conference. Eskisehir, Turkey: Anadolu University; 2008

[31] Dick W, Carey L. The Systematic Design of Instruction. New York: Scott, Foresman and Company; 1985

[32] Gustafson K. Instructional design tools: A critique and projections for the future. Educational Technology Research and Development. 2002;**50**(4):59-66

[33] Dick WC, Carey L, Carey J. The Systematic Design of Instruction. 6th ed. Boston: Pearson/Allyn and Bacon; 2005

[34] Morrison GR et al. Designing Effective Instruction. Danvers, MA: John Wiley and Sons; 2011

[35] Koksal MS. An instructional design model to teach nature of science. Asia-Pacific Forum on Science Learning and Teaching. 2009;**10**(2):1-23

[36] Beetham H, Sharpe R. Rethinking Pedagogy for a Digital Age. London: Routledge; 2007

[37] Swan K. Building learning communities in online courses: The importance of interaction. Education, Communication and Information. 2002;**2**(1):23-49

[38] McNaught C, Lam P, Cheng K. Investigating relationships between features of learning designs and student learning outcomes. Educational Technology Research and Development. 2012;**60**(2):271-286

[39] Song L et al. Improving online learning: Student perceptions of

useful and challenging characteristics. The Internet and Higher Education. 2004;7(1):59-70

[40] Patton M. Qualitative Research and Evaluation Methods. New York: Sage Publications; 2002

[41] Shea PJ, Pickett AM, Pelz WE. A follow-up investigation of "teaching presence" in the SUNY Learning Network. Journal of Asynchronous Learning Networks. 2003;7(2):61-80

[42] Benson R, Samarawickrema G. Addressing the context of e-learning: Using transactional distance theory to inform design. Distance Education. 2009;**30**(1):5-21

[43] Wilson BG, Myers KM. Situated cognition in theoretical and practical context. Theoretical Foundations of Learning Environments. 2000. January 2012

[44] Cook D. Where are we with web-based based learning in medical education? Medical Teacher. 2006;**28**(7):594-598

[45] Alexander S. E-learning developments and experiences. Education and Training. 2001;**43**(4/5):240-248

[46] Moule P. Challenging the five-stage model for e-learning: A new approach. Association for Learning Technology Journal. 2007;**15**(1):37-50

[47] Hill JR et al. Exploring research on internet-based learning: From infrastructure to interactions. In: Jonassen DH, editor. Handbook of Research on Educational Communications and Technology. Mahwah: Lawrence Erlbaum Associates; 2003. pp. 433-460

[48] Hermans C, Haytko D, Mott-Stenerson B. Student satisfaction in web-enhanced learning environments. Journal of Instructional Pedagogies. 2009;**1**:1-19

[49] Ituma A. An evaluation of students' perceptions and engagement with e-learning components in a campus based university. Active Learning in Higher Education. 2011;**12**(1):57

[50] Mason R, Weller M. Factors affecting students' satisfaction on a web course. Australian Journal of Educational Technology. 2000;**16**(2):173-200

[51] Phielix C, Prins FJ, Kirschner PA. Awareness of group performance in a CSCL-environment: Effects of peer feedback and reflection. Computers in Human Behavior. 2010;**26**(2):151-161

[52] Seddon K et al. Towards an understanding of the learning processes that occur in synchronous online seminars for the professional development of experienced educators. Education and Information Technologies. 2011;**17**(4):431-449

[53] Moule P, Ward R, Lockyer L. Nursing and healthcare students' experiences and use of e-learning in higher education. Journal of Advanced Nursing. 2010;**66**(12):2785-2795

[54] Salmon G. E-Moderating—The Key to Teaching and Learning Online. Abington, Oxon: Routledge Falmer; 2008

[55] Gunawardena CN, Lowe CA, Anderson T. Analysis of a global online debate and the development of an interaction analysis model for examining social construction of knowledge in computer conferencing. Journal of Educational Computing Research. 1997;**17**(4):397-431

[56] Harasim L. Shift happens: Online education as a new paradigm in learning. The Internet and Higher Education. 2000;**3**(1-2):41-61

[57] Laurillard D. Rethinking University Teaching: A Conversational Framework

for the Effective Use of Learning Technologies. New York: Routledge Falmer; 2002

[58] Baker J. An investigation of relationships among instructor immediacy and affective and cognitive learning in the online classroom. The Internet and Higher Education. 2004;**7**(1):1-13

[59] Knowles MS. The Adult Learner: A Neglected Species. Oxford: Gulf Publishing; 1978

[60] Eustace K. Building an effective online learning community: An ethnographic study. Communications in Computer and Information Science. 2011;**177**:226-242

[61] Bandura A. Social cognitive theory in cultural context. Applied Psychology. 2002;**51**(2):269-290

[62] Lee H, Kim JW, Hackney R. Knowledge hoarding and user acceptance of online discussion board systems in e-learning: A case study. Computers in Human Behavior. 2011;**27**(4):1431-1437

[63] West RE. Insights from research on distance education learners, learning, and learner support. American Journal of Distance Education. 2011;**25**(3):135-151

[64] Thanasoulas D. Autonomy and learning: An epistemological approach. Applied Semiotics Journal. 2000;**4**(10):115-132

[65] White C. Autonomy and strategy use in distance foreign language learning: Research findings. System. 1995;**23**(2):207-221

[66] White CJ. The metacognitive knowledge of distance learners. Open Learning: The Journal of Open, Distance and e-Learning. 1999;**14**(3): 37-46

[67] Chen YJ, Willits FK. Dimensions of educational transactions in a videoconferencing learning environment. American Journal of Distance Education. 1999;**13**(1):45-59

[68] Garland MR. The adult need for "personal control" provides a cogent guiding concept for distance education. Journal of Distance Education. 1994;**9**(1):45-59

Chapter 6

Designing a Participatory and Interactive Opera

Geoffrey Edwards, Jocelyne Kiss, Ernesto Morales, Coralee McLaren, Serge Lacasse, Marie Louise Bourbeau, Juan Nino Falcon and Jonathan Proulx Guimond

Abstract

Opera as an art form should lend itself to participatory design, given its wide variety of theatrical and musical components. Opera, however, imposes its own constraints and challenges. The problem as laid out in the early stages of the project was to design a short one-act interactive opera that could be managed within a modest budget. The source material was a science fiction manuscript currently undergoing publication by a small independent publishing house. Our research and production team included a composer, several singers/musicians, an engineer, a designer, and a choreographer/dancer as well as the writer. Furthermore, several of these had done extensive work with interactive and immersive environments. In addition to the opera itself, which incorporated both live and virtual elements, we recycled the 3d virtual designs as the substratum for an online co-creation environment that could be used to elicit public participation in the future development of our operas. We discuss both the diverse challenges involved in creating the opera and the co-creation environment, and highlight projected future work.

Keywords: opera, virtual staging, augmented virtuality, augmented reality, participatory design, choreography, libretto, scenario, 3d design, musical composition, animation, interaction, interactivity, avatars

1. Introduction

At its beginnings, dramatic art as practiced, for example, by the ancient Greeks [1], was understood to be a participatory activity. Audiences were coached and guided to participate in the chorus [2], audience members were often invited to act out a part, and the cathartic effects of drama were designed to be used as a form of social engagement [3]. Over the centuries, especially in the period leading into the Enlightenment, audiences became more passive and a separate class of professional performers emerged who were tasked with ensuring that formal performance esthetics were achieved [4], especially in music [5], although there were also contrary tendencies [6]. Today, although this remains the de facto modus operandi of most public performances, there is a growing demand on the part of a broader public to be re-integrated into the dramatic production process. The lines between professional and audience productions are blurring again. Hence video and audio recordings are "remixed" by adventurous user communities, and "mashups" that combine elements from several sources are also created and disseminated [7]. Fan fiction has become a huge industry, with countless individuals writing their own versions of popular stories, whether these remain purely literature or have been transposed from film or television series, or even stories confined to the gaming universes [8]. Ways are being found to integrate audience productions within live drama presentations, for example by integrating live camera footage of audiences into stage productions [9].

It has been noted that opera as an art form should lend itself to participatory design [10] given its wide variety of theatrical and musical components, but efforts to do so are still relatively limited. Furthermore, if one were to succeed in making opera more participatory, then this success should spill over into other performance arts where the modes of representation are more constrained. Participatory design in a broader sense has been, of course, an established practice now in research circles for several decades, addressing problem-solving in relation to a wide variety of application domains [11, 12]. Furthermore, participatory design is increasingly being used within art production practices [13–15], including the design of television episodes. Opera, however, imposes its own constraints and challenges. In our context, we had neither the budget of a television studio nor that of a major production house—instead, we had a small seed budget from the Canadian Social Science and Humanities Research Council (SSHRC) for developing the opera (the Insight Development program). How, then, to not only design a participatory opera, but also to develop a collaboration protocol that would support the design process?

As a team, we had not all worked together before, which posed its own challenges. However, some of us (particularly Edwards and Bourbeau [16]) had extensive experience working with multidisciplinary teams. Several members of our team were also highly polyvalent, that is, masters of more than one discipline (see **Table 1** which shows the different forms of expertise).

The opera project formed a natural and organic extension to the creative work of the original author and librettist for the project, Edwards [17]. His writing activity sprang out of a lifelong interest towards improving the lives of other humans that has also underlain his career as a research scientist. The themes his writing addresses bear witness to this interest—his work raises issues of tolerance and its relationship to conformity and peer pressure, gender fluidity issues, bullying and violence, disability and mental health among other thematic areas. The engagement of a broader public within his creative work is one manifestation of this abiding interest, and one that he finds particularly compelling, in that it opens the possibility to carry the writing out "into the world" in ways that are not usually accessible to writers.

2. The challenge

The problem as laid out in the early stages of the project was to design a short (20–30 min) one-act interactive opera that could be managed within our modest budget. The source material was a science fiction manuscript that Edwards wrote in 2012, which was itself the first volume of a fifteen volume opus which is now undergoing publication [17]. We had on board for the project (see **Table 1**), a composer (Lacasse), several singers/musicians (Kiss, Stévance, Bourbeau, Falcon), an engineer (Falcon), a designer (Morales), and a choreographer and dancer (McLaren) as well as the writer (Edwards). Furthermore, we had several people who had done extensive work with interactive and immersive environments (Kiss, Edwards, Bourbeau and Falcon primarily).

Hence, there were several tasks to be addressed:

- Find an appropriate scenario.
- Determine how the story should be interactive (e.g., what mix of augmented and virtual reality should be incorporated? How should individual interactions be engendered, and how should group interactions be facilitated? etc.).
- Embellish the scenario with the other components (stage design, music, choreography, and lyrics).
- Bring the elements together into a performance for presentation to diverse publics.

Figure 1 shows an example of how we viewed this taking place. Some of the details of the flow are subject to discussion, but, overall, this was our planned process.

What is important about this conception of the process, is that although there were areas where understanding was lacking, the plan followed a kind of general procedure for developing performance-based productions. The diagram also incorporates a number of assumptions: that a scenario needed to come first, and that following the scenario, the libretto and the music had to come next. In our case, the libretto was viewed as preceding the music because the two steps had to be carried out by different individuals (when carried out by the same individual, historical evidence suggests the process is much more iterative, with a constant back and forward shift of attention between music and libretto [18]). Furthermore,

Team member	Basic expertise	Complementary expertise
Geoffrey Edwards	Senior researcher	Writer (librettist, virtual reality, augmented reality, smart garments, geomatics, motion capture, fashion/costume design)
Jocelyne Kiss	Researcher in music	Virtual reality, singer (soprano), non-verbal communications
Ernesto Morales	Architect, designer	Rehabilitation, co-design
Cora McLaren	Choreographer, dancer	Rehabilitation, nursing
Serge Lacass	Composer, singer	Network communications applications
Sophie Stévance	Singer, theorist	Critical theory
Juan Nino Falcon	Student, mechatronics	Virtual and augmented reality, animation, voice
Marie Louise Bourbeau	Singer, coach	Immersive installations
Jonathan Proulx Guimond	Student, visual design	Avatar design, 3D design
Antoine Guérette	Student, architecture	3D design
Alicia Lamontagne	Student, architecture	3D design
André Dorval	Sound engineer	Experience with film, stage and TV production, concerts and studio recordings

Table 1.
The production team.

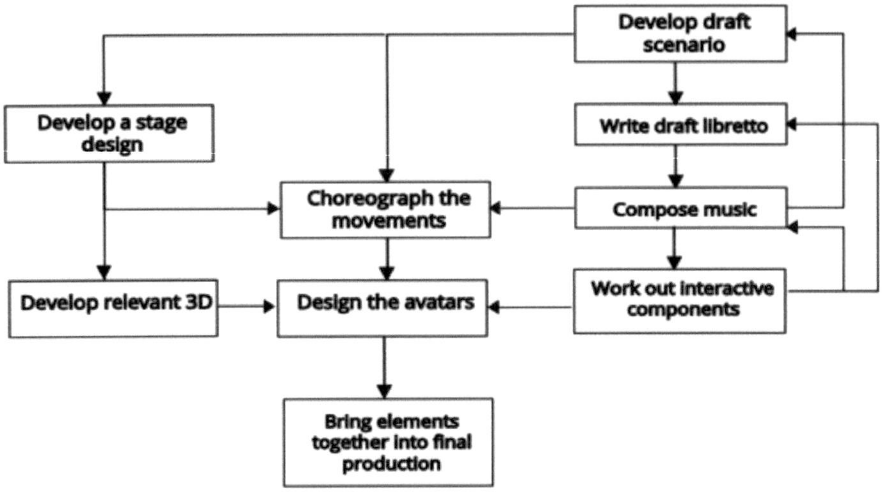

Figure 1.
Original concept of the design process.

within our original discussions about interactivity, the presence of augmented or virtual reality avatars was implicitly assumed, although exactly how these would be integrated was unclear. The diagram incorporates these assumptions.

We also viewed the process as having an addendum—in parallel to, or following, the development of the opera, we would develop an online environment for co-creation, but in our original conception, these tasks were viewed as separate. In the next section, we shall see how the design and production process actually occurred and what the differences between plan and realization taught us about these processes.

3. The production process

3.1 The libretto

Anyone who has worked on a screenplay for a film or a TV episode will attest to this fact—there is nothing "linear" about the process of developing a viable scenario in a group production enterprise. The process took about eight major iterations to arrive at something workable [19], several of these after we had made substantial progress in other areas of the production. Indeed, the scenario and its attendant libretto were still being modified during the final stages of the production, although the changes at that point were limited. The initial problem was to take a 150 page novel and extract from it a scenario that could be presented in a dramatic way within a 20 min span of time. Also, there is very little documentation that exists to guide anyone attempting to develop an opera or write a libretto. The only scholarly text we could find was a small memoire written in 1914 [18] that drew on analysis of existing, mostly nineteenth century operas to make a few suggestions, although there is also information to be gleaned from discussions concerning whether the text or the music should have primacy [20] as well as the process of bringing meraviglia into opera [15].

The original story was focused around the character of Oreph Sodenheim, a young teenager who is the main protagonist of the novel *Pinnacle: The First Book of Eng*. Oreph is a central figure for the larger cycle of 15 novels that collectively forms *The Ido Chronicles* [17]. However, in Pinnacle, he passes through a series of events that lead to the destruction of his family. The subject matter, overall, is therefore depressing. In addition, the main theme of the story is concerned with being bullied, both by conservative factions within the society of the planet called Pinnacle, and also by mysterious groups that belong to the larger civilization called the Humanitat.

As Edwards was working on the compression of the original story to its essential elements—about eight scenes were identified as key, but this remained too long for the planned production—an opportunity came up to develop a short story based on what was originally a secondary character in Pinnacle, that of Oreph's girlfriend, Relliana Sapuro. The short story that resulted from this effort provided a much better framing for the opera, and iterations #2 and #3 involved recasting the original story to include Relliana (iteration #2), and eventually to focus exclusively on Relliana's story (iteration #3). This led to a much more compact scenario, now limited to four scenes, and a story which was overall much more uplifting (although also involving conflict) and which better reflected the title Pinnacle.

In the revised version, Relliana when first encountered is complaining about a set of unusual aches and pains she is experiencing in her body, while also engaging with a friend, Aki Oneya, who is a "gender morph," that is, a person who is bi-gendered. Aki is being bullied by a group of young conformists. Later, Relliana encounters one of the bullies, Mandra Lakso, as it is revealed that her body is undergoing some sort of profound transformation, although we still do not know what this is leading to. During a performance event at the end of the story, Relliana's transformation completes itself and a dragonfly-like winged creature emerges in Relliana's place—the first stage of a new "splinter species" of the human race.

By this time, a stage design had been completed (see Section 2.2 below), and the next iteration led to a reorganization of the scenes so that all the different exchanges could take place within the same physical setting (iteration #4). In addition, the discussions concerning interactions (see Section 2.3 below) had singled out the idea of a finale that would be affected by audience participation, and so the climax of the scenario/libretto was re-written to accommodate a multiplicity of endings (iteration #5).

It should be noted that although in principle the scenario and the libretto are distinct, in practice, given the time constraints of the production schedule, a draft version of the libretto was created as early as iteration #2 of the scenario. The scenario may be viewed as the general description of unfolding events and interactions, whereas the libretto meant the full verse realization of the text to be sung or declaimed.

Interaction elements were also introduced earlier in the scenario, and it was realized that an introductory segment would be useful. As a result, an introduction was written and incorporated into the libretto (iteration #6). During the work on the music, it was realized that the libretto lacked an intimate contact with Relliana and her difficulties—as a result, a new aria was introduced into the libretto (iteration #7). The lead-up to the interactive component in the final scene also needed some adjustments (iteration #8).

The libretto itself was written in metered verse, but drawing on principles such as harnessing the natural rhythms of the English language rather than slaving the verses to its metric structure. In addition, although rhyming structures were used, they were not consistently maintained at all times, again, to break up the regularity of the resulting text. Because the scenario was science fiction, a certain amount of exposition was required—this made for relatively dense lyrical structures, that is, arias that contained significant amounts of information.

The meter and the length of lines were, however, varied across different arias and recitatives as a reflection of the emotional intensities and information being conveyed. Voice range was determined by the available singers—that is, each aria was developed as a function of the vocal range of the singers. This probably follows traditional practice in operatic production—historically, many arias were designed with particular singers in mind, although well-established composers could also pick and choose at will, permitting greater flexibility. Additional small changes were made to the lyrics during the musical composition stage (see Section 3.4 below).

Figures 2–4 show some examples of the libretto lyrics that highlight these considerations.

3.2 Stage and 3D design

As outlined earlier, the original concept was to develop a physical staging of the opera that would incorporate virtual reality or augmented reality elements in support of interactions with users. The design was developed and organized by Morales and his students based on a series of initial discussions about the scenario/libretto as well as the larger opus that framed the opera. Indeed, Morales and Edwards led several co-design sessions held at the CIRRIS[1]. The design was initially organized around the opening scene of the opera, which consisted of a ledge on the side of the airborne city called the Orr Enclave. The Orr Enclave was conceived as being roughly cubical in shape (**Figure 5**), but with numerous extensions and indentations down its sides, one of which formed the stage for the opening scene of the scenario. It became evident that the cost constraints of the production meant that we needed the one stage to support all scenes. For this to work, in addition to the ledge, we needed the main area to have sufficient depth to accommodate bully dancers, we needed a kind of gate-like area that might represent a school playground or patio, and we needed a round "portal" that would provide access to images of diverse types. One of the most important challenges was to decide which parts of the staging should be real and which virtual. We initially assumed that the production would involve both elements within an augmented reality type staging. To do this, the virtual elements needed to be fit perfectly and seamlessly with the real stage objects. We developed and tested virtual components that would operate in this way. In addition, we conceived of the use of VR goggles that could be provided to the public, and which would allow users to select among a range of display options. During the co-design sessions, Morales and Edwards generated many

AKI
It's not a simple change to make.
Six months went by while I regrew.
The moelen folds to either shape.
I can both male and female do.

My parents chose to oppose the trend,
I wish sometimes they'd been more sage
Among our friends I am content
Beyond our circle, things are frayed.
Yes, things are frayed !

Figure 2.
Lyrics sung by Aki, the "gender morph" (bi-gendered person). "Moelen" is the term given to the fold of skin that can curl to form either a pseudo-penis or pseudo-vagina as the situation calls for. The text highlights the use of metric verse and near but not perfect rhymes to break up the regularity of the poetry (e.g., "frayed" is a near rhyme to "sage").

[1] Centre interdisciplinaire de recherche en réadaptation et integration sociale.

CHORUS (the children, chanting as they walk and stamping their feet)

Don't ignore us,
Don't deplore us,
Don't be sore at us, Don't !
We're the enforcers!
Don't fight us,
Don't despise us,
Don't cry on us,
Don't,
We're the enforcers!

Life on Pinnacle's a breeze
Provided one respects the rules
Our ancient culture only serves
Those who follow all decrees.
If you do not want to play,
There's a billion worlds out there.
If you do not want to stay
Take your things and disengage!
Leave us to our old guard ways.

Figure 3.
Example of the lyrics sung by the conformist bullies—the first two verses of the song. Here the meter changes between the snappy chorus and the more substantive main verse. The rhyme scheme for the main verse is abcadeddd, so, again, some regularity and some variation, whereas the chorus is much more structured.

I told Aki of my aches,
Not sinews split in two!
Nor skin that cracks and breaks!
Or bruises black and blue!

It isn't just some odd malaise,
A momentary test,
No, some unexpected beast
Has made of me its nest!
O courage, help me in my quest !
O courage, help me in my quest !

Figure 4.
These lyrics are part of the additional aria added for Relliana to sing, to explain her own feelings about the transformation she was going through.

drawings to ensure staging ideas were clear for everyone involved. In addition, we were conscious that a complex stage would be costly to build, so we were looking for something simple.

Figure 5.
The Orr Enclave, the floating city that serves as the main setting for the events that take place in both Pinnacle: The First Book of Eng (the original novel) and Pinnacle: A One Act Participatory Opera (the opera).

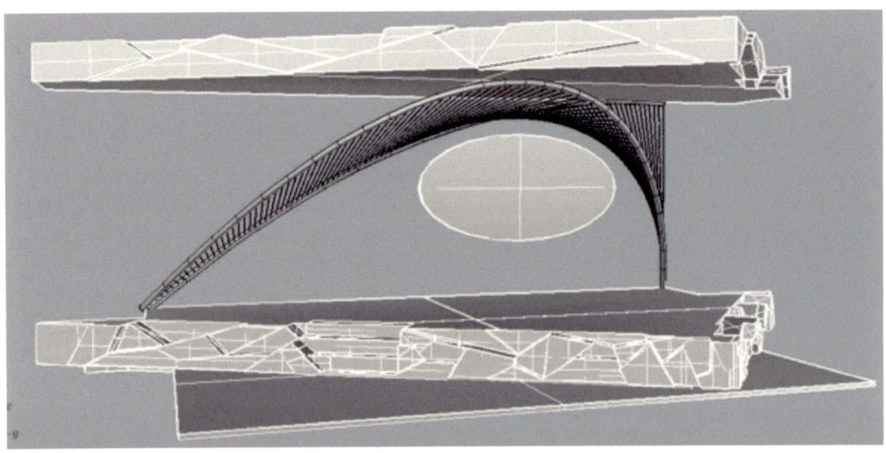

Figure 6.
The basic stage design. The set consisted of a ledge on the side of the city, an oval area onto which images could be projected, a fabric structure (the curved form), and steps from the main stage to the protrubing lower ledge where the nemo plants were to be situated.

The early designs therefore incorporated these different factors (see **Figure 6**).

Since it is supposed that the city itself was composed largely of fabric materials along with some structural, weight bearing elements (that is, because the city floats in the atmosphere, it must be made out of light materials), the final stage design incorporated fabric, cord and aluminum struts into an elegant design that could be relatively inexpensive to construct. Different variants of the ledge structure and upper area were proposed—only one of these is shown in **Figure 6**. Further along we shall show the staging area used in the final production.

The production almost stalled when it was realized that our budget was probably not adequate to cover the stage construction costs. It was at this point in the development that the team decided to go with a virtual staging which was much easier to manage within the context of the grant monies, even though the final costs may have been roughly commensurate to those involved in a physical staging. The difference was that the costs of the virtual production went primarily towards paying students rather than into the construction materials themselves, which would have required storage, which needed to be dismantled and then rebuilt and so robust against such manipulations, and so forth. No doubt a more experienced production team would have known how to circumvent these issues more effectively, although the budget was fixed and rather modest.

The advantage of shifting the production towards a virtual staging meant that the two initiatives, which were initially viewed as separate, could be merged together into common development protocols—that is, the construction of the opera and the construction of an online co-creation environment. The latter effort had been focused towards the creation of a 3D version of the "cube city." Edwards had initially developed some rudimentary 3D models of the city (see **Figure 7**) that showed both its internal structure and the locations of key scenes. Drawing on the architectural expertise of students such as Alicia Lamontage, under guidance from Edwards, a rough design for the top of the "cube city" was developed. Within this structure, several key features that were present in the original novel (*Pinnacle*: *The First Book of Eng*) were given a detailed structure—the Agora space in which major events took place, the sunken Concourse area where the final performance was originally planned, the Portal building, where information about other planets and habits could be accessed, and the threader stations where the spindle-like transport vehicles, which moved within dedicated tubes, could be boarded. In addition, for the online co-creation environment, an additional location was eventually introduced, a monument space along the front edge of the city top (**Figure 8**).

The disadvantage with the shift from a physical to a virtual production was that we needed to work harder to find ways to bring "embodiment issues" back into the production of what would be essentially a virtual opera (see next section). We felt

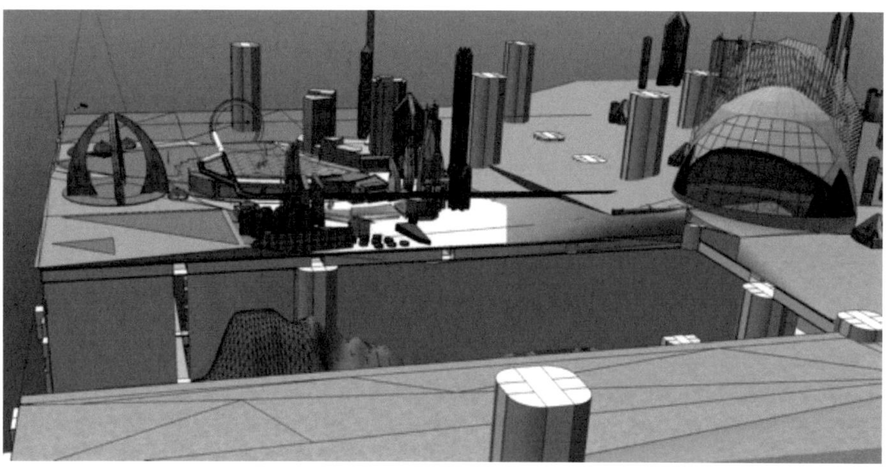

Figure 7.
Early design for the top surface of the cube-shaped city of Orr Enclave; the cleft is the location of the concourse, the blue dome at the right is the Agora and the arched shape at the left is the monument.

Figure 8.
(Above) The monument site and the threader transport system (tubes), in the early design, and (below) as later implemented within Unity in the co-creation environment, along with the user avatar (labeled) and the dancing avatars.

from the beginning that the opera needed to be "embodied"—part of both Edwards' and Kiss' larger research programs concern how to enhance embodiment effects within environments that may be partially or wholly virtual. Indeed, our use of live singing/declaiming was also an attempt to enhance the feelings of presence and embodiment ([21], see also Section 2.4 below).

Furthermore, to return to the opera staging, the 3D city design allowed us to stage the opera on the ledge on the side of the city. Rather than redesign this area, the design of the physical stage was simply incorporated into the 3D city design, resulting in the final "stage" for the virtual opera (**Figure 9**). This elegant solution meant that if, at some future occasion, we should want to physically stage the opera, we could do so with no substantive changes to the overall set design. Furthermore, the approach used aligns with cognitive design principles [22, 23].

Figure 9.
Virtual stage for the opera, incorporated into the 3D city design. Shown is the scene with the bully dancers, with Aki (in blue) and Relliana in gray and brown next to hir.

The final virtual rendition of the stage was carried out by a visual arts student, Jonathan Proulx Guimond. As we shall discuss further on, Jonathan also did extensive development, in tandem with our engineering student, Juan Nino Falcon, of the more extensive virtual environment used for the co-creation endeavor (see Section 2.10 below).

3.3 Interactive components

As might be expected, designing and incorporating interactive elements into the opera posed enormous challenges to the production team. The problem was to allow the audience to influence the unfolding story in manageable ways that were thematically compelling in the frame of the story itself. Hence, for example, many potential interactions discussed were discarded either because they would have been too costly to do effectively or alternatively, because they allowed game-like interactions that were, however, poorly integrated with the story line.

Any attempt to use the audience's interactions to modify the story potentially runs into the problem of combinatorics. If a choice of two outcomes is introduced, then two stories need to be constructed. If a second choice of two outcomes is introduced, at another point of the story, then four versions of the story need to be determined. For a third decision point, we are now at eight versions of the story, and so on. This quickly becomes unmanageable. Therefore a "management strategy" needs to be developed to allow variation without leading to such combinatory effects. For example, audiences could be given the ability to modify aspects of the staging that concern appearance (i.e., esthetics) but which do not substantially influence the plot itself.

Early on in the design process, even during the stage when we were considering a physical staging with additional virtual elements via augmented reality techniques, we developed an approach where each audience member could have their own "access device" within which they could be given more flexibility for customization than in the common staging, whether the latter be physical or virtual. Possibilities discussed for these devices included introducing virtual flora and fauna that could be influenced by the audience member (**Figure 10**), superimposing a photograph of the audience member's face on one of the actor's (or avatar's) faces so that the

Figure 10.
The nemo plants (blue) emit particles that enhance airborne buoyancy and in addition that respond to audience input (via either voice or breath).

audience member could experience an enhanced identification with a character of their choice (early experimentation showed this to be possible—see **Figure 11**), and introducing new (virtual) avatars that moved between the actors and which could be influenced by audience members. Furthermore, Kiss believed the possibility existed to incorporate voices from the audience members as well, although this possibility was never fully fleshed out. ... In addition, even for a physical staging of the opera, we realized that it would be possible to "add in" the side of the city around the physical stage using augmented reality techniques—again, early experimentation showed this could be achieved sufficiently well to create the impression that the action was taking place on the side of the floating city.

Of course, once we abandoned the idea of doing a physical staging, the integration of virtual elements into the staging was greatly facilitated—we no longer had to worry about anchoring virtual elements into the physical stage (even though we had demonstrated to our own satisfaction that this was feasible).

There were concerns even from the early discussions about the intrusive nature of "viewing technologies," whether these be expensive devices like VR or AR glasses, or cheaper devices such as tablets or smartphones. Among alternatives we discussed (and tested) were the use of simple smart garments—and in the end we did develop and test an interactive belt device.

Another interest was to generate interactive possibilities that allowed audience members to work together to affect the opera, and not merely opportunities for individual customization. Finding an interactive modality that would not corrupt the opera's story line remained a challenge throughout these discussions. Any attempt to provide users with some form of access to or control over avatars on the stage seemed to mean disrupting the way the story evolved. Of course, one option could have been to abandon any effort to control the storyline, and this might have been an interesting endeavor, but having taken the time to select a scenario and construct a libretto, this seemed self-defeating. We therefore sought mechanisms for interaction that preserved the story-line or allowed only for limited variations.

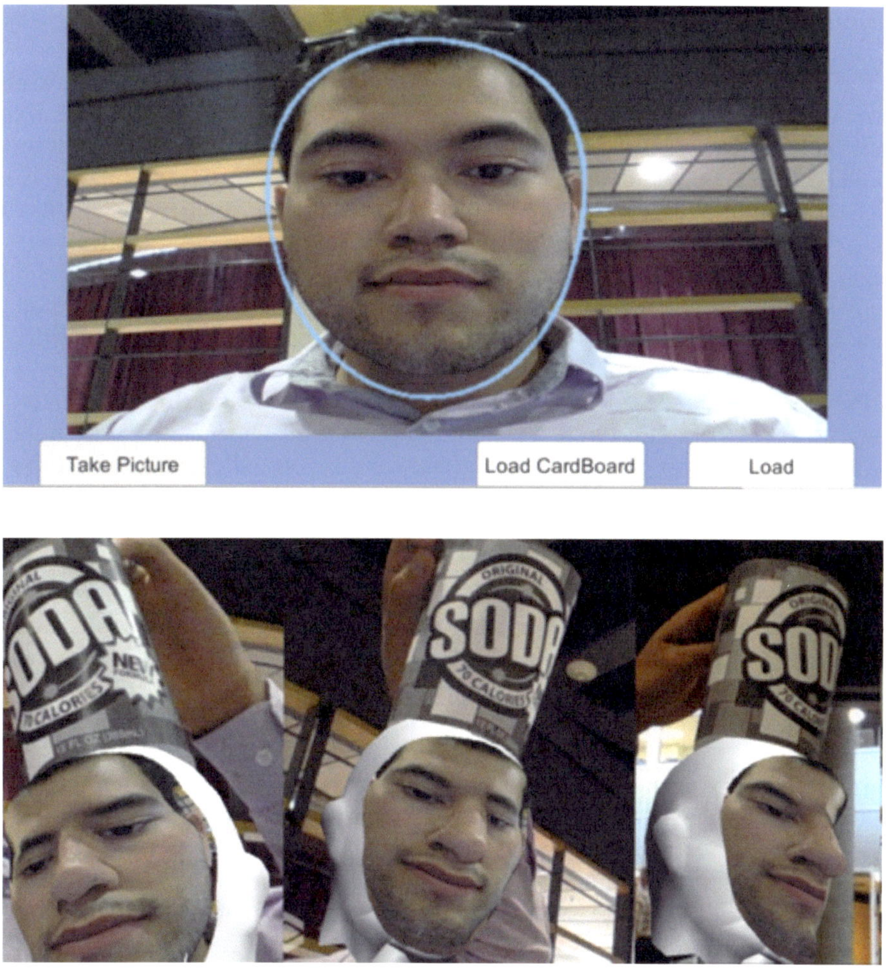

Figure 11.
Superimposing a photographed face onto an avatar; above—the software used to capture the image of the face; below—the rendered virtual face using the soda can as the directional reference object (normally, the reference object would be invisible or more discrete!).

Our solution to the problem of allowing audience members to introduce elements that could affect the story in limited ways that nonetheless felt "organic" was to focus on the flora and fauna that form an essential background to the stage setting (in fact, to the world being presented via the staging), and could be allowed to influence the unfolding of the story even if such influences had not been present in the original version (the source novel). The world portrayed in the larger opus (*The Ido Chronicles*) is situated in the far future, at a time when ecosystems are essentially constructed by humans. These constructed ecosystems are designed to provide utilitarian functionality to support a range of human activities as well as to function with each other in ecological ensembles. Among the plants and animals described in the Chronicles are plants called "nemos" and animal hybrids such as "doskies" (combining features of flying squirrels and dogs) or adapted animal species such as "jonahs" (modified sperm whales). Nemos are plants derived from sea anemones that bush outwards via tendril-like leaves that collect water droplets from the air, while "spiners" are adapted from spiders to spin structural elements for buildings. Doskies are a kind of flying or gliding domestic pet. Jonahs have been modified to function in interstellar vacuum and can transport people or freight between planets or habitats inside a solar system.

For the purposes of the opera, we decided that nemos could emit some kind of particle that would provide buoyancy to someone attempting to float or glide in the air. In addition, we assumed they could sense and mimic vocal tones, and that they would emit their buoyant particles following vocal stimulation. By populating the ledge on which the stage is set with nemos, we could introduce virtual elements that could be controlled by humans. We explored several interaction modalities—as suggested in the previous sentences, vocal activation was one of these, and the one we eventually retained. But in an earlier effort, we also developed a belt that activated the nemos via a person's breathing. Both of these interaction modalities were attempts to re-introduce embodied interactions into the opera.

We modified the scenario to accommodate these interactions. In the original scenario, a group of bullies were intimidating the two principal characters, Oreph and Relliana, in the opening scene, and these would eventually be pushed off the city. However, they both wore "windplanes," a kind of glider that allowed them to escape falling to the distant ground. In the early scenario modifications, we determined that if the nemos were activated enough, then the two characters would not fall at all, they would fly up. Later, however, as we simplified the story line to fit it into a sufficiently short time from (less than 30 min), we used the same idea in the final scene of the opera. Now, however, it was the transformed Relliana, with her nascent wings, that was to be supported by the audience interaction. If they successfully supported her, she flew away upwards. If they failed, she eventually fell downwards.

In addition, we posited the existence of a plant species we called "phramae," which could organize into physical forms that mimic, in a ghost-like manner, the movement of real creatures, human or otherwise. These phramae were used in the bully sequence to make a number of additional dancers than the small number of actual bullies, and they were also used in the on-line co-creation environment to provide added control to users to "create" their own dancing avatars (see Section 2.10 below).

3.4 Music

Developing the music for this opera posed several challenges. For reasons that are too complex to go into here, Lacasse was not as available to do as much composing as had been originally planned. The libretto, which as outlined earlier went through many different versions, incorporated relatively early on a "bully song," to be sung by a main "bully" and his/her troops as they underwent a "bully dance." Lacasse developed quickly a successful musical rendition of the bully song, drawing on both pop culture musical ideas as well as more traditional opera constructions. The result was compelling in interesting ways. The bullies in the scenario are complex individuals in the sense that they are not simply "bad guys." They promote a kind of conformism, but they are in some sense supported by the ambient culture, and their ideas are not unsympathetic. Lacasse captured these ambiguities in his musical rendition, giving them a positive energy offset by the negative sentiments to some extent expressed in the lyrics.

Following this initial effort, however, Lacasse was no longer available to develop the remainder of the songs or the musical introduction. Kiss, who has no claims to be a composer, drew on a process of combining public domain royalty-free samplings, some recordings she had from an earlier collaboration with violincellist Haruko Kido, and a knack for bringing disparate elements from the creative commons together into a musical rendition which while not as "characteristically individualistic" as Lacasse's work had been, resulted in a musical soundtrack that supported the opera in appropriate and interesting ways. She and Edwards worked in tandem on this, Edwards for overall direction and Kiss for the creative musicality of the ensemble. In addition, we consulted with Marie Louise Bourbeau, another collaborator with extensive experience in lyric singing and musical production, who helped guide us through some of the difficult choices we had to make at that point in the production.

3.5 Choreography

Once Serge Lacasse had produced the music for the bully song, we solicited our choreographic collaborator, Coralee McLaren, to develop a musically-responsive dance work. At that time, we were still orienting towards a physical staging, so we were looking for movement that could be performed by a small group of dancers on stage. However, we also imagined using virtual avatars in addition to actual dancers. As such, we organized a movement session with Motion Capture equipment available to us through Edwards' engagement with the Centre interdisciplinaire de recherche en réadapation et intégration sociale (CIRRIS), a research center in rehabilitation. Dr. McLaren flew from Toronto to Quebec City to carry out this work. In preparation, she created a number of movement phrases that complimented Lacasse's rhythms and melodies. Drawing on these phrases, McLaren responded physically to spontaneous feedback called out from the team, and modified/refined her movement in response to fast changing, verbal cues. This resulted in an unparalleled collaborative movement experience and invaluable methodological insight, with each "audience" member providing input that reflected his or her own sensorial expertise or movement preferences (e.g., as singer, stage designer, writer, composer, etc.). The final outcome was a dance that enhanced Lacasse's dynamically rich score, and a subsequent Motion Capture sequence of movement was digitally applied to the avatars during the virtual staging (**Figure 12**). Furthermore, as we shall discuss below, the dance sequences were included within the co-creation environment in interesting ways.

3.6 Animation

Once we had opted for a purely virtual staging, the major issues became the process of developing and animating the avatars that would represent the characters in the story. There were a number of issues that affected this process. As mentioned earlier we were experimenting with the idea of applying a user's face to the avatars,

Figure 12.
Matching the motion capture recorded movements to the avatar movements.

and so, at least in the preliminary version of the opera, we used our own faces. There are three main characters in the opera, and we applied an image of our faces to each of these characters—Kiss's face was applied to Relliana, Falcon's face to Mandra, the leader of the bullies, and Edwards' face to Aki, Relliana's friend. Aki is a bi-gendered character—neither female nor male. Therefore, we chose a neutral morphology for the avatar, used Edwards' masculine face, and chose dress-like clothing which resulted in an avatar which is successfully ambiguous in terms of gender. In follow-up work on the opera we propose to modify the user interface so that the process of assigning the face to the avatar could be carried out by any member of the audience for their private interface. The calibration process that allows this to occur has already been developed, tested and programmed (see **Figure 11**).

The Unity game engine underwent several improvements over the course of the project which allowed us to improve the animations. Initially, the work was quite onerous. In general, gestures, postures and movements were chosen from banks of animation data in appropriate formats that were publically available and these were looped or integrated with other animations to generate movements that would appear (we hoped) as natural as possible. Originally, all the timing of the animations had to be implemented manually. However, after our first public performance, Unity installed a new module called Timeline that enabled a more organic and systemic control of the timing between different events, greatly facilitating the subsequent animation efforts. A second major challenge was the development of appropriate lip-synching. Finding a reliable and robust method to develop lip-synching of the avatars with the singing proved to be a substantial challenge, and was never solved to our complete satisfaction.

Another problem with the use of avatars and a virtual reality environment, of course, is that the sense of embodiment, of embodied actors is largely lost. Since the themes incorporated into the opera were at least partially resonant with issues of embodiment, this was a significant deception for the production team, and we worked hard to re-introduce elements of embodiment to compensate for this loss.

The fourth element that needed to be mastered to create a compelling operatic experience, beyond the appearance of the avatars, their programmed movements, and the lip-synching, was the development of camera zooming and panning sequences that could also be used to enhance the drama. Because the opera was presented in a "streaming" Unity environment, in principle the means to control the camera could have been left in the hands of the user/observer. However, since camera movements can significantly enhance or detract from dramatic tension, we retained control of these elements in our first version of the opera.

3.7 Bringing the components together

Additional elements that needed to be managed included the opening sequence, the closing sequence, and the introductory remarks and organization. Indeed, because the opera presented the audience with a number of new elements, explanations needed to be provided along with some basic "training." We organized the material into several formats for different presentation protocols. In most of our presentations, we performed the singing live in addition to the prerecorded music.

Hence, during our first presentation, we used belts that tracked the singer's breathing and used the breath as a way to "operate" the interactive plants so that they opened wide under deeper and more expansive breathing and spread more of the buoyant particles into the air. The belts were designed using "flex bands," that is, sensors that convert elastic stretch into a capacitance measurement that can be read off by a computer chip. However, although we achieved one working prototype, the second failed to operate correctly. Given the difficulties ensuring robust measurements from the belts, we developed a second interaction method which used a centrally placed microphone to capture the audience singing and used the intensity of the voice to open the nemos and create more buoyant particles. This solution was much more robust and repeatable, and so we eventually adopted this solution within our final production.

3.8 Public performances

The initial staging was done using the Unity Game Engine in interactive mode projected onto a shared screen, following a predetermined script that determined avatar movements, virtual camera movements, music soundtracks, and that tracked voice production on the part of the audience. In addition, the two main live performers, Kiss and Edwards, sang (in Edwards' case, declaimed) the lyrics along with the pre-recorded lyrical tracks. The second and third times we presented the opera, we used a video recording of the scripted Unity staging along with the live performers and the voice-interaction module. This allowed us to incorporate subtitles in either English or French translation to assist audiences in understanding the sung or spoken text, as well as facilitating the complexity of the staging. In the final public presentation, we used a different real-time streaming version designed using the 360 view capabilities made available in the more recent version of Unity, with a view to giving the user greater flexibility using VR glasses to change view directions. For this fourth presentation, we had refined the avatar and camera movements, and had done more work on the lip-synching. This fourth staging could, in principal, accommodate changes to scripting possibilities and potentially allows for multiple endings. In the second, third and fourth stagings, we trained the audience to sing a small melodic line that could be used to guide the protagonist towards her more hopeful outcome.

3.9 Post-performance discussions

Each time we presented the opera to a public, we engaged in a post-performance discussion to both assess reactions on the part of audience members concerning content and staging, but also to discuss technical aspects of the production that might interest audience members. One of the goals of the development of this opera was to engage audiences around content issues, that is, the need to be more tolerant towards others who are different from ourselves, especially in the light of peer pressures towards greater conformity, but also to recognize that even tolerant communities may include individuals or groups who are less tolerant, and that communities that may at first appear to be intolerant may include elements who are more tolerant if one only paid more attention.

Overall, audiences reacted favorably to the opera as staged, and during the discussion it became clear that the conformity-tolerance issues were accepted and interesting discussions ensued. These were mostly scientific audiences, although they included practitioners from a broad variety of public health contexts, including disability studies, mental health, social justice, and so on.

3.10 The co-creation environment

Originally conceived to be a tool to enable public engagement in the process of producing the opera (and this is still our long term goal), it was necessary to simplify to some extent the design of the environment to fit for the budget and time constraints of the project. Essentially, we had funding for 3 years and the process of developing the opera itself took most of the first 2 years, leaving a little over a year to develop the co-creation environment (talesfromthehumanitat.com) with, by that point, greatly reduced funding.

We used the 3d design developed for the opera as the substratum for the co-creation environment—although we also substantially embellished the environment to provide more virtual experiences in much greater detail, drawing on both information provided by the original novel and extended notes by the author (Edwards). While the setting for the opera itself was a platform on the side of the floating city, we used the top surface of the city to define four areas for the co-creation environment. Each of these areas showcases a different set of co-creation tools. **Table 2** presents the main features of these four sites.

In addition to the sites themselves, we implemented a transport system. This was part of the fictional world on which the opera was based. Transport vehicles are called "threaders"—they are elongated spindle-like structures that move in closed tubes. The user of the co-creation environment may move by foot between the four sites, or may use a transport.

Furthermore, we framed the experience for the online co-creation environment within a game. Hence the user, upon entry, is presented with the task of collecting five medallions, representing the five different factions (EngFax, DeoFax, UmaFax, EcoFax and IdoFax), each of which is located at one of the co-creation stations. Note that the images used for the five medallions were designs developed by Morales at the request of Edwards in support of the novel cycle. The first medallion is provided to begin with, and the user must visit each of the co-creation stations to find the other medallions. Furthermore, they must activate the co-creation mechanisms to gain access to the medallion. The location of the medallion is indicated once the station's particular co-creation modality is engaged by a rising stream of red particles. Once all five medallions are collected, the user must find the final stream of particles to bring the five medallions together, and this liberates a final surprise interaction, which consists of access to an oracular service.

Hence, in a typical gaming encounter, a user would visit the dance zone and create a choreography with as many dancers as they chose (**Figure 13a**), would visit the Concourse and capture sung or whistled melodies that would be reproduced by the nemos when avatars passed nearby (**Figure 13b**), would visit the Agora and interact with the jonahs through their breathing, (**Figure 13c**) and would visit the Portals and either view/read or post a document of their choosing (**Figure 13d**), and would do these activities in any order. Moving between the sites could be done either on foot or via the transport system. Having visited and activated each of the four sites, the user could then access the oracular system, which is based on another of the 15 volumes that make up the *Ido Chronicles* (**Figure 14**). The interactive music components incorporated design principles developed by Kiss and her students [24] for the VR staging of music.

In addition to ensuring the esthetics of the 3d design of the co-creation environment, our visual designer, Jonathan Proulx Guimond worked on optimizing the rendition to make the complex 3d structure digitally more compact so as to

Site name	Plant/animal	Site building	Co-creation skills
Dance zone	Phramae	Monument	Dance
Concourse	Nemos	Concourse	Singing
Agora	Jonahs	Agora	Video
Portals	Spiners	Portal	Text

Table 2.
Co-creation stations.

Figure 13.
The four stations of the online co-creation environment. (a) The dance zone; (b) the concourse; (c) the Agora; and (d) the portals.

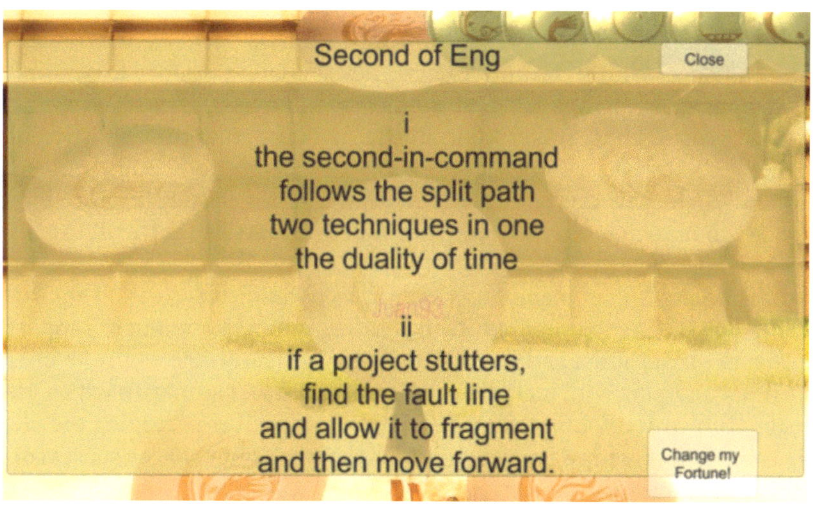

Figure 14.
Accessing the oracular function of the online co-creation environment.

ensure faster loading times and better dynamics. For example, objects were sorted in terms of visibility for each scene, and objects not visible in any of the principal scenes were suppressed. Furthermore, details for objects that were far from camera positions were also suppressed. Objects were also grouped together where possible to diminish rendering times for complex structures. The colors were processed to incorporate atmospheric absorption and the effects of distance were also included in the quality of the rendering.

4. Discussion

The participatory opera we designed and implemented has both strengths and weaknesses. On the positive side of the ledger, we developed a viable staging from a complex story and setting that is understood and appreciated by audiences (given the far future setting and the science fiction components, this is itself a net achievement). The story is perceived as being engaging and intense, as well as having undeniable poetic and esthetic qualities. Furthermore, as we desired, the opera raises interesting and nuanced questions and elicits discussion about tolerance and conformity.

On the other hand, none of the current (virtual) staging efforts was fully successful. Indeed, despite several attempts to re-introduce embodied elements into the opera via interactive components, for example, audience identification with the avatars remains weaker than we would have preferred. For example, the bully dance, which was brilliantly choreographed, remains of muted impact because the dance movements are applied to the small figures of the animated dancers. To have more impact, the animations of individual dancers should vary slightly from one dancer to the next, and means should be provided to view "up close" the dance sequences. The integration of live lyrics with the pre-recorded or scripted scenarios helped give the opera a more effective impact [23], but the integration of the live, virtual and pre-recorded components remains a challenge.

The incorporation of subtitles into the staging was easier to do using the pre-recorded scenarios than in the scripted scenarios. Although the scripted staging offers in principle greater flexibility, in practice most members of the audience were not even aware of the difference between the two options, and the pre-recorded option is much easier to manage since it consists only of running video footage (rather than triggering Unity scripts that have to work together).

The interaction via the plant ecosystem appears to be a successful strategy for engaging audiences within the unfolding action. It allows the story to be influenced in "organic" ways without these being overly intrusive. However, the actual interaction as carried out remains of limited scope (affecting the final success of the protagonist's flight). We would like to provide more varied opportunities for interaction—again, this was part of our original concept but our resource limitations made full implementation of more complex interactions difficult to achieve, even within the virtual staging.

We also successfully implemented a multiplayer online co-creation environment, although we have as yet not fully harnessed the environment to support the ongoing work on the opera and its potential sequels. The online environment allows users to input and play with melodies, movement and text scenarios with a view to influencing future development of related operas, as well as providing the means to explore other aspects of the "world building" that contribute to the success of the Ido Chronicles universe.

Validation remains an issue that has not been adequately addressed. The effort to develop the opera was itself so demanding that we had little time or resources left over to work out a viable evaluation protocol. Coming up with assessment modalities is part of the ongoing work we are looking into. Indeed, assessment needs to address several contexts: the success of the opera as an artistic achievement, its success in raising pertinent issues for discussion, and the success of particular technical features of the opera design.

In the introduction, the value of the opera project to the writer (Edwards) was described. Although the project is by no means finished, and the full engagement with the public has yet to be achieved, the work to date has led to the opening of significant areas for further development. In particular, Edwards has begun work on a second context, that of the passage of trauma across generations, within the context of the impacts of the Second World War. Drawing on the existing work within the opera project and its online co-creation environment, we are now beginning the development of an additional co-creation environment dealing with this other context, hence creating extended value for engendering transformation within broader publics.

Furthermore, the story of *Pinnacle: The First Book of Eng* was substantially modified to support the development of the opera script and its corresponding libretto. Given that the *Ido Chronicles* itself is still undergoing publication [17], this presents an opportunity to "update" the story of Pinnacle to bring it into alignment with the opera. Note that one of Edwards' goals in writing the *Ido Chronicles* was to allow for a certain level of inconsistency to exist between the different versions of the same story, that is, emphasizing that multiple truths are needed to describe human experiences, not all of them consistent with each other. Nonetheless, the opera represents a dramatic change and hence some effort to reduce the level of inconsistency is being attempted. *Pinnacle: The First Book of Eng* required revision in any case, for other reasons, but the rewriting will include paying attention to the need to bring the text within the broad framework provided by the operatic version of the text. Hence the work on the opera has enriched the writing of the source story in substantive and interesting ways.

5. Conclusion

Our team remains convinced that participatory opera is viable despite skepticism on the part of some practitioners [25]. Our project, in many ways, only scratched the surface of what could be achieved. Participation could potentially involve many different modalities, up to and including direct insertion of audience members, e.g., as avatars, into the unfolding scenario of the opera. However, such direct insertion poses challenges for managing the story line that results. We found a more organic means of having audiences influence the unfolding action by allowing them to control flora and fauna, that is, peripheral elements within the current set design that nonetheless may affect the story line.

We also noted that it is possible to provide a kind of "local" interaction that individual observers may see—through, for example, a virtual or augmented reality device without affecting the shared perspective—that is, they may control the virtual appearance (e.g., esthetics) of many of the scene elements without necessarily affecting the story line itself. These esthetic considerations/interactions will also affect the final perception by the participant of the opera. Indeed our work highlights these two distinct modalities for participation, one involving the private customization of the esthetics of the presentation via personal devices, and the other collecting reactions (i.e., gestures, voice) so as to ensure their cumulative effect on the shared action as it unfolds.

Although we remain convinced that augmented reality productions are a viable performance modality, our experience of augmented virtuality constitutes a useful and significantly less costly performance alternative. We use the term "augmented virtuality" to highlight the fact that although our opera was virtual, it included live performance elements that enhanced what would otherwise be a pure VR experience [26]. For opera designed to be presented to small audiences in, for example, educational settings, virtual opera is a feasible product, where a fully developed stage production or even a reduced augmented reality staging would be prohibitively expensive.

Now that the opera and the online co-creation environment are both complete, we will be using these to reach out to a range of audiences in order to address issues of tolerance, change, conformity, disability and other relevant issues raised by these productions. We are also planning to extend the capabilities of the online co-creation environment and to encourage its use as a means to engage audiences in the production process, that is, the development of new operas, or in support of other collective ventures. Finally, it is worth noting that as a collaborative effort this was an extraordinary adventure at the intersection between artistic creation, technological innovation and the science of audience engagement.

Acknowledgements

We gratefully acknowledge the financial support of the Canadian Social Sciences and Humanities Research Council (SSHRC) via its Insight Development Program, and also we thank Sophie Stévance, Erin Manning, Adel Elmaghraby, Alicia Lamontagne, Antoine Guérette, Afnen Arfaoui and André Dorval for their contributions to this work.

Author details

Geoffrey Edwards[1,2*], Jocelyne Kiss[1,3], Ernesto Morales[1,4], Coralee McLaren[5], Serge Lacasse[3], Marie Louise Bourbeau[6], Juan Nino Falcon[1] and Jonathan Proulx Guimond[1]

1 Centre Interdisciplinaire de Recherche en Réadaptation et Integration Sociale (CIRRIS), Québec, Canada

2 Département des Sciences Géomatiques, Faculté de Foresterie, Géographie et Géomatique, Université Laval, Québec, Canada

3 Faculté de Musique, Université Laval, Québec, Canada

4 Département de Réadaptation, Faculté de Médicine, Université Laval, Québec, Canada

5 Daphne Cockwell School of Nursing, Ryerson University, Toronto, Ontario, Canada

6 Bourbeau Voice Dynamics, Montréal, Québec, Canada

*Address all correspondence to: geoffrey.edwards@scg.ulaval.ca

References

[1] Forment B, editor. (Dis) Embodying Myths in Ancient Regime Opera: Multidisciplinary Perspectives. Leuven, Belgium: Leuven University Press; 2012

[2] Daly C. Revue générale de l'architecture et des travaux publics. Paris; Volume 5. 1844. pp. 160-162

[3] Mégevand M. L'éternel retour du chœur, Littérature, N°131, Masques, intertextes. 2003. pp. 105-122

[4] Patin G. Études sur les tragiques grecs: livre III. In: Théâtre de Sophocle. Paris, France: Hachette; 1981. p. 177

[5] Goehr L. The Imaginary Museum of Musical Works: An Essay in the Philosophy of Music. Oxford: Oxford University Press; 1992

[6] Anna D et al. The "Do-It-Yourself" Artwork: Articipation from Fluxus to New Media. Manchester: Manchester University Press; 2010

[7] Sonvilla-Weiss S. Introduction: Mashups, remix practices and the recombination of existing digital content. In: Mashup Cultures. Heidelberg, Germany: Springer; 2010. pp. 8-23

[8] Harrigan P, Wardrip-Fruin N. Third Person: Authoring and Exploring Vast Narratives. Cambridge: MIT Press; 2009. p. 496

[9] Cheok AD, Weihua W, Yang X, Prince S, Wan FS, Billinghurst M, et al. Interactive theatre experience in embodied+ wearable mixed reality space. In: Mixed and Augmented Reality, 2002. ISMAR 2002. Proceedings. International Symposium on. Darmstadt, Germany: IEEE; pp. 59-317

[10] Novitz D. Participatory art and appreciative practice. The Journal of Aesthetics and Art Criticism. 2001;**59**(2):153-165

[11] Morales E, Gauthier V, Edwards G, Guerette A. Co-designing sex toys for adults with motor disabilities. Sexuality and Disability Journal. 2017;**35**(3):1-10

[12] Morales E, Rousseau J, Passini R. Using a co-design methodology for research on environmental gerontology. Journal of Gerontology & Geriatric Research. 2012;**106**(1):1-10

[13] Bishop C. Artificial Hells: Participatory Art and the Politics of Spectatorship. London, UK: Verso Books; 2012

[14] Kafai YB, Peppler KA. Youth, technology, and DIY: Developing participatory competencies in creative media production. Review of Research in Education. 2011;**35**(1):89-119

[15] Tanay D. The birth of opera and the new science. The European Legacy. 2006;**11**(7):753-764

[16] Edwards G, Bourbeau ML, Dupéré R, Ligozat G, Duguay D. Exploring and reasoning about perceptual spaces for theatre, new media installations and the performing arts. In: Frank A, Mark D, editors. Cognitive and Linguistic Aspects of Geographic Space—New Perspectives on Geographic Information Research. Berlin: Springer Verlag; 2010

[17] Edwards G. The Ido Chronicles. Boulder, Colorado: Untimely Books; 2020. (in press)

[18] Istel E. The Art of Writing Opera-Librettos: Practical Suggestions. Whitefish, Montana, US: Kessinger Publishing; 1914

[19] Pinnacle EG. A One Act Opera: The Libretto. 2018. https://www.geoffreyedwards.org/pinnacle-a-one-act-opera-libretto

[20] Brown HM. Ut musica poesis: Music and poetry in France in the late

sixteenth century. Early Music History. 1994;**13**:1-63

[21] Kiss J. The perception of the vocality with through a virtual 3D interface within the framework of an interactive opera. In: FIRT-IFTR International Conference: The Director in the Theatre World; 22-27 May; St Petersburg. 2004

[22] Edwards G. A virtual test bed in support of cognitively-aware geomatics technologies. In: International Conference on Spatial Information Theory. Berlin: Springer Verlag; 2001

[23] Yaagoubi R, Edwards G. Cognitive design in action: Designing assistive technology for situational awareness in the blind. Disability and Rehabilitation: Assistive Technology. 2008;**3**(5):1-252

[24] Kiss J, Nino J. Mixed-reality game for enhancing uniqueness of user creation in a collaborative music practice environment. In: Proceedings Asian Conference Design and Digital Engineering; Oct. 25-28; Jeju, Korea. 2016

[25] Almenberg G. Notes on Participatory Art: Toward a Manifesto Differentiating it from Open Work, Interactive Art and Relational Art. Bloomington, Indiana, US: Author House; 2010

[26] Dubois E, Nigay L, Troccaz J, Chavanon O, Carrat L. Classification space for augmented surgery, an augmented reality case study. In: Sasse A, Johnson C, editors. Proceedings of Interact'99. Edinburgh (UK): IOS Press; 1999. pp. 353-359

Section 3

Interactive Multimedia and Medicine

Chapter 7

The Graphical Access Challenge for People with Visual Impairments: Positions and Pathways Forward

Jenna L. Gorlewicz, Jennifer L. Tennison, Hari P. Palani and Nicholas A. Giudice

Abstract

Graphical access is one of the most pressing challenges for individuals who are blind or visually impaired. This chapter discusses some of the factors underlying the graphics access challenge, reviews prior approaches to addressing this long-standing information access barrier, and describes some promising new solutions. We specifically focus on touchscreen-based smart devices, a relatively new class of information access technologies, which our group believes represent an exemplary model of user-centered, needs-based design. We highlight both the challenges and the vast potential of these technologies for alleviating the graphics accessibility gap and share the latest results in this line of research. We close with recommendations on ideological shifts in mindset about how we approach solving this vexing access problem, which will complement both technological and perceptual advancements that are rapidly being uncovered through a growing research community in this domain.

Keywords: haptics, touchscreen-based accessibility, vibrotactile displays, multimodal interfaces, information-access technologies

1. Introduction

Lack of access to graphical information represents one of the most pervasive information access challenges faced by people who are blind and visually impaired (BVI). Although graphical information is ubiquitous in today's digital world, the vast majority of this content is highly visual, regardless of setting. For instance, consider looking at graphs in a work report, diagrams in a classroom, figures in a magazine article, images on the internet, photographs of friends on social networking sites, or maps for determining your location and finding routes through an unfamiliar building or city. All of these scenarios consist of highly visual, digital information that is often only conveyed via graphical formats, often excluding low- and no-vision individuals from the content. While many of these visual products can be accessed through alternative means—figures have captions, web-based images have labels, social media photos are tagged, and so on—these text-based descriptions are only sometimes present, and often do not tell the whole story as they are not designed to do so. Unfortunately, their inclusion is more often the exception than the rule and when available, the description is generally short and imprecise, failing to capture much of the information conveyed by the graphical rendering. One need only to read a few alt tags of graphics on the web to demonstrate how poorly these text descriptions convey what is represented in the graphical depiction. Diversification of design to meet a range of accessibility needs in the digital space can make the information given more valuable to users who must access information in a different way [1]. With more content moving to the electronic space, it is paramount that new solutions for graphical information access are explored in the digital domain.

The aim of this chapter is to discuss some of the factors underlying the graphics access problem faced by people who are BVI and to describe the latest class of technologies and techniques that we believe have the most potential to mitigate the problem. We first characterize the persistent challenges that have perpetuated this long-standing information access issue. We then describe some general approaches developed throughout the years to address this challenge. We specifically focus on the role of touchscreen-based smart devices (e.g., phones and tablets), which our group believes is a promising solution moving forward. We then discuss some of the advantages and disadvantages of these devices and share a few ideological positions that we believe must be advanced if we are to truly address the graphical access challenge in the context of new technology development. This chapter sets forth a clear position on the efficacy of this class of information access technology (IAT) and advocates some paradigm shifts in the way that we think about addressing this vexing access problem. It is also meant to serve as a reference for researchers and developers interested in promoting graphical accessibility via new technologies such as touchscreens.

2. Graphical access for people with visual impairments

2.1 The persistent challenge of graphical access

We start by highlighting an important distinction of nonvisual information access between textual and nontextual information sources. Access to printed, text-based material has largely been solved for BVI individuals owing to significant advances over the past 30 plus years in the development of screen-reading software using text-to-speech engines (e.g., JAWS for Windows [2] or VoiceOver for the Mac and iOS-based devices [3]). Indeed, long before these digital speech-based solutions, the Braille code provided a robust system for conveying alpha-numeric information, as well as other literary, mathematical, and musical symbols that are embossed on hardcopy paper (for a review of the history of Braille, see [4]). The development of dynamic, refreshable Braille-display technologies since the 1970s has provided access to the braille code for real-time access to text, often in conjunction with synthetic speech via the aforementioned screen reader software packages. These hardware and software solutions differ widely in their form factor, connectivity, available features, and languages supported but they share a common shortcoming--they are limited to only providing access to textual information. The crux of the problem is that graphical information is almost exclusively rendered visually. In contrast to accessing text-based material, there is no analogous low-cost, intuitive, and commercially available solution for providing individuals who are BVI with dynamic access to visually rendered graphical content. Compounding the problem, compared to the wealth of knowledge that exists about human visual information processing, there is far less basic research addressing the sensory, perceptual, and cognitive factors that are critical for accurate encoding, interpretation, and representation of graphical information rendered using nonvisual channels such as audition or touch. While earlier studies have evaluated many human information processing characteristics for tangible graphics (i.e., pressure based physical stimuli) [5–9], these results cannot ensure saliency when adopted for rendering digital graphical elements on touchscreen interfaces (see [10, 11] for discussion). The reason stems from the nature of the stimuli and its mechanism of delivery. Vibrations from flat touchscreens provide no direct cutaneous cues as are afforded with traditional raised tangible graphics, and they trigger different sensory receptors compared to what is used when encoding traditional "raised" tactile graphics or models.

Lack of access to graphical material is more than a mere frustration or hindrance. Indeed, we argue that it represents one of the biggest challenges to the independence and productivity of individuals who are BVI and has had significant detrimental effects on the educational, vocational, and social prospects for this demographic. In support, consider troubling statistics that have estimated that up to 30% of blind people do not travel independently outside of their home [12], that only ~11% of persons who are BVI have a bachelor's degree [13], and that over 70% of this demographic is unemployed or under-employed [14, 15]. This is not an isolated problem: over 12 million people in the U.S. and 285 million people worldwide are estimated as having some form of significant and uncorrected visual impairment [16]. Unfortunately, this problem is rapidly growing, and the current information gap will likely widen without a tractable solution as: (1) the incidence of people experiencing visual impairment is projected to double by 2030 owing to the aging of our population [17], (2) graphics are increasingly being used as the preferred medium of information exchange, and (3) print-based content is rapidly moving to the digital space. The growing reliance on graphical content is especially evident in educational contexts, where it has been estimated that scientific textbooks and journals contain 1.3 graphical representations per page [18]. The inability for students who are BVI to access this rich graphical content certainly helps explain the particularly low inclusion and success of this demographic in STEM disciplines [19, 20]. Outside of information access in education, the lack of accessibility of many sources of information used in daily life also inevitably contributes to the greater social isolation and depression experienced by individuals who are BVI [21]. Without question, a significant component of improving these statistics (and more importantly, benefitting the lives of BVI individuals at large) involves solving the long-standing information gap caused by lack of access to graphical materials in these domains.

2.2 Current solutions for graphical access

Traditional approaches to creating accessible, tangible graphics, include the use of: (1) a tactile embosser to produce hardcopy raised graphics (e.g., the Tiger embosser [22]); (2) renderings made on heat-sensitive swell paper (e.g., [23]); (3) physical manipulatives that are pinned or velcroed to a board [24]; or more recently, (4) 3D-printed models or manipulatives [25]. **Figure 1** provides examples of these materials.

While these techniques certainly work, they also have several significant shortcomings that limit their efficacy as a robust and broadly applicable solution. The principle drawbacks of these solutions include: (1) the authoring process is often slow and cumbersome and typically requires an individual skilled in creating tactile graphics, (2) the equipment can be prohibitively expensive (e.g., a Tiger embosser

Figure 1.
Examples of traditional methods used to convey graphics (e.g., swell paper, embosser, Wikki Stix).

can cost between $5,000 and $15,000, see [22]), (3) the technology is based on single-purpose hardware often requiring individuals to use an "army of devices" in their daily life, (4) the output is a static representation that can quickly become obsolete and is neither easy nor quick to update, and (5) the output is largely restricted to a single modality (i.e., touch). A lengthier discussion of these limitations and the challenges they pose can be found in Ducasse, Brock, and Jouffrais' review of maps for individuals with BVI [26].

Some of these barriers have been addressed through technology development, with the biggest benefit coming from the use of dynamic touch-based interfaces. For instance, a host of refreshable tactual technologies have been developed based on force feedback, refreshable pin arrays, micro fluidics, and moldable alloys. The thorough review by O'Modhrain and colleagues details the pros and cons of each of these approaches [27]. While such technology developments are pushing the boundaries of new haptic technologies as a means for access, these solutions are not widely available nor broadly adopted. This is likely due to several factors including the high cost and lack of commercial availability associated with most of the haptic systems, the in-depth manufacturing and fabrication process required for some of the technologies, and the need for additional hardware that only adds to the host of access devices and technologies already used by BVI persons.

The promise of low-cost, large-format, dot-based graphic displays has been made for decades and some examples are or were commercially available, such as the DotView from KGS Corporation [28] or the Graphic Window by Handytech [29, 30]. Other approaches have exploited auditory solutions, converting the visually-based information into an acoustic format that employs different sonification techniques and auditory parameters (e.g., pitch, loudness, timbre, or tempo) to convey the graphical content [31–33]. Additional efforts have explored utilizing language-based descriptions to convey graphical information [34, 35]. Auditory and verbal approaches, however, are not optimal as they are based on an interpretive medium that requires cognitive mediation and greater maintenance in attention [36]. Such feedback can also be distracting when accessing information in quiet environments such as classrooms or in a meeting while simultaneously trying to listen to presenters. In addition, we argue that these auditory/linguistic approaches are not as suited to conveying spatial graphics as are touch-based solutions because they do not directly specify spatial relations or provide the necessary kinesthetic feedback that enables spatial organization of information.

The above notable approaches have certainly pushed the possibilities of graphical access, yet it is important to note that simply providing dynamic nonvisual information is not sufficient for conveying and learning graphical materials. In order to effectively meet the larger purpose of what is needed to truly solve the information gap, it is necessary to consider design characteristics that will lead to user acceptance and adoption by the BVI community. These factors include being inexpensive, multi-purpose, multimodal, and readily available. Indeed, many of the solutions discussed above are generally relegated to highly specialized applications and require purpose-built equipment that is designed for specific users, to support specific tasks or needs, in a specific situation or environment. This specificity means that most haptic IATs, even if effective, are too expensive, too limited in their usage applications, too cumbersome, and unduly subject to obsolescence to be viable, long-term information-access solutions for BVI users. There are a growing number of new technologies coming to market that build upon previous work, such as the Graphiti, American Printing House (APH)'s dynamic touch-sensitive pin array [37]; the BLITAB tablet, which is capable of a full page of braille [38]; shapeShift, a refreshable multi-height pin display that can render 3D objects and dynamic movement [39]; and microfluidic-based tablets that are capable of refreshable, raised dots on tablets (e.g., [40, 27]) (see **Figure 2**). Most of these devices, however, are still in the research phase, and many still suffer from high component costs or reliance on hardware-specific platforms, thereby reducing the likelihood of such devices becoming a mainstream solution.

While the above innovative approaches have various benefits, we posit that a more broadly adoptable solution is to use technology that: (1) provides direct perceptual access to the graphical content, as is the case via visual access, (2) is (or could be) mass marketed and readily available among end users, and (3) is based on a computational platform that can be leveraged for other functions/activities. We argue that this is best accomplished using dynamic touch-based (or multimodal) displays implemented on smart devices (phones/tablets). We believe that interfaces leveraging direct touch access are critical in solving the graphical access problem as touch has much in common with visual spatial perception, sharing many parallels with the visual pathways in the brain (e.g., [41, 42]). For example, both modalities extract the basic features and spatiality of an object in the environment and integrate this information to form a complete, coherent representation of the object

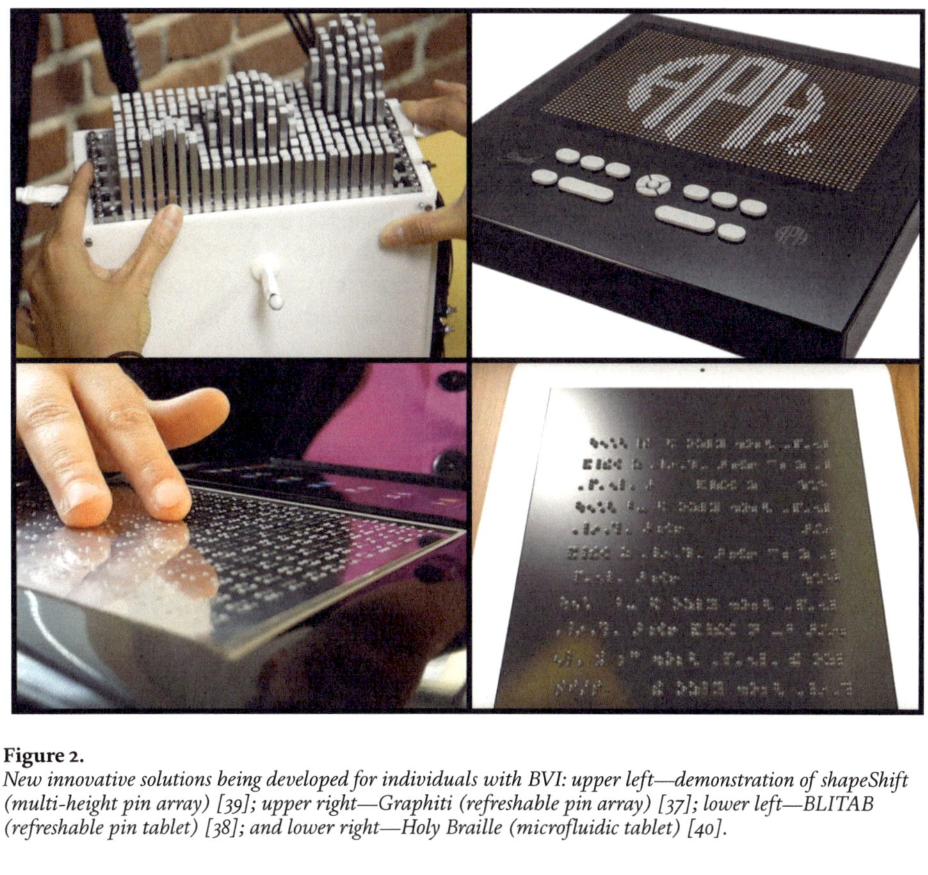

Figure 2.
New innovative solutions being developed for individuals with BVI: upper left—demonstration of shapeShift (multi-height pin array) [39]; upper right—Graphiti (refreshable pin array) [37]; lower left—BLITAB (refreshable pin tablet) [38]; and lower right—Holy Braille (microfluidic tablet) [40].

formed in memory. This lends credence to parallel or shared channels in perception [43, 44]. Further, auditory and verbal approaches often involve more cognitive effort and are thus less "perceptual" than touch-based or visually-based information displays [45]. This is not to say that auditory and verbal approaches should be ignored. To the contrary, we believe in synergizing all available modalities, as is done in some capacity on current vibrotactile touchscreen platforms today, and leveraging the appropriate constituent inputs for best supporting the information to be rendered and the task to be performed. While there are various types of haptic displays, each with their own strengths and weaknesses, the position advanced in this paper is that vibrotactile stimulation, when paired with a touchscreen equipped smart device (e.g., phone or tablet) and other output channels, is a highly promising approach for solving the nonvisual graphics access problem. We believe this platform is quickly becoming the de facto gold standard for IAT and offers a solution that has a high likelihood of being accepted and adopted among its end users, which should be the goal of any IAT design.

2.3 Why vibrotactile, touchscreen-based smart solutions?

We have all experienced our phone vibrating in our pocket to indicate an incoming call or to alert us of an upcoming meeting. However, beyond soliciting our attention, providing simple alerts, signaling a confirmation or error, or any number of other instances of secondary or tertiary cuing, people rarely consider the role of vibrotactile feedback as a primary interaction style. On the one hand, this is surprising given the multitude of common interactions we experience that involve vibration in one capacity or another. Consider the slight detents you feel when spinning the scroll wheel on your computer mouse or the volume dial on your car radio, the signal from your electric toothbrush indicating to brush in another location, the rumble from your game controller indicating an undesired behavior, the alert from the buzzer indicating that your party is being summoned at a restaurant, the vibrating seat in your car indicating that you are backing up near an obstruction, and a myriad of other haptic implementations in current technologies that employ vibrotactile cues for nonvisually conveying relevant information. On the other hand, even if informative, this information is usually either an unintended byproduct of an action, (e.g., vibration from approaching an obstacle), or a secondary cue that is part of a primary interface, (e.g., detents that simply provide frictional control over a spinning wheel/dial). They are often not necessary for its function or primary operation. Indeed, rarely is vibrotactile cuing considered as a primary interaction style. In this chapter, we argue that this need not be the case and that vibrotactile feedback is not only vastly underutilized in current interface design but that vibration can serve as a primary mode of user interaction, especially in conditions where visual access is not possible, such as for use by individuals who are BVI or in eyes-free applications (e.g., driving). We now summarize the current state of research on vibrotactile touchscreen displays before sharing four positions our group believes are needed toward addressing the graphical access challenge moving forward.

2.4 Research brief on vibrotactile touchscreen displays

A growing body of research has demonstrated the efficacy of using touchscreen-based devices and vibrotactile or vibrotactile plus auditory information as a primary interaction style for conveying graphical information. Choi and Kuchenbecker provide an excellent review of vibrotactile displays from both a perceptual and technological perspective, summarizing foundational knowledge in this area and providing implementation guidelines for exemplary applications

[46]. Brewster and colleagues have also done extensive work exploring tactile feedback, particularly from mobile platforms, and have demonstrated important findings illustrating how structured tactile messages (Tactons) can be used to communicate information using different vibration features [47–49]. Other research has demonstrated that vibrotactile feedback enables users to complete scrolling and inputting tasks faster on a mobile device compared to interfaces that lack such feedback [50, 51], and can improve textual reading in braille (e.g., [52–55]). More recent examples have focused on using vibrotactile touchscreen platforms for conveying graphics. A recent project has shown that lines (linear and non-linear) and basic shapes (e.g., circles, triangles, squares) can be successfully interpreted and followed nonvisually through haptic, audio, and haptic-audio access on the touchscreen [5]. Further examples demonstrating the efficacy of this approach were shown when exploring grids [56], graphs [57], maps [58], and nonvisual panning and zooming of large format vibrotactile maps that extended beyond the device's display [11, 59]. In aggregate, this research clearly illustrates the broad potential of this multimodal approach. Work with a prototype system, called a vibro-audio interface (VAI), based on a commercial tablet, has shown near identical accuracy between use of the VAI and hardcopy tactile stimuli for graph interpretation, pattern detection, and shape recognition [60]. In corroboration, studies by Gorlewicz and colleagues have demonstrated no significant differences in the interpretation of a variety of graphics including bar graphs, pie charts, tables, number lines, line graphs, and simple maps that were presented in embossed form and displayed multimodally on a touchscreen created by Vital [61, 62]. Not only do these studies show the efficacy of this interface, but also that this multimodal platform can achieve similar performance to the gold standard of hardcopy graphics. More recent work by our group has also explored the effect of screen size on the

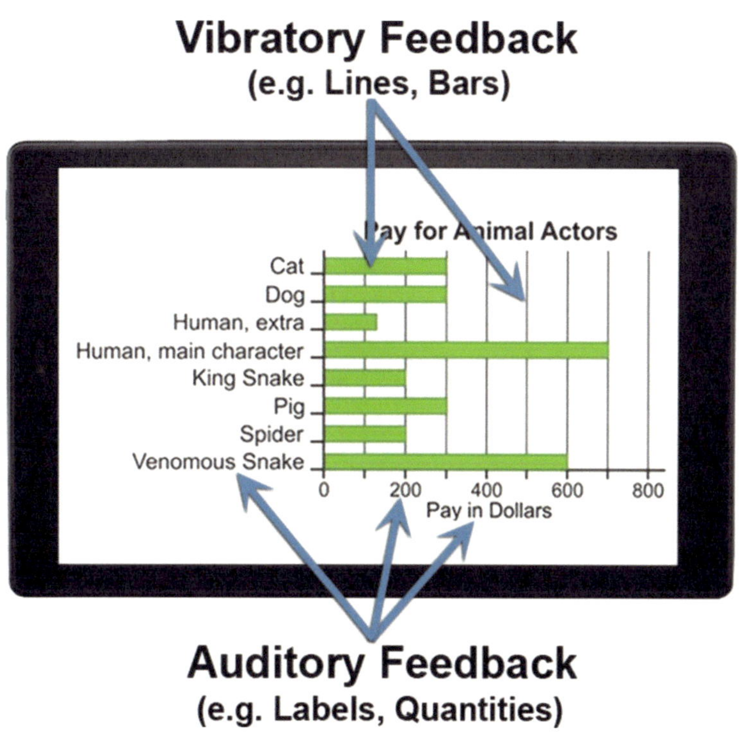

Figure 3.
Touchscreens can leverage both auditory and vibrotactile feedback to convey rich information without the need to look at the screen.

success of these tasks (e.g., tablets versus smaller mobile platforms), and we have shown that performance on a pattern matching task is equivalent across small and large screen sizes [63]. Even though this is a low resolution output mode, these data show that vibrotactile graphics can still be used effectively and accurately when rendered on the smaller form factor of phone-sized smart devices. This is a positive finding, as the majority of BVI users of smart devices are using mobile phones. A recent review by Grussenmeyer and colleagues provides a thorough survey of how touchscreen-based technologies have been used to support information access by people who are BVI and reiterates the prevalent challenges that exist to bring full inclusion to this population [64]. In short, many of these projects suggest promising pathways forward for vibrotactile touchscreens, supported with empirical evidence and positive qualitative feedback of their capacity to convey multimodal information for the interpretation of visual graphics. Moreover, these platforms offer several significant advantages to one-off information access hardware, with the primary benefits being portability, multi-functional use, relative affordability, and widespread adoption and support by the BVI demographic. Indeed, vibrotactile touchscreens provide a robust multimodal framework, which if continually developed in conjunction with advances in touchscreen-based smart devices, has the potential to become the de-facto, universal means for accessing graphics in a multimodal, digital form (for example, see **Figure 3**). A universal, multimodal platform that is widely available is not only beneficial for the BVI population but extends to many others who benefit from multimodal learning platforms and the brain's capacity to process both redundant and complementary information from different senses.

2.5 Positions and pathways forward

While there are promising pathways forward, the graphical access challenge for BVI individuals remains a vexing and largely unsolved problem. We argue that the solution requires advancements on several fronts, including ideological, technological, and perceptual. While there has been significant research advancing our understanding of the technological and perceptual pieces (as illustrated in the vibrotactile touchscreen use case presented here), we also want to call the community to consider new ideological perspectives that will advance the field as a whole. Specifically, we present four positions that our group views as necessary for moving closer to addressing the graphical access challenge and that we see as being best addressed by vibrotactile touchscreen technology:

1. A shift in thinking of assistive technologies as single-purpose, specialized hardware solutions to considering mainstream technologies (and simple adaptations to them) as a first choice for a development platform.

2. A shift in the traditional approach of retrofitting existing technologies for accessibility to embedding universal design in technologies from the onset.

3. A shift in using unimodal feedback as a primary mode of interaction to leveraging all modalities available for primary interactions.

4. A shift in designing based on features and capabilities to a principled design approach driven by end user needs that is scoped by practical guidelines supporting efficient and effective usage/implementation.

We briefly elaborate on these positions below.

2.6 Ideological requirements

2.6.1 A shift from using single-purpose, specialized hardware solutions to considering mainstream, multi-use technologies

To truly advance this class of technology, we need a shift from thinking of assistive technologies as being specialized, single-purpose hardware/software supporting a single (niche) user group to being incorporated in a commercial platform supporting multiple functions that can be used by a broad range of people. Of course, specialized equipment is necessary in certain instances—if you want a hardcopy page of braille or to emboss a physical tactile map, you will need a specialized Braille/graphics embosser. However, in many instances, nonvisual access to information can be delivered using standard commercial devices, which has the advantage of vastly decreasing the development costs and purchase price, thereby increasing actual adoption by BVI users. One example of this is text-to-speech engines, which provide access to visually-based textual information on the screen via speech output. While an intervening software layer is needed to efficiently analyze the video model and represent this information in an intuitive manner for auditory output, the requisite hardware involving a sound card and speaker output is already available on almost all commercial devices. Adding speech input requires a mic, which is also on all smart devices, as is embedded speech-to-text software. In the spirit of this chapter, this idea can be extended to include tactile feedback. Many current touchscreen displays have vibration capabilities in some form. Using the standard vibration motor can open pathways to a whole new universe of haptic information that can augment, complement, or completely replace other modes of feedback.

As such, the traditional notion of developing highly specialized assistive technology for specific groups of users (e.g., BVI users) as a completely separate process from mainstream technology needs to be reconsidered. This shift is more about a mindset than the technology itself. That is, designers of assistive technology should start with the goal of using commercial hardware and existing software platforms when possible. They should first consider how to creatively use the built-in components of the system and the existing feature set of the interface to solve the problem before resorting to the use of specialized one-off hardware or software development. Using existing hardware, computational platforms, sensors, and other components when possible and making the access layer as implemented in software as possible betters the overall commercial product while also reducing the price of developing accessible technologies at large.

2.6.2 A shift from retrofitting existing technologies to embedding universal design from the onset

We posit that mass market companies (and researchers) developing mainstream products should embrace the notion of universal and inclusive design in their R&D process, as this not only results in products that will benefit the greatest number of users (thereby increasing their pool of potential customers) but will also have many unintended positive results that will better support core users. Consider Apple, who developed a completely inaccessible product (the iPhone) in 2007. Although touchscreen technology has been around for a long time, Apple's 2007 introduction of the iPhone brought them to the mass market. Initially, this was considered a huge set back to accessibility for blind consumers, as this new disruptive technology was based around a flat, featureless glass surface with no screen reader to provide text-to-speech. As such, blind users were completely unable to access the native input or output functions with these devices. However, in 2009, Apple released the iPhone 3GS, which included the VoiceOver screen reader and a host of associated interactive gestures as part of the native operating system (iOS 3.0). Overnight, this release propelled Apple from a company who had ostensibly abandoned their long history supporting BVI users to the leader of mobile accessibility. TalkBack, the Android analog to VoiceOver, was also released in 2009, though it has been slower to gain momentum among the BVI community compared with iOS-based devices. Almost immediately, the iPhone became one of the most accessible pieces of assistive technology even though it was not designed to be an assistive technology in and of itself. For example, VoiceOver was designed to assist BVI users on the iPhone, but it was built-in to the native OS, rather than requiring an expensive, separate, stand-alone software package, as is the traditional model of selling screen-reader software. In addition to this universal design aspect, VoiceOver's inclusion had many unintended benefits to other markets that would have not been realized if it had not been included. For instance, self-voicing benefits people using English as a second language, it helps those with learning disabilities, and it is used regularly by individuals for proof reading. This revealed further pathways, where app developers leveraged features like the Siri personal assistant and other built-in sensors to develop apps that support accessibility in a wide variety of applications. Examples of these include apps that can read barcodes, can tell you about your surroundings, can describe a picture to you, can read money to you, and so on [65]. The exponential growth and broad-based proliferation of touchscreen-based devices has been an amazing boon for access technology. For the first time, it is now possible to incorporate most of the expensive, stand-alone devices that were previously required for information access, as fully accessible apps on the phone. The rapid development of apps harnessing this power, mobile flexibility, diversity of usage scenarios, and user groups means that all roads (at least from a computing standpoint) lead to incorporating some aspect of these technologies, and this has broad-based benefits that extend across demographics. Further, the incorporation of multimodal feedback—visual, aural, and touch—expands the possibilities and capabilities that can be achieved through these new developments. To maximize the broader impacts possible when incorporating inclusive/universal design, we strongly encourage developers to leverage all communication channels available from the onset of the design and implementation process.

2.6.3 A shift from relying on unimodal feedback to leveraging all modalities available for primary interactions

Many hardware platforms today rely heavily on unimodal feedback. Even if they have multimodal capabilities, many of these multimodal interactions are significantly underutilized and sparsely implemented. Additionally, many of them are only implemented as a means for input or output, but not both, with additional modalities being used only for secondary or tertiary cueing. For example, touchscreens currently can provide visual, auditory, and vibrotactile information, yet they are generally only thought of as visual input/output interfaces. Despite having built-in vibration capabilities, vibrotactile cues are usually only used for conveying information about alerts or confirmation of an operation, not as a primary mode of extracting key information during user interactions or as input to the system. Acknowledging and enabling multimodal information as a primary means of input and output interaction is an important design consideration moving forward. This chapter provides several examples of research illustrating the benefits of leveraging all modalities available on touchscreens, with a specific focus on its potential to address the graphical access problem for BVI individuals. We note that there are likely several other unintended positive outcomes that would result should such an approach be adopted with touchscreens and other technologies if multimodal capabilities were leveraged equally in the user experience.

2.6.4 A shift from designing based on interface features to designing based on end-user needs

A critical first step here is overcoming the engineering trap, i.e., designing based on maximizing features and developer interests. The better approach is adopting a principled user-based design philosophy from the onset that considers the most relevant features ensuring the greatest functional utility for the end-user. The context of the technology implementation, how it will be deployed and used, how it compares to current tools, and where it falls short or excels are all worthy investigations that need to be explored. Most importantly, adhering to standards and guidelines to scope when and where a given technology is (or is not) appropriate are necessary. Success here often requires interdisciplinary research that cuts across several domains, involves multiple stakeholders in the process, and incorporates iterative end user assessment and participation. While advancements in technology will certainly open up new pathways, we, as designers, must also be open and cognizant to the reality that more advanced technology does not necessarily mean an immediately better solution. New technologies and advancements should be probed from multiple perspectives and should be situated and contextualized in practical use case scenarios that consider known perceptual and cognitive capabilities. While this approach may not be the fastest or the easiest path, it is certainly the one that will best inform when and how a new product will be most successful and when and where it will not work. Our group has come together to do this for vibrotactile touchscreens, and we are encouraged by the growing number of teams who are also adopting this design approach. We acknowledge that this user-centered, needs-based, principled design model takes a great deal of time and resources, and that all technology developments begin with feasibility studies. We are hoping to encourage communities of researchers and technology developers to come together to extend these inquiries and tackle this challenge from multiple perspectives, with the shared goal of driving it to its full potential. We further encourage researchers to disseminate and share their work, and when possible, to open SDK's, API's, and hardware platforms for community access, contribution, and growth.

3. Conclusions and future research

We believe that a principled solution to graphical access, designed from the onset to maximize the perceptual and cognitive characteristics of nonvisual and multimodal information processing, while also meeting the most pressing information access needs of the target demographic, could have broad and immediate societal impact. In this chapter, we highlight both the challenges and the vast potential of touchscreen-based smart devices as a platform for alleviating the graphics accessibility gap. We review the state of the art in this line of research and present positions and pathways forward for addressing the graphical access challenge from multiple perspectives. We do this specifically from an ideological standpoint, which will complement both technological and perceptual advancements that are rapidly being uncovered through a growing research community in this domain. Despite the need for more research, we see vibrotactile touchscreen platforms as a promising springboard for bringing multimodal, nonvisual graphical access into the hands of individuals everywhere. Because of their portability, availability, capabilities, and wide adoption among the BVI community, multimodal touchscreen interfaces are poised to serve as a model for universally designed consumer technologies that are also effective assistive technologies. These multimodal interfaces are also poised to close the accessibility gap while serving as a model for how we think about accessibility in the context of a new technological era.

Acknowledgements

This material is based upon work by the National Science Foundation Grant No. 1425337 and Grant No. 1644471. Any opinions, findings, and conclusions or recommendations expressed in this material are those of the authors and do not necessarily reflect the views of the National Science Foundation.

Conflict of interest

Jenna Gorlewicz is also Co-Founder and President of JLG Innovations, LLC. Hari Palani is also Co-Founder and President for Unar Lab, LLC. Nicholas Giudice is also Co-Founder and Director of Research for Unar Lab, LLC.

Author details

Jenna L. Gorlewicz[1], Jennifer L. Tennison[1], Hari P. Palani[2] and Nicholas A. Giudice[2*]

1 Saint Louis University, Saint Louis, MO USA

2 University of Maine, Orono, ME USA

*Address all correspondence to: nicholas.giudice@maine.edu

References

[1] Metatla O, Serrano M, Jouffrais C, Thieme A, Kane S, Branham S, et al. Inclusive education technologies: Emerging opportunities for people with visual impairments. In: Extended Abstracts of the 2018 CHI Conference on Human Factors in Computing Systems; ACM. 2018. p. W13

[2] Freedom Scientific [Internet]. 2018. Available From: https://www.freedomscientific.com/ [Accessed: 2018-09-08]

[3] Apple. Accessibility [Internet]. 2018. Available from https://www.apple.com/accessibility/mac/vision/ [Accessed: 2018-09-08]

[4] Foulke E. Reading braille. Tactual Perception: A Sourcebook. Cambridge [Cambridgeshire], New York: Cambridge University Press; 1982. p. 168

[5] Tennison JL, Gorlewicz JL. Toward non-visual graphics representations on vibratory touchscreens: Shape exploration and identification. In: International Conference on Human Haptic Sensing and Touch Enabled Computer Applications. Cham: Springer; 2016. pp. 384-395

[6] Craig JC. Grating orientation as a measure of tactile spatial acuity. Somatosensory & Motor Research. 1999;**16**(3):197-206

[7] Johnson KO, Phillips JR. Tactile spatial resolution. I. Two-point discrimination, gap detection, grating resolution, and letter recognition. Journal of Neurophysiology. 1981;**46**(6):1177-1192

[8] Loomis JM. Tactile pattern perception. Perception. 1981 Feb;**10**(1):5-27

[9] Loomis JM, Lederman SJ. Tactual perception. In: Handbook of Perception and Human Performances. 1986;**2**:2

[10] Loomis JM, Klatzky RL, Giudice NA. Sensory substitution of vision: Importance of perceptual and cognitive processing. In: Assistive Technology for Blindness and Low Vision. Boca Raton, Florida: CRC Press; 2012. pp. 179-210

[11] Palani HP. Principles and guidelines for advancement of touchscreen-based non-visual access to 2D spatial information [thesis]. Orono: Maine University of Maine; 2018

[12] Clark-Carter DD, Heyes AD, Howarth CI. The efficiency and walking speed of visually impaired people. Ergonomics. 1986;**29**(6):779-789

[13] Erickson W, Lee C, von Schrader S. Disability Statistics from the 2011 American Community Survey (ACS). Ithaca, NY: Cornell University Employment and Disability Institute (EDI); 2012. Retrieved June 28, 2018 from www.disabilitystatistics.org

[14] Chua B, Mitchell P. Consequences of amblyopia on education, occupation, and long term vision loss. British Journal of Ophthalmology. 2004;**88**(9):1119-1121

[15] Kaye SH, Kang T, LaPlante MP. Mobility Device Use in the United States. Washington, DC; 2000

[16] World Health Organization. Visual impairment and blindness. Fact Sheet No. 282. 2011. Available from http://www.who.int/mediacentre/factsheets/fs282/en/ [Accessed: 2012-06-02]

[17] Friedman DS, O'Colmain BJ, Munoz B, Tomany SC, McCarty C, De Jong PT, et al. Prevalence of age-related macular degeneration in the United States. Archives of Ophthalmology. 2004;**122**(4):564-572

[18] Roth WM, Bowen GM, McGinn MK. Differences in graph-related

practices between high school biology textbooks and scientific ecology journals. Journal of Research in Science Teaching: The Official Journal of the National Association for Research in Science Teaching. 1999;**36**(9):977-1019

[19] National Federation of the Blind. Statistical Facts about Blindness in the United States. 2017. Available from: https://nfb.org/blindness-statistics [Accessed: 2018-09-08]

[20] Moon NW, Todd RL, Morton DL, Ivey E. Accommodating Students with Disabilities in Science, Technology, Engineering, and Mathematics (STEM). Atlanta, GA: Center for Assistive Technology and Environmental Access, Georgia Institute of Technology; 2012

[21] Nyman SR, Gosney MA, Victor CR. Psychosocial impact of visual impairment in working-age adults. British Journal of Ophthalmology. 2010;**94**(11):1427-1431

[22] View Plus. 2018. Available from: http://www.viewplus.com [Accessed: 2018-09-08]

[23] American Thermoform. Swell Touch Paper. 2018. Available from: http://www.americanthermoform.com/product/swell-touch-paper/ [Accessed: 2018-09-08]

[24] Polly E. Tactile Graphics. New York: American Foundation for the Blind; 1992

[25] Buehler E, Kane SK, Hurst A. ABC and 3D: Opportunities and obstacles to 3D printing in special education environments. In: Proceedings of the 16th international ACM SIGACCESS conference on Computers & Accessibility; Oct 20; ACM. 2014. pp. 107-114

[26] Ducasse J, Brock AM, Jouffrais C. Accessible interactive maps for visually impaired users. In: Mobility of Visually Impaired People. Cham: Springer; 2018. pp. 537-584

[27] O'Modhrain S, Giudice NA, Gardner JA, Legge GE. Designing media for visually-impaired users of refreshable touch displays: Possibilities and pitfalls. IEEE Transactions on Haptics. 2015;**8**(3):248-257

[28] KGS Corporation. 2018. Available from: http://www.kgs-jpn.co.jp/ [Accessed: 2018-09-08]

[29] Help Tech. Handytech. 2018. Available from: https://handytech.de/en/welcome [Accessed: 2018-09-08]

[30] Vidal-Verdú F, Hafez M. Graphical tactile displays for visually-impaired people. IEEE Transactions on Neural Systems and Rehabilitation Engineering. 2007;**15**(1):119-130

[31] Nees MA, Walker BN. Auditory interfaces and sonification. In: Stephanidis C, editor. The Universal Access Handbook. New York: CRC Press; 2009. pp. 507-521

[32] Walker BN, Cothran JT. Sonification Sandbox: A Graphical Toolkit for Auditory Graphs. Georgia Institute of Technology

[33] Walker BN, Mauney LM. Universal design of auditory graphs: A comparison of sonification mappings for visually impaired and sighted listeners. ACM Transactions on Accessible Computing (TACCESS). 2010;**2**(3):12

[34] Ferres L, Lindgaard G, Sumegi L, Tsuji B. Evaluating a tool for improving accessibility to charts and graphs. ACM Transactions on Computer-Human Interaction (TOCHI). 2013;**20**(5):28

[35] Ferres L, Parush A, Roberts S, Lindgaard G. Helping people with visual impairments gain access

to graphical information through natural language: The igraph system. In: International Conference on Computers for Handicapped Persons. Berlin, Heidelberg: Springer; 2006. pp. 1122-1130

[36] Giudice NA, Palani HP, Brenner E, Kramer KM. Learning non-visual graphical information using a touch-based vibro-audio interface. In: Proceedings of the 14th International ACM SIGACCESS Conference on Computers and Accessibility; 2012 Oct 22; ACM. pp. 103-110

[37] American Printing House for the Blind. Graphiti. 2018. Available from http://www.aph.org/graphiti/ [Accessed: 2018-09-08]

[38] Blitab Technology. 2018. Available from: http://blitab.com/ [Accessed: 2019-09-08]

[39] Siu AF, Gonzalez EJ, Yuan S, Ginsberg JB, Follmer S. Shapeshift: 2D spatial manipulation and self-actuation of tabletop shape displays for tangible and haptic interaction. In: Proceedings of the 2018 CHI Conference on Human Factors in Computing Systems; Apr 21; ACM. 2018. p. 291

[40] Russomanno A, Gillespie RB, O'Modhrain S, Burns M. The design of pressure-controlled valves for a refreshable tactile display. In: World Haptics Conference (WHC); 2015 Jun 22; IEEE. 2015. pp. 177-182

[41] Martino G, Marks LE. Cross-modal interaction between vision and touch: The role of synesthetic correspondence. Perception. 2000;**29**(6):745-754

[42] Thesen T, Vibell JF, Calvert GA, Österbauer RA. Neuroimaging of multisensory processing in vision, audition, touch and olfaction. Cognitive Processing. 2004;**5**(2):84-93

[43] Pensky AE, Johnson KA, Haag S, Homa D. Delayed memory for visual—Haptic exploration of familiar objects. Psychonomic Bulletin & Review. 2008;**15**(3):574-580

[44] Ricciardi E, Bonino D, Gentili C, Sani L, Pietrini P, Vecchi T. Neural correlates of spatial working memory in humans: A functional magnetic resonance imaging study comparing visual and tactile processes. Neuroscience. 2006;**139**(1):339-349

[45] Giudice NA. 15. Navigating without vision: Principles of blind spatial cognition. In: Handbook of Behavioral and Cognitive Geography. 2018. p. 260

[46] Choi S, Kuchenbecker KJ. Vibrotactile display: Perception, technology, and applications. Proceedings of the IEEE. 2013;**101**(9):2093-2104

[47] Hoggan E, Anwar S, Brewster SA. Mobile multi-actuator tactile displays. In: International Workshop on Haptic and Audio Interaction Design. Berlin, Heidelberg: Springer; 2007. pp. 22-33

[48] Hoggan E, Brewster SA, Johnston J. Investigating the effectiveness of tactile feedback for mobile touchscreens. In: Proceedings of the SIGCHI Conference on Human Factors in Computing Systems; ACM. 2008. pp. 1573-1582

[49] Hoggan E, Kaaresoja T, Laitinen P, Brewster SA. Crossmodal congruence: The look, feel and sound of touchscreen widgets. In: Proceedings of the 10th International Conference on Multimodal Interfaces; ACM. 2008. pp. 157-164

[50] Poupyrev I, Maruyama S, Rekimoto J. Ambient touch: Designing tactile interfaces for handheld devices. In: Proceedings of the 15th Annual ACM

Symposium on User Interface Software and Technology; ACM. 2002. pp. 51-60

[51] Yatani K, Truong KN. Sem feel: A user interface with semantic tactile feedback for mobile touch-screen devices. In: Proceedings of the 22nd Annual ACM Symposium on User Interface Software and Technology; ACM. 2009. pp. 111-120

[52] Nicolau H, Guerreiro J, Guerreiro T, Carriço L. UbiBraille: Designing and evaluating a vibrotactile braille-reading device. In: Proceedings of the 15th International ACM SIGACCESS Conference on Computers and Accessibility. 2013. p. 23

[53] Al-Qudah Z, Doush IA, Alkhateeb F, Al Maghayreh E, Al-Khaleel O. Reading braille on mobile phones: A fast method with low battery power consumption. In: 2011 International Conference on User Science and Engineering (i-USEr); IEEE. 2011. pp. 118-123

[54] Jayant C, Acuario C, Johnson W, Hollier J, Ladner R. V-braille: Haptic braille perception using a touch-screen and vibration on mobile phones. In: Proceedings of the 12th International ACM SIGACCESS Conference on Computers and Accessibility; ACM. 2010. pp. 295-296

[55] Rantala J, Raisamo R, Lylykangas J, Surakka V, Raisamo J, Salminen K, et al. Methods for presenting braille characters on a mobile device with a touchscreen and tactile feedback. IEEE Transactions on Haptics. 2009;**2**(1):28-39

[56] Gorlewicz JL, Burgner J, Withrow TJ, Webster IIIRJ. Initial experiences using vibratory touchscreens to display graphical math concepts to students with visual impairments. Journal of Special Education Technology. 2014;**29**(2):17-25

[57] Klatzky RL, Giudice NA, Bennett CR, Loomis JM. Touch-screen technology for the dynamic display of 2D spatial information without vision: Promise and progress. Multisensory Research. 2014;**27**(5-6):359-378

[58] Poppinga B, Magnusson C, Pielot M, Rassmus-Gröhn K. TouchOver map: Audio-tactile exploration of interactive maps. In: Proceedings of the 13th International Conference on Human Computer Interaction with Mobile Devices and Services; ACM. 2011. pp. 545-550

[59] Palani HP, Giudice U, Giudice NA. Evaluation of non-visual zooming operations on touchscreen devices. In: International Conference on Universal Access in Human-Computer Interaction. Cham: Springer; 2016. pp. 162-174

[60] Giudice NA, Palani HP, Brenner E, Kramer KM. Learning non-visual graphical information using a touch-based vibro-audio interface. In: Proceedings of the 14th International ACM SIGACCESS Conference on Computers and Accessibility; Oct 22; ACM. 2012. pp. 103-110

[61] ViTAL. 2018. Available from: https://www.vital.education/ [Accessed: 2018-09-08]

[62] Hahn ME, Mueller CM, Gorlewicz JL. The comprehension of STEM graphics via a multi-sensory tablet in students with visual impairment. Journal of Visual Impairment and Blindness. 2018. In Press

[63] Tennison JL, Carril ZS, Giudice NA, Gorlewicz JL. Comparing haptic pattern matching on tablets and phones: Large screens are not necessarily better. Optometry and Vision Science. 2018;**95**(9):720-726

[64] Grussenmeyer W, Folmer E. Accessible touchscreen technology

for people with visual impairments: A survey. ACM Transactions on Accessible Computing (TACCESS). 2017;**9**(2):6

[65] Braille Works. 5 Top Mobile Apps for the Blind. 2015. Available from: https://brailleworks.com/5-top-mobile-apps-for-the-blind/ [Accessed: 2018-09-08]

Chapter 8

Training Reading, Writing and Spelling Fluency: Centre-Periphery Dissemination through Interactive Multimedia

Charles Potter

Abstract

This chapter focuses on a reading, writing and spelling programme based on Luria's theories of automaticity, which uses repetitive paired reading and phonological referencing to develop fluency in reading, writing and spelling. All materials used in programme implementation are electronic and are currently delivered using email and cellphone technologies. The results have been promising, and the programme has a number of therapists, teachers, tutors parents and institutional users, both in South Africa and its neighbouring territories, as well as in the United Kingdom. Programme usage is supported via electronic manuals as well as an eight-module training course based on use of multimedia including email, cellphone and use of computer-based electronic material. The first half of the chapter describes the theoretical basis of the programme, and the methods used in its implementation. The second half focuses on the modular training course and its aims, and the centre-periphery model of development and evaluation used in disseminating the programme. The dissemination model is both evidence-based and interactive in its emphasis on assessment and evaluation and will increasingly involve the use of interactive website-based technologies as the programme grows in scale.

Keywords: reading fluency, writing and spelling fluency, phonological referencing, phonological recoding, automaticity, learning disabilities, centre-periphery dissemination, multimedia

1. Introduction

An estimated 20% of children have reading difficulties or have not learned to read fluently. This chapter describes a reading, writing and spelling programme based on a series of ebooks, which form part of a fluency-based intervention which is being used in work with children with reading difficulties by therapists, teachers and parents. The ebooks are based on the theories of the Russian neuropsychologist Luria [1–3], who proposed that automaticity is necessary for any acts (including reading, writing and spelling) to become fluent. Fluent acts then form the basis for higher level processing.

Following Luria, the ebooks are designed to be used with a form of oral impress procedure based on paired reading. This is simple to implement and differs from the type of paired reading procedures documented in the literature, as the method involves additional repetition to develop phonic associations, rapid naming ability and automaticity in reading. The ebooks are set in large print with wide spaces between words to circumvent and provide maximal visual cues and also to prevent crowding, which has emerged in recent literature as a factor affecting reading in dyslexic children. The oral impress procedure also builds in visual tracking to maintain visual attention.

Once observable differences in reading fluency are noted, methods involving use of these materials for repetitive paired reading are combined with phonological referencing methods based on print-to-sound recoding, as the basis for developing fluency in writing and spelling. The results have been promising and indicate that the combined use of methods is effective in developing automaticity in reading, while at the same time building skills in print-to-sound translation, which can then be used both for improving word attack and for developing the working memory skills involved in writing and spelling both individual words, and words in sequence.

Gains in reading, spelling and sequential spelling scores indicate that combining paired reading with the teaching of phonics and with the teaching of phonological referencing leads to optimal results. Repetition is also necessary in implementation to enable the learner to acquire the phonic skills necessary for accurate visual word recognition, as well as the detailed orthographic representations necessary to write and spell individual words, and words in sequence. As these skills develop, this has effects on reading accuracy and rate of reading, as well as accuracy in writing and spelling. Reading comprehension also improves as the child's reading, writing and spelling become more fluent.

2. Developing automaticity in reading, writing and spelling

Luria [1–3] conceptualised higher mental processes as complex reflex activities, responsible for reflecting and working with the outside world. Following Vygotsky [4, 5, 67], Luria suggested that these reflex processes were social in origin, mediate in structure, and volunteer in mode of function ([1], p. 32).

In terms of Luria's conceptualisation of the development of higher mental processes, the development of automaticity in reading would be essential for its use in the hierarchical processing of information by the working brain. Following Luria [1], automaticity would be developed in reading, writing and spelling when there has been sufficient practice to enable these complex functional acts to become fluent enough to form the basis for higher mental processing.

Our fluency-based programme has been developed based on these principles. The processes of reading, writing, spelling and comprehension are conceptualised as linked on a functional level, with basic phonological and phonic skills initially being taught as a foundation for use in the processes of reading, writing, spelling and comprehension [61–63]. The use of repetitive paired reading is then combined with the teaching of phonics to provide the basis for developing reading fluency. Once observable difference in reading fluency is noted, the child is taught how to phonologically reference from print to sound to provide a metacognitive basis for developing fluency in writing and spelling.

In each case where this type of linked intervention across different areas and components has taken place, there has been steady and even progress. There has also been evidence of a backwash effect from application of the methods used in teaching phonological referencing skills into proficiency in one word reading ability as well as fluency in reading sequentially, as well as reciprocal effects from use of reading fluency methods into competencies in writing and spelling. The indications would thus be that there is commonality of influence across the different areas of the fluency-based intervention programme described in this chapter.

3. Paired reading

One of the most successful methods for developing automaticity in reading has been what is called 'paired reading', which is based on the methods pioneered by Heckelman [6, 7] in the 1960s and the information processing model proposed by Laberge and Samuels [8, 9] in the 1970s. Based on positive results, paired reading has been widely used for developing reading ability (e.g. [10–17]) and forms the basis for developing reading fluency in our own programme.

The literature on paired reading reflects some differences in preferred methodology [18], as well as some differences between recommendations concerning the type of materials felt to be most appropriate for use in the process. Overall, however, there is consensus concerning the value of paired reading, with all of the studies indicating the potential of including parents as well as peer tutors as partners in the process of teaching children to read fluently.

Difficulty level of materials is an important variable to consider in developing paired reading programmes, but here there is a lack of consensus. Certain authorities suggest the value of fun reading materials, others the value of instructional level reading materials and others the value of reading material chosen to be at or near frustration level [18].

What is clear from the literature, however, is that the quality of scaffolding and support in paired reading is important, especially where difficult materials are chosen for use in paired reading programmes. How reading errors are corrected would appear to be less important, as the literature suggests that a wide variety of strategies have been used for doing so, particularly by teachers. It would, however, be important that the procedures used in paired reading are clear enough to be consistently used by parents, tutors and teachers, and that recommended procedures for correcting the errors made by children are also defined.

These principles have informed the development of our materials and methods for developing reading fluency, which are described in the section following.

4. Our reading fluency programme

Our programme for developing reading fluency involves use of a paired reading method called the 3 × 3 oral impress method, which involves the reading of paragraphs repetitively. The method is designed to be used with a series of phonically based, large-print books. The books are graded and are written in a way that builds repetition into the words used, as well as phrases used in sentences. They are also printed in a way that aims to avoid clutter [19–21].

Our materials thus aim to present the letters and letter strings associated with particular sounds and to present these visually in an uncluttered format. The 3 × 3 oral impress method is used to ensure that large-print phonically based material is presented to the child repeatedly. Repetitive oral reading is used to develop the association between the visual configuration of the letters within phonically regular words and their sounds as used in the written language the child sees, the spoken language the child hears and the words read by both adult and child.

Luria [1–3] suggests that cerebral organisation would be enhanced by this type of repetitive process, and this was also Heckelman's view when he pioneered the use of paired reading as a procedure. Heckelman [6, 7] reported that 24 students involved in using what he called 'the neurological impress method' made exceptional gains in reading ability. The mean gain in reading comprehension was 1.9 grade levels after using the method daily for 15 minutes (a total of seven and a quarter hours) over a 6-week period. On the basis of these results, Heckelman suggested that paired reading is 'one of the most direct and fundamental systems of reading' involving a 'combination of reflexive neurological systems'.

Other subsequent researchers (e.g. [8–17, 22–25]) have reported positive effects of use of paired reading methods on reading ability. We have reported similar positive results [18, 26, 27] based on use of repetitive paired reading.

The results to date indicate gains in word reading, sentence reading, as well as gains in spelling and sequential spelling test scores when our 3 × 3 oral impress method has been used with large-print phonically based material and combined with the teaching of phonics as well as with the methods of phonological referencing described later in this chapter. Our work with children with reading, writing and spelling difficulties would support Heckelman's view that gains made are based on increasing neurological integrity [64].

Following Dehaene [28], what the 3 × 3 oral impress method does when used with our phonically based large-print reading fluency books is to present the visual word form area in the brain with strings of letters representing sounds repeatedly. This would have the effect of strengthening the connections between the visual areas in the brain and the areas of the brain involved in processing sounds and oral language, thus enabling the child first to read and then to read fluently.

The model for developing using the phonically based, large-print reading materials to develop reading fluency would be conceptualised as based on the coding and recoding of phonic associations and can be represented as in **Table 1**:

FUNCTIONAL LEVEL	CENTRAL PROCESSING LEVEL
Phonically Regular Reading Material	
↓	
Repetitive Paired Reading Methods	*Visual-Occipital and Parietal Processing Areas linked to Phonological and Language Processing Areas through Visual Word Form Area*
↓	↕
Rapid Naming Ability for Individual Words and for Words in Sequence	*Visual-Occipital and Parietal Processing Areas linked to Phonological and Language Processing Areas and Cortical Areas Involved in Phonological, Morphological and Semantic Working Memory*
↓	
Fluency based on Automaticity in Coding and Recoding	

Table 1.
Model for reading fluency development.

DOI: http://dx.doi.org/10.5772/intechopen.82812

From the model presented in **Table 1**, it can be seen that use of our phonically based large-print materials for the development of reading fluency is based on repetitive paired reading with the aim of developing rapid and accurate naming of words, and words in sequence. On a central level, the repetitive paired reading methods would involve both forward and reverse processing from the visual and occipital areas of the cortex through the visual word form area to the areas of the cortex involved in phonological and language processing.

The procedures used in our programme are documented in a user's manual, which includes both theory and the methods used in programme implementation [29], as well as in a parent implementer's manual, which presents a step-by-step approach to implementation [30]. The theory is based on Luria [1–3] who conceptualised reading as a linguistic process in which repetition would be intrinsic to the development of automaticity in the recognition and naming of phonic associations. Following Luria, reading fluency would be developed through repeated stimulation of the areas of the cortex involved in phonological and language processing as well as the areas of the cortex involved in the phonological, morphological and semantic working memory used for reading individual words, and words in sequence.

The methods followed in our programme focus on developing accurate and rapid naming ability for individual words and words in sequence as an intrinsic part of the repetitive methods used to develop automaticity in reading. The procedures used involve initial work with phonically regular words and sentences and then on the rapid reading of a wider range of reading material.

Based on Luria's theories of automaticity [31], repetition would thus be intrinsic to the development of fluency in reading. The aim of our programme would to use repetitive paired reading to develop the coding, recoding and working memory abilities necessary for fluent and accurate reading and for self-teaching. Once observable differences in reading fluency have been noted and a child has attained a reading and spelling age at around the 8-year level (Note 1), work on developing writing and spelling fluency would be commenced using the phonological referencing and recoding procedures described in the next section.

5. Developing automaticity in writing and spelling

Fluency in writing and spelling is addressed in our programme through a variety of methods involving not only training in phonics and basic skills in writing and copying, but also by teaching the child phonological referencing skills. This involves teaching the child how to work from print to sound, how to analyse words based on phonic analysis of how words work and how to use the letters and letter combinations used to represent the vowels in words as the basis for remembering how words are spelled both individually and in sequence.

The aim is to build phonological, orthographic and morphological awareness through this process, which we call 'phonological referencing'. This is introduced through the Seven Vowel Phonic Analysis System, which is a procedure for teaching children through activities involving mapping the combinations of letters used in writing words to the sounds made when those words are spoken orally. It focuses in particular on developing skills in word attack as well as in spelling, through focusing on the letters and letter combinations used to represent the vowel sounds in words.

Following Luria [1–3], the Seven Vowel Phonic Analysis System is applied repetitively. This has effects in improving word attack in reading, as well as providing the phonic analysis skills and phonic associations on which spelling accuracy can be built. This is done by working from printed word to sound and from sound back to print. These phonological recoding skills provide the building blocks on which writing and spelling fluency can be developed.

FUNCTIONAL LEVEL	CENTRAL PROCESSING LEVEL
Copying of Phonically Regular Material	*Visual-Occipital and Parietal Processing Areas linked to Phonological and Language Processing Areas Involved in Reading and Writing of Individual Words and Words in Sequence*
Mapping Written Text to Sounds of Oral Language through Repetitive Phonological Referencing	*Visual-Occipital and Parietal Processing Areas linked to Phonological and Language Processing Areas Involved in Phonemic Analysis of Individual Words and Words in Sequence*
Use of Working Memory in Learning Letter Combinations Used in Words and Sequences of Words in Written Text	*Visual-Occipital and Parietal Processing Areas linked to Phonological and Language Processing Areas and Additional Cortical Areas Involved in Phonological, Morphological and Orthographic Memory for Individual Words and Words in Sequence*
Fluency based on Automaticity in Coding and Recoding	

Table 2.
Model for writing and spelling fluency development.

The model for using our phonically based, large-print materials for developing writing and spelling fluency would also be conceptualised as based on the coding and recoding of phonic associations and can be represented as in **Table 2**.

From the model presented in **Table 2**, it can be seen that use of our phonically based, large-print materials for the development of writing and spelling fluency is based on repetitive coding and recoding of phonic associations. As the recoding process involves both working from printed word to sound and from sound back to print, the use of our methods of phonological referencing would be based on widely distributed central processing. This would involve the visual and occipital areas of the cortex, the areas of the cortex involved in phonological and language processing and the areas of the cortex involved in phonological, morphological and orthographic working memory for words when written individually and for words when written in sequence.

Following Luria, repetition would be intrinsic to the development of automaticity in writing and spelling fluency. As with reading fluency, the aim would be to develop the coding, recoding and working memory abilities necessary for fluent and accurate writing and spelling and for self-teaching. This would be done through phonological referencing, using our Seven Vowel Phonic Analysis System.

6. What is phonological referencing?

The notion of phonological referencing has its basis in the 'self-teaching' model proposed by Jorm and Share [32–35]. According to this model, phonological recoding (print-to-sound translation) performs a self-teaching function enabling the learner to acquire the detailed orthographic representations necessary for fast, efficient visual word recognition.

As Share [36] suggests, at p. 96:

> *'Although direct whole-word instruction and contextual guessing have also been proposed as options for developing orthographic knowledge, both theoretical and practical considerations suggest that only phonological recoding offers a viable route to printed word learning (see [34]). According to the self-teaching hypothesis, each successful identification decoding) of a new word in the course of a child's independent reading of text is assumed to provide an opportunity to acquire the word-specific orthographic information on which skilled visual word recognition is founded. Relatively few exposures appear to be sufficient for acquiring orthographic representations, both for skilled readers [37] and for young children [38–41]. In this way, phonological recoding acts as a self-teaching device or built-in teacher enabling a child to independently develop the word-specific orthographic representations essential to skilled reading and spelling'.*

Shahar-Yames and Share [42] suggest that spelling fulfils a self-teaching function in the acquisition of orthographic knowledge because, like decoding in reading, accurate spelling requires close attention to letter order and identity as well as to word-specific spelling-sound mapping. This highlights an additional dimension of reading-writing reciprocity in the compilation of word-specific orthographic representations.

Following the theories proposed by Share and his colleagues, our methods focus on teaching the child to map the associations between the letters and letter strings used in the printed word, and the sounds used in speaking the word orally. Our methods then focus on teaching the child to recode these phonic associations back into the writing and typing of both individual words and words in sequence. Working memory is then invoked in teaching and testing spelling, using revisualisation techniques.

The Seven Vowel Phonic Analysis System is used for this purpose, and the procedures used are documented in a user's manual, which includes both theory and the methods used in programme implementation [43], as well as in a parent implementer's manual, which presents a step-by-step approach to implementation [44]. The theory is based on the evidence of a common linguistic awareness manifesting in phonological, orthographic and morphological awareness as suggested by Berninger et al. (2010), and of a universal phonic principle manifesting across different orthographies as suggested by Perfetti et al. (1992). Following McCutchen (1988), it aims to develop linguistic awareness through the metacognitive strategies involved in phonological referencing.

The methods used are based on the research of Share and his colleagues [32, 34, 35] and Perfetti and his colleagues [45], which indicates that the coding and recoding of phonic associations is involved in both reading and spelling. They are also based on the insights of Sister Mary Caroline [46] concerning the value of including the /y/ and /w/ as vowels in phonic analysis, as well as the research of Ellis and Hooper [47] and Spencer and Hanley [48] on the comparative ease of decoding Welsh orthography using systems of phonic analysis and association based on seven vowels, as opposed to systems of phonic association based on five vowels.

In summary, the Seven Vowel Phonic Analysis System focuses on teaching the child to phonologically reference the letters and letter combinations used to represent the vowel sounds from print to sound and from sound back to print. This is done initially by referencing the letters used to represent the vowel sounds in written words back to the sounds made when the words are spoken orally. The letters used to represent the vowel sounds are then analysed and colour-coded, as a basis for improving both word attack ability and for developing and memorising the phonic associations on which writing and spelling fluency can be built.

The logic of mapping phonological associations is outlined in the following sections, while the use of seven vowels as opposed to five vowels is linked to the research on which it is based.

7. Teaching the child to map phonological associations

As certain children battle to establish the relationships between sounds and letters, what we call 'phonological referencing' is designed to teach the child how to map the associations between the letters used in written words, and the sounds made when the words are spoken orally. The process is designed to work on a metacognitive level (McCutchen, 1988).

Like many other programmes based on current research in the field, the methods used in the Seven Vowel Phonic Analysis System are based on the evidence from the work of the National Reading Panel in the United States that English should be phonically taught (Ehri, 2004), and that the teaching of phonics should be systematic (i.e. planned and taught in a particular order). The Seven Vowel Phonic Analysis System is thus introduced at a particular stage in the child's learning of phonic associations and rules. It is then accompanied by ongoing systematic phonics instruction, based on the errors made in the child's writing and spelling.

The Seven Vowel Phonic Analysis System teaches the child to map the correspondence between the letters and letter combinations used to represent the vowel sounds in written words and the sounds made when the words are spoken orally. The reason for focusing on this is that there is convergent evidence indicating that children, no matter what language they speak or how it is written, go through a process where they attempt to match the sounds they hear in the spoken word to the letters or symbols they see when the language is written.

The research of Perfetti and his colleagues (Perfetti et al., 2003; [45]), for example, indicates that Chinese children will attempt at the earliest stage possible to relate the pictographs in their written language to the language they speak, and the sounds on which their spoken language is based. Similar results are found in children learning those languages in which letters (as opposed to pictures) are used to map the sounds in spoken language into writing.

8. Transparent versus opaque written languages

A number of studies have indicated that children find it easiest to learn to read and spell when the system of mapping the sounds they hear in the spoken word to the letters or symbols they see in written language is transparent and easy to understand and use, as opposed to opaque and more difficult to understand and use [49–52].

In Wales in the United Kingdom, there are schools in which reading is taught in Welsh (an orthographically transparent language), as well as schools in which reading is taught in English (an orthographically opaque language). A study conducted by Ellis and Hooper [47] in Northern Wales, for example, demonstrated that the consistency of spelling-to-sound patterns in Welsh allowed children to rapidly learn the Welsh alphabetic code, leading to rapid reading acquisition based on a strategy of letter-sound decoding. Conversely, children learned the more ambiguous English orthographic code more slowly, and it failed to generalise well to other words. Similar results were reported by Spencer and Hanley [48], working with Northern Welsh children.

South Africa is also a country in which both transparent and opaque orthographies are taught in schools. There are schools in which children are taught to read in Afrikaans (an orthographically transparent language) and schools in which reading is taught in English (an orthographically opaque language). De Sousa et al. [53]

reported that bilingual English- and Afrikaans-speaking children showed greater spelling accuracy in the spelling of Afrikaans words and non-words compared to their spelling of English words and non-words. The bilingual children's ability to spell in Afrikaans and English was correlated, signifying a cross-language relationship for spelling both languages, but with language background and orthographic depth exerting an influence on the nature and development of spelling strategies used to spell in an orthographically different first language and second language.

These results would support Perfetti and Zhang's claim [54] that learning to read is learning how one's writing system encodes one's language. As Perfetti and Dunlap [45] suggest, children need to work out how the graphic forms work and how these map on to spoken language. This is the departure point of the Seven Vowel Phonic Analysis System.

The Seven Vowel Phonic Analysis System focuses on the mapping of phonic associations and on the particular letters and combinations used to represent the vowel sounds in English. It attempts to make the task of mapping the sounds children hear in words on to the letters used when the words are written clear, logical, consistent and easy. This is done by teaching the child how to phonologically reference the letters and letter combinations used in written words back to the sounds made when the words are spoken orally.

Use of the Seven Vowel Phonic Analysis System does not need changes in the way words are spelled. It is a system for enabling the way in which words are written and spelled in English to become more transparent, easier to map, and easier to learn and remember. Following Luria [1–3], the system is applied repetitively, working from print to sound, and from sound back to print, as the basis for developing fluency in writing and spelling.

9. The logic of the Seven Vowel Phonic Analysis System

The logic of the Seven Vowel Phonic Analysis System is based on research, which indicates that ease in learning to write and spell is associated with the phonic complexity of words in English [55–57]. In terms of this evidence, a system of phonic analysis that makes written English more transparent for children, and therefore easier to understand and use, makes sense logically.

It has also made sense empirically with the children and parents with whom I have worked, who have found the Seven Vowel Phonic Analysis System logical, easy to understand, and easy to apply and use. Used repetitively, it has effects on word attack, thus increasing fluency in reading. It can also form the basis for developing fluent writing and spelling.

These conclusions are based on clinical evidence, both from initial case studies and from subsequent implementation of the Seven Vowel Phonic Analysis System with a number of children with reading, writing and spelling difficulties. These results are outlined in the previous publications in the programme [58–60], as well as in the section following.

In summary, the Seven Vowel Phonic Analysis System works on the assumption that understanding of phonic associations can be enhanced by working back from the printed word to the sounds made when the word is spoken orally. This is done through a process of phonological referencing, in which the child is taught how to map these associations.

Once these associations have been mapped from print to sound, they can then be used as the basis for recoding from sound back to print. As the child becomes more rapid and accurate in the phonological referencing and recoding processes involved, the process of usage can become automatic. And once usage has become automatic, it can then be used as the basis for self-teaching involving the process of phonological recoding referred to by Share and his colleagues [32, 34, 35, 42].

10. Results

Phonological referencing in our programme is a taught process, which is not implemented at the outset, but is introduced after the child has established phonological and phonemic awareness, and has also been involved in foundation level programmes in which the child has been introduced to reading, writing and spelling through systematic phonics teaching. Once a basic level of competence has been established in reading and spelling phonically based material, the child is then taught how to map the associations between the letters and letter combinations used in printed words and the sounds in spoken language.

Following Jorm and Share (1985), not all children would need to be taught phonological referencing, as certain children would develop phonological recoding as well as the working memory associations for letters and strings of letters without

---

Child 1

Pretest date: March 2014	Pretest age scores			
Grade at school: 3 gender male	One word reading	Sentence reading	One word spelling	Sequential spelling
Age at pretest : 8 yrs 4 mths	7 yrs 0 mth	7 yrs 7 mth	7 yrs 5 mth	7 yrs 0 mth
Post-test date: June 2016	Post-test age scores			
Grade at school	One word reading	Sentence reading	One word spelling	Sequential spelling
Age at post-test: 10 yrs 8 mths	10 yrs 1 mth	9 yrs 10 mth	9 yrs 7 mth	8 yrs 10 mth

Number of therapy sessions: 84
Number of reading fluency books covered: 11
Number of writing/spelling fluency paragraphs covered: 18

Child 2

Pretest date: July 2015	Pretest age scores			
Grade at SCHOOL: 4 Gender female	One word reading	Sentence reading	One word spelling	Sequential spelling
Age at pretest 9 yrs 9 mths	**9 yrs 2 mth**	**9 yrs 10 mth**	**9 yrs 8 mth**	**7 yrs 0 mth**
Post-test date: November 2015	Post-test age scores			
Grade at school: 4	One word reading	Sentence reading	One word spelling	Sequential spelling
Age at post-test 10 yrs 2 mths	**10 yrs 10 mth**	**11 yrs 10 mth**	**9 yrs 9 mth**	**13 yrs 1 mth**

Number of therapy sessions: 22
Number of reading fluency books covered: 5
Number of writing/spelling fluency paragraphs covered: 10

Child 3

Pretest date: November 2014	Pretest age scores			
Grade at school: 3 gender male	One word reading	Sentence reading	One word spelling	Sequential spelling
Age at pretest : 7 yrs 7 mth	**7 yrs 4 mth**	**7 yrs 3 mth**	**7 yrs 0 mth**	**< 6 yrs 0 mth**
Post-test date: November 2016	Post-test age scores			
Grade at school	One word reading	Sentence reading	One word spelling	Sequential spelling
Age at post-test : 9 yrs 7 mth	**10 yrs 8 mth**	**9 yrs 10 mth**	**9 yrs 4 mths**	**9 yrs 6 mth**

Number of therapy sessions: 73
Number of reading fluency books covered: 8
Number of writing/spelling fluency paragraphs covered: 10

Child 4

Pretest date: November 2015	Pretest age scores			
Grade at school: 5 gender female	One word reading	Sentence reading	One word spelling	Sequential Spelling
Age at pretest : 11 yrs 5 mth	**10 yrs 8 mth**	**9 yrs 5 mth**	**10 yrs 9 mth**	**9 yrs 6 mth**
Post-test date: July 2016	Post-test age scores			
Grade at school: 6	One word reading	Sentence reading	One word spelling	Sequential spelling
Age at post-test 12 yrs 1 mth	**12 yrs 9 mth**	**12 yrs 1 mth**	**11 yrs 1 mth**	**10 yrs 9 mth**

Number of therapy sessions: 30
Number of reading fluency books covered: 6
Number of writing/spelling fluency paragraphs covered: 11

Child 5

Pretest date: April 2014	Pretest age scores			
Grade at school: 7 gender male	One word reading	Sentence reading	One word spelling	Sequential spelling
Age at pretest : 14 yrs 0 mth	**8 yrs 2 mth**	**8 yrs 6 mth**	**6 yrs 8 mth**	**6 yrs 9 mth**
Post-test date: November 2016	Post-test age scores			
Grade at school: 9	One word reading	Sentence reading	One word spelling	Sequential spelling
Age at post-test: 16 yrs 7 mth	**12 yrs 4 mth**	**11 yrs 0 mth**	**8 yrs 8 mth**	**8 yrs 8 mth**

Number of therapy sessions: 121
Number of reading fluency books covered: 9
Number of writing/spelling fluency paragraphs covered: 31

Child 6

Pretest date: November 2015	Pretest age scores			
Grade at school: 3 gender female	One word reading	Sentence reading	One word spelling	Sequential spelling
Age at pretest : 9 yrs 7 mth	**7 yrs 9 mth**	**8 yrs 3 mth**	**8 yrs 4 mth**	**7 yrs 0 mth**
Post-test date: November 2016	Post-test age scores			
Grade at school: 4	One word reading	Sentence reading	One word spelling	Sequential spelling
Age at post-test : 10 yrs 7 mth	**10 yrs 9 mth**	**9 yrs 5 mth**	**8 yrs 7 mth**	**8 yrs 0 mth**

Number of therapy sessions: 42
Number of reading fluency books covered: 5
Number of writing/spelling fluency paragraphs covered: 15

Child 7

Pretest date October 2015	Pretest age scores			
Grade at school: 2 gender male	One word reading	Sentence reading	One word spelling	Sequential spelling
Age at pretest : 8 yrs 11 mth	7 yrs 7 mth	8 yrs 3 mth	7 yrs 3 mth	7 yrs 3 mth
Post-test date: August 2016	Post-test age scores			
Grade at school: 3	One word reading	Sentence reading	One word spelling	Sequential spelling
Age at post-test: 9 yrs 6 mths	9 yrs 5 mth	9 yrs 10 mth	8 yrs 8 mth	8 yrs 6 mth

Number of therapy sessions: 34
Number of reading fluency books covered: 2
Number of writing/spelling fluency paragraphs covered: 4

Child 8

Pretest date: June 2014	Pretest age scores			
Grade at school: 3 gender female	One word reading	Sentence reading	One word spelling	Sequential spelling
Age at pretest : 9 yrs 1 mth	**6 yr 10 mth**	**7 yrs 2 mth**	**5 yrs 6 mth**	**< 6 yrs 0 mth**
Post-test date: November 2016	Post-test age scores			
Grade at school: 5	One word reading	Sentence reading	One word spelling	Sequential spelling
Age at post-test: 11 yrs 7 mth	**8 yrs 11 mth**	**8 yrs 0 mth**	**7 yrs 7 mth**	**7 yrs 11 mth**

Number of therapy sessions: 78
Number of reading fluency books covered: 9
Number of writing/spelling fluency paragraphs covered: 11

Child 9

Pretest date: March 2016	Pretest age scores			
Grade at school: 4 gender male	One word reading	Sentence reading	One word spelling	Sequential spelling
Age at pretest" 10 yrs 6 mth	**7 yrs 10 mth**	**8 yrs 6 mth**	**7 yrs 4 mth**	**6 yrs 9 mth**
Post-test date: November 2016	Post-test age scores			
Grade at school: 4	One word reading	Sentence reading	One word spelling	Sequential spelling
Age at post-test: 11 yrs 3 mth	**10 yrs 0 mth**	**8 yrs 11 mth**	**8 yrs 2 mth**	**7 yrs 11 mth**

Number of therapy sessions: 27
Number of reading fluency books covered: 6
Number of writing/spelling fluency paragraphs covered: 8

Child 10

Pretest date: August 2016	Pretest age scores			
Grade at school: 2 gender female	One word reading	Sentence reading	One word spelling	Sequential spelling
Age at pretest: 8 yrs 10 mth	**8 yrs 5 mth**	**7 yrs 7 mth**	**7 yrs 6 mth**	**< 6 yrs 0 mth**
Post-test date: November 2016	Post-test age scores			
Grade at school: 2	One word reading	Sentence reading	One word spelling	Sequential spelling
Age at post-test: 9 yrs 1 mth	**9 yrs 3 mth**	**9 yrs 2 mth**	**8 yrs 1 mth**	**8 yrs 6 mth**

Number of therapy sessions: 17
Number of reading fluency books covered: 3
Number of writing/spelling fluency paragraphs covered: 6

Child 11

Pretest date: October 2015	Pretest age scores			
Grade at school: 1 gender male	One word reading	Sentence reading	One word spelling	Sequential spelling
Age at pretest: 7 yrs 4 mth	**6 yrs 10 mth**	**7 yrs 5 mth**	**6 yrs 6 mth**	**< 6 yrs 0 mth**
Post-test date: November 2016	Post-test age scores			
Grade at school: 2	One word reading	Sentence reading	One word spelling	Sequential spelling
Age at post-test: 8 yrs 4 mth	**8 yrs 4 mth**	**8 yrs 8 mth**	**7 yrs 9 mth**	**8 yrs 4 mth**

Number of therapy sessions: 29
Number of reading fluency books covered: 4
Number of writing/spelling fluency paragraphs covered: 12

Child 12

Pretest date: June 2016	Pretest age scores			
Grade at school: 5 gender male	One word reading	Sentence reading	One word spelling	Sequential spelling
Age at pretest: 10 yrs 8 mth	**8 yrs 5 mth**	**8 yrs 3 mth**	**6 yrs 9 mth**	**< 6 yrs 0 mth**
Post-test date: November 2016	Post-test age scores			
Grade at school: 5	One word reading	Sentence reading	One word spelling	Sequential spelling
Age at post-test: 11 yrs 4 mth	**10 yrs 1 mth**	**9 yrs 10 mth**	**9 yrs 6 mth**	**8 yrs 10 mth**

Number of therapy sessions: 25
Number of reading fluency books covered: 4
Number of writing/spelling fluency paragraphs covered: 2

Child 13

Pretest date: April 2016	Pretest age scores			
Grade at school: 5 gender female	One word reading	Sentence reading	One word spelling	Sequential spelling
Age at pretest: 8 yrs 10 mth	**8 yrs 6 mth**	**8 yrs 0 mth**	**6 yrs 6 mth**	**6 yrs 0 mth**
Post-test date: November 2016	Post-test age scores			
Grade at school: 5	One word reading	Sentence reading	One word spelling	Sequential spelling
Age at post-test: 9 yrs 1mth	**9 yrs 1 mth**	**9 yrs 5 mth**	**7 yrs 6 mth**	**7 yrs 0 mth**

Number of therapy sessions: 26
Number of reading fluency books covered: 9
Number of writing/spelling fluency paragraphs covered: 7

Child 14

Pretest date: October 2015	Pretest age scores			
Grade at school: 1 gender male	One word reading	Sentence reading	One word spelling	Sequential spelling
Age at pretest: 7 yrs 4 mth	**6 yrs 6 mth**	**6 yrs 9 mth**	**6 yrs 8 mth**	**< 6 yrs 0 mth**
Post-test date: November 2016	Post-test age scores			
Grade at school: 2	One word reading	Sentence reading	One word spelling	Sequential spelling
Age at post-test: 8 yrs 4 mth	**8 yrs 7 mth**	**9 yrs 2 mth**	**9 yrs 7 mth**	**8 yrs 6 mth**

Number of therapy sessions: 29
Number of reading fluency books covered: 4
Number of writing/spelling fluency paragraphs covered: 17

Child 15

Pretest date: June 2017	Pretest age scores			
Grade at school: 4 gender male	One word reading	Sentence reading	One word spelling	Sequential spelling
Age at pretest: 10 yrs 2 mth	**10 yrs 9 mth**	**9 yrs 2 mth**	**9 yrs 0 mth**	**8 yrs 0 mth**
Post-test date: December 2018	Post-test age scores			
Grade at school: 5	One word reading	Sentence reading	One word spelling	Sequential spelling
Age at post-test: 11 yrs 8 mth	**>12 yrs 6 mth**	**12 yrs 9 mth**	**10 yrs 3 mth**	**12 yrs 0 mth**

Number of therapy sessions: 58
Number of reading fluency books covered: 2
Number of writing/spelling fluency paragraphs covered: 18

Child 16

Pretest date: April 2018	Pretest age scores			
Grade at school: 3 gender female	One word reading	Sentence reading	One Word spelling	Sequential spelling
Age at pretest: 8 yrs 8 mth	**8 yrs 10 mth**	**8 yrs 8 mth**	**7 yrs 9 mth**	**6 yrs 11 mth**
Post-test date: December 2018	Post-test age scores			
Grade at school: 3	One word reading	Sentence reading	One word spelling	Sequential spelling
Age at post-test: 9 yrs 4 mth	**12 yrs 0 mth**	**10 yrs 1 mth**	**9 yrs 2 mth**	**8 yrs 6 mth**

Number of therapy sessions: 28
Number of reading fluency books covered: 2
Number of writing/spelling fluency paragraphs covered: 12

Child 17

Pretest date: May 2018	Pretest age scores			
Grade at school: 3 gender male	One word reading	Sentence reading	One word spelling	Sequential spelling
Age at pretest: 8 yrs 9 mth	**6 yrs 8 mth**	**6 yrs 9 mth**	**6 yrs 9 mth**	**No score**
Post-test date: December 2018	Post-test age scores			
Grade at school: 3	One word reading	Sentence reading	One word spelling	Sequential spelling
Age at post-test: 9 yrs 4 mth	**8 yrs 7 mth**	**8 yrs 3 mth**	**7 yrs 1 mth**	**< 6 yrs 0 mth**

Number of therapy sessions: 24
Number of reading fluency books covered: 5
Number of writing/spelling fluency paragraphs covered: 1

Child 18

Pretest date: March 2018	Pretest age scores			
Grade at school: 2 gender male	One word reading	Sentence reading	One word spelling	Sequential spelling
Age at pretest: 7 yrs 7 mth	**7 yrs 7 mth**	**7 yrs 10 mth**	**7 yrs 1 mth**	**< 6 yrs 0 mth**
Post-test date: November 2018	Post-test age scores			
Grade at school: 2	One word reading	Sentence reading	One word spelling	Sequential spelling
Age at post-test: 8 yrs 3 mth	**9 yrs 6 mth**	**9 yrs 7 mth**	**8 yrs 1 mth**	**8 yrs 7mth**

Number of therapy sessions: 32
Number of reading fluency books covered: 5
Number of writing/spelling fluency paragraphs covered: 12

Child 19

Pretest date: May 2018	Pretest age scores			
Grade at school: 2 gender male	One word reading	Sentence reading	One word spelling	Sequential spelling
Age at pretest: 8 yrs 4 mth	**7 yrs 6 mth**	**7 yrs 7 mth**	**7 yrs 4 mth**	**6 yrs 5 mth**
Post-test date: November 2018	Post-test age scores			
Grade at school: 2	One word reading	Sentence reading	One word spelling	Sequential spelling
Age at post-test: 8 yrs 8 mth	**8 yrs 0 mth**	**9 yrs 2 mth**	**8 yrs 5 mth**	**6 yrs 11 mth**

Number of therapy sessions: 21
Number of reading fluency books covered: 6
Number of writing/spelling fluency paragraphs covered: 1

Child 20

Pretest date: February 2018	Pretest age scores			
Grade at school: 4 gender male	One word reading	Sentence reading	One word spelling	Sequential spelling
Age at pretest: 10 yrs 10 mth	**8 yrs 1 mth**	**8 yrs 11 mth**	**8 yrs 8 mth**	**7 yrs 6 mth**
Post-test date: December 2018	Post-test age scores			
Grade at school: 4	One word reading	Sentence reading	One word spelling	Sequential spelling
Age at post-test: 11 yrs 8 mth	**10 yrs 1 mth**	**9 yrs 7 mth**	**9 yrs 8 mth**	**8 yrs 6 mth**

Number of therapy sessions: 28
Number of reading fluency books covered: 3
Number of writing/spelling fluency paragraphs covered: 8

Note that in the above table, the pre- and post-test scores for each child have been highlighted and accentuated in larger font size to enable case-by-case visual inspection of the data for each type of assessment test used, as well as profile interpretation across different areas of the assessment. Case aggregation is possible, as all children have been diagnosed as learning disabled against the DSMIV criteria (the tests of basic reading, writing and spelling skills conducted falling well below would be expected in terms of age level as well as overall level of cognitive performance, enabling diagnosis of a reading disorder under DSM-IV code 315.0013 and a disorder of written expression in terms of the diagnostic criteria for DSM-IV code 315.2.14). Case contrast is also possible, using the therapy and method indicators quoted for each child. All 20 children have been exposed to reading fluency materials and methods implemented with parent involvement. Child 17 and Child 19 have not yet been exposed to the writing and spelling fluency methods used in the programme, as each child commenced this side of the programme in November 2018.

Table 3.
Results of children who have worked on phonological and phonic skills, reading fluency, as well as writing and spelling fluency materials and methods.

being specifically taught these basic skills. However, the evidence from using the Seven Vowel Phonic Analysis System would suggest that a number of children have benefitted from being taught how to reference the letters and letter combinations involved in print-to-sound translation and then how to use working memory to recode these associations from sound back to print.

The results presented in **Table 3** have been drawn on a case-by-case basis from the files of children in my practice. All of the 20 children have had reading, writing and spelling difficulties, and in each of the 20 cases, reading fluency work has been undertaken in conjunction with phonic instruction and also in conjunction with phonological referencing focused on developing fluency in writing and spelling.

The results presented in **Table 3** indicate that there has been a backwash effect from application of the methods used in teaching phonic analysis into both proficiency in one word reading ability and fluency in reading sequentially, as well as reciprocal effects from use of reading fluency methods into competencies in writing and spelling (and vice versa). The indications would thus be that there is commonality of influence across the different areas of the fluency-based intervention programme described in this chapter. These underpin the results presented in this chapter, as well as the individual case studies, aggregated case study results and case contrasts presented in previous chapters on the programme [18, 26, 27].

11. Discussion of results

Following Luria [1–3], the reason for commonality of influence across the different areas and components in our programme would be that the various language, reading, writing and spelling interventions are dependent on the mediation of speech processes. They would thus be dependent on the development of both phonological and phonic abilities, which would need to be the core skills taught in the language and reading comprehension, the reading fluency, as well as the writing and spelling fluency areas of intervention in the programme, as well as across different components within each of these areas, on a functional level.

In terms of more recent literature, commonality of influence could also be cited as evidence of a common linguistic awareness manifesting in phonological, orthographic and morphological awareness as suggested by Berninger et al. (2010), and of a universal phonic principle manifesting across different orthographies as suggested by Perfetti et al. (1992). Difficulties in developing linguistic awareness and the universal phonic principle would have been assisted, as suggested by McCutchen (1988), by introducing metacognitive strategies such as the Seven Vowel Phonic Analysis System.

The results to date indicate positive effects in children with whom both reading fluency and writing and spelling fluency methods have been implemented [18, 26, 27]. Following Berninger and McCutcheon's theories, greater metacognitive control as opposed to simply increasing encapsulated automaticity would account for the backwash effects from writing and spelling into reading, as well as the steady progress across different areas of the fluency-based programme observed by users of our programme.

12. Effectiveness of the programme

From first interventions using large-print phonically based materials in the 1990s to the present, positive results have been obtained using the programme described in this chapter [18, 26, 27]. Evidence has been drawn from the files of children in my practice with whom reading fluency work as well as writing and spelling fluency work has been conducted, and also from the files of children in the practice for whom there has been one or other systematic variation in the way in which the programme has been implemented.

Based on this evidence, three implementation variables are likely to affect the successful implementation of the programme. These variables are as follows:

- consistent and regular exposure to phonological and phonic instruction to provide a foundation of basic skills on which the fluency interventions in the programme can be built;

- consistent implementation of methods designed to improve both reading fluency and writing and spelling fluency to produce the greatest likelihood of positive effects; and

- consistent support from parents in programme implementation to produce the greatest likelihood of positive effects.

These conclusions are based on the aggregation of case studies conducted by the author over a number of years and are also supported by case contrast analysis [26, 27]. They are also supported by the experience and evaluations of an increasing number of users of the programme's methods and materials.

The development of the first series of books occurred over a 5-year period in the 1990s [66], while over the last 6 years since 2012, a large number of additional graded reading books have been written. These are about a set of animal characters with stories set in a variety of settings and have been workshopped and used with South African children of different ages, and from different cultural backgrounds, whose parents report that they find them enjoyable. They are also being used by children in England, as well as in other countries adjacent to South Africa, whose parents are reporting that their children are learning to read more fluently and at the same time enjoying the stories.

Similarly, the writing and spelling methods used in the programme have been developed and modified over time, have been implemented clinically for a number of years and have over the past 6 years been implemented with an increasing number of children of different ages and cultural backgrounds. There is evidence indicating that other therapists working with children diagnosed as having learning disabilities have used these methods successfully. There is also evidence from the network of parents, teachers, therapists, and schools currently using the materials that others are able to use these methods successfully at home, in their practices, in reading centres, as well as in the classroom.

The evidence on the programme to date is thus based on the work of an expanding network of users and would support Luria's view that, like any other skill, reading, writing and spelling need to become fluent to be of maximal use and that automaticity in reading, writing and spelling is a function of repetitive use. Following Dehaene [28], the use of the 3 × 3 oral impress method together with the large-print, phonically based materials in our reading fluency programme would be effective in stimulating the visual word form area in the left temporal cortex repeatedly and repetitively, thus developing the connections necessary to read fluently.

Once observable differences in reading fluency are noted, phonological referencing methods are introduced. Following Jorm and Share [32, 34, 35], the repetitive phonological referencing methods used in the Seven Vowel Phonic Analysis System would be based on the teaching of skills for phonological recoding (print-to-sound translation, as well as translation of sound back to print). Working memory for the phonic associations developed through phonological referencing would then enable the learner to acquire the detailed orthographic representations necessary for fast, efficient visual word recognition, as well as the detailed orthographic representations necessary to spell both individual words and words in sequence.

In essence, the methods used in our fluency-based programme are based on use of a combination of repetitive paired reading and repetitive phonological referencing. The evidence from aggregated case studies of children who have worked with a combination of these methods indicates that there are benefits in improvement in reading, spelling individual words and spelling words in sequence, with backwash effects occurring across these areas. Case contrasts indicate lessened effects from programme implementation where there has been systematic variation in either the implementation of repetitive paired reading or repetitive phonological referencing using the methods described in this chapter and in previous chapters on the programme [18, 26, 27].

13. Linked delivery of materials and methods

At this stage in the development of the programme, there is a database of materials, a set of tried and tested methods that are theoretically based, experience in usage of both the reading fluency and the writing and spelling areas of the programme and promising results. Our phonically based, large-print materials are also being increasingly used by other therapists and teachers, who are reporting positive evaluations from parents as well as improved reading, writing and spelling results in children.

There is thus potential for wider usage of the programme and for implementation at greater scale than at present. The materials are in electronic form and provide a form of elearning, which can be used in contact, as well as at distance. The ebooks are designed to be used by parents and can also be used by therapists, teachers and schools to develop fluent reading. As the books are large-print and phonically based, they can also be used for developing writing and spelling fluency.

The programme can thus be described as a fluency-based intervention, which can be used to introduce children to reading as well as develop the reading, writing and spelling skills necessary to reading fluently, and writing and spelling fluently. As all materials in the database are electronic, the programme can be implemented through use of multimedia, including email, cellphone as well as computer-based access and delivery.

Assessment and evaluation are built into the programme's structure, linked to an awards system for children using the materials. The model is both evidence-based and interactive in its emphasis on assessment and evaluation.

14. Availability of materials in our database

Both the repetitive paired reading methods used for developing reading fluency and the methods of repetitive phonological referencing used for developing writing and spelling fluency are based on use of the resource of phonically regular, large-print materials in our database. These materials are used for the development of fluency, which is conceptualised as based on the coding and recoding of phonic associations.

There are over 80 phonically based large-print ebooks in our database. These are graded according to reading level and divided into different libraries of materials. The individual books as well as the libraries of materials are presented in a format in which they can be made available electronically at low cost to others.

There are also particular methods we have developed to implement both the reading fluency and the writing and spelling fluency areas of our fluency-based programme. These are presented in a number of manuals, which are also made available at low cost to those working with our materials.

15. Training of therapists, teacher and parents, and outreach to schools

The books in the 'The Tales of Jud the Rat' reading fluency programme were originally developed in a form in which they could be delivered by email and then downloaded and used by parents at home. As the reading fluency materials were designed to complement the sessional work done in contact sessions in my practice, parents were provided with tutorial support by email, as well as questions and answers by cellphone.

The aim was to provide a large body reading fluency materials, which were appropriately graded, which were readily available and inexpensive and which could be used daily at home. As the materials were written to meet the needs of parents of children in my practice who had rate of work problems linked to reading fluency difficulties, parents became partners in the learning process through use of the materials in the practice's database.

As the programme evolved and other therapists, teachers and tutors who were working with the children also saw promising results [65], there were requests from outside my practice to use the materials and methods. This led to the development of a set of manuals to be used with the materials, to be used by those working with the materials either at home, or in reading centres, or in tutoring centres, or in schools.

This led to demand for more formal training to complement the informal support provided to users of the programme's materials and methods, and an implementer training course for therapists, teachers and parents.

16. The implementer training course

The implementer training course has eight modules, as follows:

a. *Module 1: Introductory module.* This focuses on course orientation and on the theory underpinning the programme.

b. *Module 2: Assessment.* This module focuses on work with the four core tests used in the programme to establish needs for fluency-based work, as well as assessment of pre-reading skills at the foundational level.

c. *Module 3: Reading fluency.* This module focuses on use of our 3 × 3 oral impress method to address reading fluency needs at basic and intermediate levels in the programme. A pdf library is also provided with the module, consisting of 12 reading fluency books (6 at basic and 6 at intermediate levels in the programme).

d. *Module 4: Foundational skills for reading, writing and spelling.* This focuses on work with children having difficulties establishing the basics of reading, as a basis for intervention using our foundational level materials. A pdf library is also provided with this module, consisting of 15 foundational level reading books and 6 activity books.

Participants who have completed Module 4 are awarded a certificate for successful completion of the reading fluency side of the implementer training course. At this point, participants are competent in working with the reading fluency area of our programme and also have a library of 27 reading books and 6 activity books with which to work at foundation, basic and intermediate reading levels. The methods and materials can then be used for learning support with individual children and groups of children, as well as for the development of classroom-based reading fluency programmes and reading clubs.

a. *Module 5: Assessment of phonic skills.* This focuses on assessment of phonic skills and phonic difficulties. The module focuses in particular on use of phonic inventories to establish needs for phonic instruction, as well as needs for work in the writing and spelling fluency area of the programme.

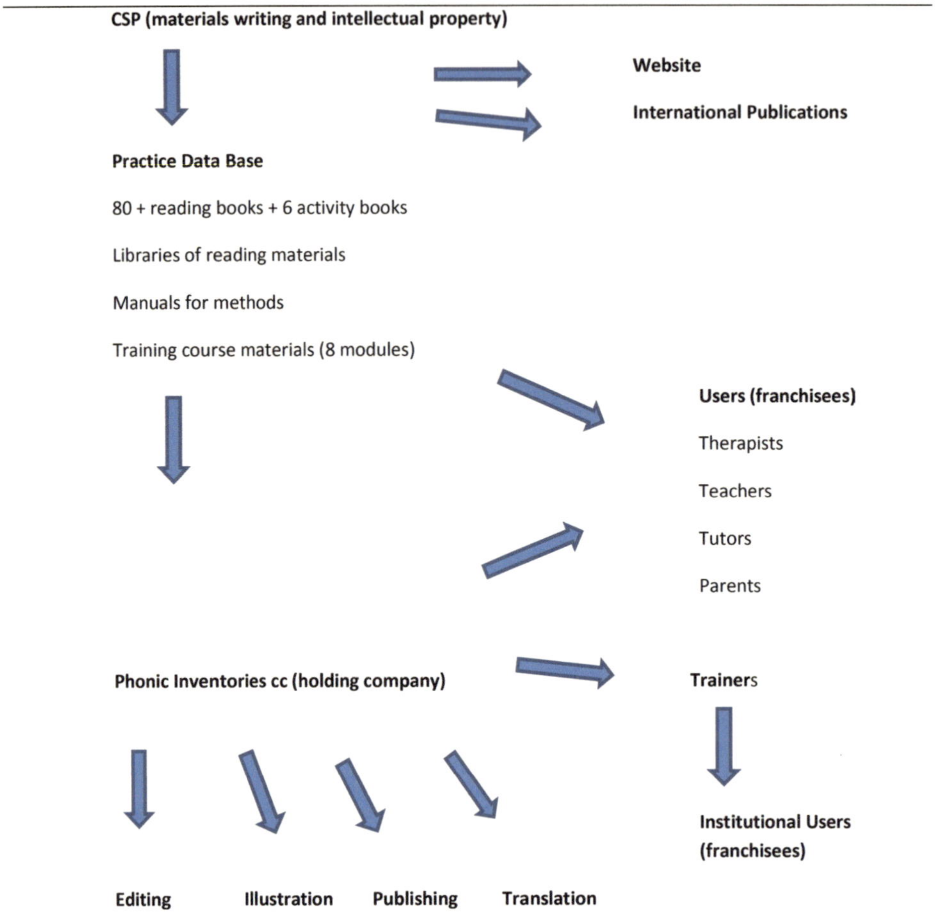

Table 4.
Operational model of Dr. Charles Potter's Reading Fluency Programme.

b. *Module 6: Writing and spelling fluency.* This focuses on work with writing and spelling fluency. The module focuses in particular on use of the Seven Vowel Phonic Analysis System, based on results that indicate that optimum results are achieved where work in reading fluency is accompanied by work using this method.

c. *Module 7: Sequentialisation and working memory for words in sequence.* This focuses on work with sequential spelling difficulties. The module focuses in particular on use of the Targeted Analysis, Revisualisation and Sequential Spelling Programme, which integrates the training of sequential memory skills into writing and spelling fluency work.

d. *Module 8: Language and reading comprehension:* This is the final course module. It focuses on ways in which fluency-based work can be contextualised in language and reading comprehension activities, as well as the types of language and reading comprehension work being done in the classroom at school.

After completing Module 8, participants are awarded a certificate for successful completion of the writing and spelling fluency side of the course. This is accompanied by a letter that states that at this point, participants have successfully completed all eight course assignments and are competent in working with both the reading fluency area and the writing and spelling fluency area of our programme.

Assignments are completed with each of the eight modules, and these are designed so that after completing all eight modules, participants are competent to work with our materials in learning support work and in the integration of our methods and materials into the classroom. The methods and materials can then be used to support fluency-based work with individual children and groups of children, as well as to support classroom-based spelling, sequential spelling, language and reading comprehension programmes.

The course as a whole is implemented flexibly and is designed to fit in with the programme user's other commitments. This is done by negotiation of deadlines for each module, which are doable, within an agreed time framework.

17. Outreach to schools, reading centres and tutoring schemes

Outreach to schools, reading centres and tutoring schemes involves provision of a library of 27 reading fluency books and 6 activity books, which are leased from the programme. Training is then provided on how to use the materials and methods to optimal effect. This focuses on providing information about the potential uses of our materials and methods, as well as training key members of staff in use of our materials and methods.

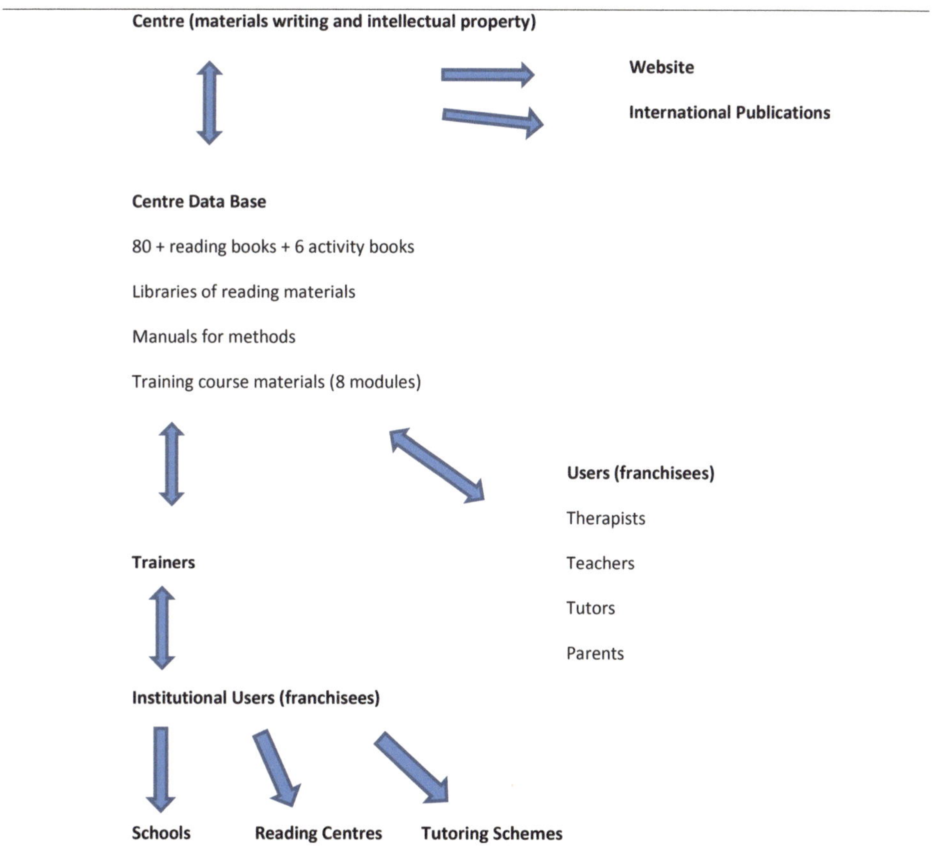

Table 5.
Centre-periphery model of Dr. Charles Potter's Reading Fluency Programme.

This is based on the following operational model involving provision of training courses for staff of schools, reading centres and tutoring schemes, combined with involvement of those members of staff with a learning support function in our eight-module implementer training course.

To date, the model in **Table 4** has been based on a centre-periphery approach to materials development and dissemination. In the operation of the programme, external demand for materials and methods developed centrally and implemented as part of my practice as an educational psychologist has been met through training. The training involves use of electronic materials supported by email and cellphone contact. This is supported by open-source publication of the theory behind the programme, the initial case studies on which the methods and materials were based, as well as its subsequent results in wider application.

This currently involves use of multiple forms of electronic media suited to working with users at distance. However, as demand grows, use of multimedia will become increasingly necessary as expansion of the programme takes place. In the process, the model will need to change. Delivery of the programme's materials and methods will need to become increasingly website-based, while at the same time involving use of interactive multimedia for evaluative purposes, as the programme grows in scale.

18. Use of multimedia in programme development and implementation

A feature of the programme's development to date has been the use of distance educational methods involving computer-based writing and delivery of materials, combined with email and cellphone interaction with programme users. This has enabled centre-periphery dissemination of materials and methods at small scale, and regular centre-periphery and periphery-centre contact as well as evaluative feedback.

This model has enabled publication of evidence in the form of case studies, as well as aggregated case studies [18, 26, 27]. It has also enabled usage of the programme's methods and materials by an increasing number of both individual users and institutional users.

The programme has reached a scale where the next stage in the programme's development will need to involve work with training partners. This will attempt to expand what is already taking place to larger scale, based on use of the programme's materials and methods in training both individual and institutional users. In the next stage, this will also need to be expanded to the training of trainers, based on the use of multimedia to carry the programme's central message outwards concerning its methods and electronic materials, and use of multimedia to carry evaluative evidence concerning usage.

19. Training in use of materials and methods

The programme is both research- and evidence-based. The central message from centre to periphery focuses on optimal use of methods and materials, based on theory drawn from the literature, as well as evidence concerning effective implementation.

This centre-periphery approach to carrying the message can be modelled as in **Table 5**.

It will be evident from the above that the model is evidence-based, in which the output of the media is developed on the basis of evidence drawn from published research, as well as evidence based on implementation. Both delivery and evaluative feedback are currently dependent on email and cellphone-based technologies. The challenges for work at greater scale will involve keeping channels of two-way evidence-based communication open, while at the same time increasing use of website-based delivery.

20. Summary

This chapter has focused on a reading, writing and spelling programme, which has been developed for working with children with reading, writing and spelling difficulties. As all materials are electronic, the programme has been implemented via email and cellphone technologies. Based on promising results, a number of therapists, teachers, tutors and parents as well as institutions are currently using the methods and materials, both in South Africa and its neighbouring territories, as well as in the United Kingdom. There are also a number of therapists, teachers, tutors and parents involved in an eight-module training programme based on use of multimedia.

The first half of the chapter has described the theoretical basis of the programme, as well as the methods used in its implementation. The second half of this chapter has focused on the modular training course and its aims, as well as the centre-periphery model of development and evaluation used in disseminating the programme through use of multimedia, including email, cellphone and use of computer-based electronic material. The model is both evidence-based and interactive in its emphasis on assessment and evaluation. It is currently delivered by email supported by email and cellphone contact and will increasingly involve use of interactive website-based technologies as the programme grows in scale.

Author details

Charles Potter
Educational Psychologist in Private Practice, Johannesburg, South Africa

*Address all correspondence to: pottercs@gmail.com

References

[1] Luria AR. Higher Cortical Functions in Man. London: Tavistock Publications; 1966

[2] Luria AR. The Working Brain: An Introduction to Neurospychology. Harmondsworth: Penguin Education; 1973

[3] Luria AR. Basic Problems of Neurolinguistics. Vol. 73. Berlin: Walter de Gruyter; 1976

[4] Vygotsky LS. Selected Psychological Investigations. Moscow: Izdstel'sto Pedagogical Academy; 1956

[5] Vygotsky LS. Razvitie vysshikh psikhicheskikh funktsii [Development of the Higher Mental Functions]. Moscow: Publishing House of the R.S.F.S.R. Academy of Pedagogical Sciences; 1960. pp 13-223

[6] Heckelman RG. A Neurological Impress Method of Reading Instruction. Merced CA: Merced County Schools Office; 1962

[7] Heckelman RG. A neurological-impress method of remedial-reading instruction. Academic Therapy. 1969;**4**(4):277-282

[8] Laberge D, Samuels JS. Toward a theory of automatic information processing in reading. Cognitive Psychology. 1974;**6**(2):293-323

[9] Samuels SJ. The method of repeated readings. The Reading Teacher. 1979;**32**(4):403-408

[10] Hollingsworth PM. An experiment with the impress method of teaching reading. The Reading Teacher. 1970;**24**(2):112-114

[11] Morgan R, Lyon E. Paired reading—A preliminary report on a technique for parental tuition of reading retarded children. Journal of Child Psychology and Psychiatry. 1979;**20**(2):151-160

[12] Overett J, Donald D. Paired reading: Effects of a parent involvement programme in a disadvantaged community in South Africa. British Journal of Educational Psychology. 1998;**68**(3):347-356

[13] Topping K. Paired reading: A powerful technique for parent use. The Reading Teacher. 1987;**40**(7):608-614

[14] Topping K. Peer tutored paired reading: Outcome data from ten projects. Educational Psychology: An International Journal of Experimental Educational Psychology, 7. 1987;**2**: 133-145

[15] Topping K. Peer tutoring and paired reading: Combining two powerful techniques. The Reading Teacher. 1989;**42**:488-494

[16] Topping K. Paired, Reading, Spelling and Writing: The Handbook for Teachers and Parents. London: Cassell; 1995

[17] Vanwagenen MA, Williams RL, Mclaughlin TF. Use of assisted reading to improve reading rate, word accuracy, and comprehension with ESL Spanish-speaking students. Perceptual and Motor Skills. 1994;**79**(1):227-230

[18] Potter CS. Using phonically based E-books to develop Reading fluency. In: Gradinarova B, editor. E-Learning—Instructional Design, Organizational Strategy and Management. Rijeka: InTech; 2015. DOI: 10.5772/61607. Available from: http://www.intechopen.com/books/e-learning-instructional-design-organizational-strategy-and-management/using-phonically-based-e-books-to-develop-reading-fluency

[19] Martelli M, Di Filippo G, Spinelli D, Zoccolotti P. Crowding, reading, and developmental dyslexia. Journal of Vision. 2009;**9**(4). Article 14

[20] Spinelli D, De Luca M, Judica A, Zoccolotti P. Crowding effects on word identification in developmental dyslexia. Cortex. 2002;**38**(2):179-200

[21] Yu D, Cheung S, Legge GE, Chung STL. Effect of letter spacing on visual span and reading speed. Journal of Vision. 2007;**7**(2). Article 2

[22] Chomsky C. After decoding: What? Language Arts. 1976;**53**(3):288-296

[23] Hoskisson K, Krohm B. Reading by immersion: Assisted reading. Elementary English. 1974;**51**(6):832-836

[24] Lam S, Chow-Yeung K, Wong BPH, Kiu Lau K, In Tse S. Involving parents in paired reading with preschoolers: Results from a randomized controlled trial. Contemporary Educational Psychology. 2013;**38**(2):126-135

[25] MacDonald P. Paired reading: A structured approach to raising attainment in literacy. Support for Learning. 2010;**25**(1):15-23

[26] Potter CS. Developing automaticity in children with learning disabilities: A functional perspective part one: Theory and assessment. In: Ryan C, editor. Learning Disabilities. London: InTech; 2017. Available from: https://www.intechopen.com/books/learning-disabilities-an-international-perspective/developing-automaticity-in-children-with-learning-disabilities-a-functional-perspective-part-one-the

[27] Potter CS. Developing automaticity in children with learning disabilities: A functional perspective part two: Programme methods and materials. In: Ryan C, editor. Learning Disabilities. London: InTech; 2017 Available from: http://www.intechopen.com/articles/show/title/developing-automaticity-in-children-with-learning-disabilities-a-functional-perspective-part-two-pro

[28] Dehaene S. Reading in the Brain. New York: Penguin Books; 2009

[29] Potter CS. The 3 x 3 Oral Impress System: A Manual. 2012. http://www.charlespotter.org. Electronic copy available from my practice by emailing me at pottercs@gmail.com

[30] Potter CS. Introducing the 3 x 3 Oral Impress Method: A manual for parent implementers. 2016. http://www.charlespotter.org. Obtainable from the author by email to pottercs@gmail.com

[31] Luria AR, Simernitskaya EG, Tubylevich B. The structure of psychological processes in relation to cerebral organization. Neuropsychologia. 1970;**8**(1):13-19

[32] Jorm A, Share D. Phonological recoding and reading acquisition. Applied PsychoLinguistics. 1983;**4**:103-147

[33] Jorm A, Share D, Maclean R, Matthews R. Phonological recoding skills and learning to read: A longitudinal study. Applied PsychoLinguistics. 1984;**5**:201-207

[34] Share DL. Phonological recoding and self-teaching: Sine qua non of reading acquisition. Cognition. 1995;**55**(2):151-218

[35] Share DL, Jorm AF. Segmental analysis: Co-requisite to reading, vital for self-teaching. Cahiers de Psychologie Cognitive/Current Psychology of Cognition. 1987;**7**(5):509-513

[36] Share DL. Phonological recoding and orthographic learning: A direct test of the self-teaching hypothesis. Journal of Experimental Child Psychology. 1999;**72**:95-129

[37] Brooks L. Visual pattern in fluent word identification. In: Reber AS, Scarborough DL, editors. Toward a Psychology of Reading. Hillsdale, NJ: Erlbaum; 1977. pp. 143-181

[38] Ehri LC, Saltmarsh J. Beginning readers outperform older disabled readers in learning to read words by sight. Reading and Writing: An Interdisciplinary Journal. 1995;7:295-326

[39] Manis FR. Acquisition of word identification skills in normal and disabled readers. Journal of Educational Psychology. 1985;77:78-90

[40] Reitsma P. Printed word learning in beginning readers. Journal of Experimental Child Psychology. 1983;**36**:321-339

[41] Reitsma P. Orthographic memory and learning to read. In: Aaron PG, Joshi RM, editors. Reading and Writing Disorders in Different Orthographic Systems. Dordrecht/Norwell, MA: Kluwer Academic; 1989. pp. 51-73

[42] Shahar-Yames D, Share DL. Spelling as a self-teaching mechanism in orthographic learning. Journal of Research in Reading. 2008;**31**(1):22-39

[43] Potter CS. The Seven Vowel Phonic Analysis System: A manual. 2014. http://www.charlespotter.org. Electronic copy available from my practice by emailing me at pottercs@gmail.com

[44] Potter CS. Introducing the Seven Vowel Phonic Analysis System: A manual for parent implementers. 2018. http://www.charlespotter.org. Obtainable from the author by email to pottercs@gmail.com

[45] Perfetti CA, Dunlap S. Learning to read: General principles and writing system variations. In: Koda K, Zehler A, editors. Learning to Read across Languages. New York: Routledge; 2008. pp. 13-38

[46] Caroline SM. Breaking the Sound Barrier: A Phonics Handbook. New York: Macmillan; 1960

[47] Ellis NC, Hooper AM. Why learning to read is easier in Welsh than in English: Orthographic transparency effects evinced with frequency-matched tests. Applied PsychoLinguistics. 2001;**22**:571-599

[48] Spencer LH, Hanley JR. Effects of orthographic transparency on reading and phoneme awareness in children learning to read in Wales. British Journal of Psychology. 2003;**94**:1-28

[49] Frost R, Katz L, Bentin S. Strategies for visual word recognition and orthographical depth: A multilingual comparison. Journal of Experimental Psychology: Human Perception and Performance. 1987;**13**:104-115

[50] Seymour PH, Aro M, Erskine JM. Foundation literacy acquisition in European orthographies. British Journal of Psychology. 2003;**94**(2):143-174

[51] Ziegler JC, Bertrand D, Tóth D, Csépe V, Reis A, Faísca L, et al. Orthographic depth and its impact on universal predictors of Reading: A cross-language investigation. Psychological Science. 2010;**21**(4):551-559

[52] Ziegler JC, Goswami U. Reading acquisition, developmental dyslexia, and skilled reading across languages: A psycholinguistic grain size theory. Psychological Bulletin. 2005;**131**:3-29

[53] De Sousa D, Greenop K, Fry J. Cross-language transfer of spelling strategies in English and Afrikaans grade 3 children. International Journal of Bilingual Education and Bilingualism. 2011;**14**(1):49-67

[54] Perfetti CA, Zhang S. Very early phonological activation in Chinese

reading. Journal of Experimental Psychology: Learning, Memory, and Cognition. 1995;**21**(1):24-33

[55] Spencer K. Predicting word-spelling difficulty in 7- to 11-year-olds. Journal of Research in Reading. 1999;**22**(3):283-292

[56] Spencer K. Is English a dyslexic language? Dyslexia. 2000;**6**(2), Special Issue: Multilingualism and Dyslexia (Part 2)):152-162

[57] Spencer K. Differential effects of orthographic transparency on dyslexia: Word reading difficulty for common English words. Dyslexia. 2001;**7**(4), Special Issue: 5th BDA International Conference Selected Papers (Part 2)):217-228

[58] Potter CS. Using phonically based E-books to develop reading fluency. In: Gradinarova B, editor. E-Learning—Instructional Design, Organizational Strategy and Management. Rijeka: InTech; 2015. DOI: 10.5772/61607. Available from: http://www.intechopen.com/books/e-learning-instructional-design-organizational-strategy-and-management/using-phonically-based-e-books-to-develop-reading-fluency

[59] Potter CS. Developing Automaticity in Children with Learning Disabilities: A Functional Perspective Part One: Theory and Assessment. 2017. Available from: http://www.intechopen.com/books/learning-disabilities-an-international-perspective/developing-automaticity-in-children-with-learning-disabilities-a-functional-perspective-part-one-the

[60] Potter CS. Developing Automaticity in Children with Learning Disabilities: A Functional Perspective Part Two: Programme Methods and Materials. 2017. Available from: http://www.intechopen.com/articles/show/title/developing-automaticity-in-children-with-learning-disabilities-a-functional-perspective-part-two-pro

[61] Ehri L. Linguistic insight: Threshold of reading acquisition. In: Waller TG, MacKinnon GE, editors. Reading Research: Advances in Theory and Practice. Vol. 1. New York: Harcourt Brace; 1979. pp. 63-114

[62] Ehri L. Systematic phonics instruction: Findings of the national reading panel. In: Paper Presented at the Invitation Seminar Organised by the Standards and Effectiveness Unit, Department for Education and Skills, British Government (London, England, March 17). 2003

[63] Ehri LC. Learning to read words: Theory, findings and issues. Scientific Studies of Reading. 2005;**9**:167-188

[64] Heckelman RG. N.I.M. revisited. Academic Therapy. 1986;**21**(4):411-420

[65] Ravenscroft G. Remedial instructional techniques: Assessing the effectiveness of high imagery teaching techniques in the remedial environment [unpublished master's thesis]. Johannesburg: University of the Witwatersrand; 2008

[66] Sfetsios N. The use of mental imagery in the treatment of a child with severe learning disabilities. In: Honours Research Report. Johannesburg: University of the Witwatersrand, Department of Psychology; 2002

[67] Vygotsky L. Thought and Language. Trans. E. Hanfmann and G. Vakar. Cambridge MA: MIT Press; 1934

Chapter 9

Digital Pathology: The Time Is Now to Bridge the Gap between Medicine and Technological Singularity

Consolato M. Sergi

Abstract

Digitalization of the imaging in radiology is a reality in several healthcare institutions worldwide. The challenges of filing, confidentiality, and manipulation have been brilliantly solved in radiology. However, digitalization of hematoxylin- and eosin-stained routine histological slides has shown slow movement. Although the application for external quality assurance is a reality for a pathologist with most of the continuing medical education programs utilizing virtual microscopy, the abandonment of traditional glass slides for routine diagnostics is far from the perspectives of many departments of laboratory medicine and pathology. Digital pathology images are captured as images by scanning and whole slide imaging/virtual microscopy can be obtained by microscopy (robotic) on an entire histological (microscopic) glass slide. Since 1986, services using telepathology for the transfer of images of anatomic pathology between detached locations have benefited countless patients globally, including the University of Alberta. The purpose of specialist recertification or re-validation for the Royal College of Pathologists of Canada belonging to the Royal College of Physicians and Surgeons of Canada and College of American Pathologists is a milestone in virtual reality. Challenges, such as high bandwidth requirement, electronic platforms, the stability of the operating systems, have been targeted and are improving enormously. The encryption of digital images may be a requirement for the accreditation of laboratory services—quantum computing results in quantum-mechanical phenomena, such as superposition and entanglement. Different from binary digital electronic computers based on transistors where data are encoded into binary digits (bits) with two different states (0 and 1), quantum computing uses quantum bits (qubits), which can be in superpositions of states. The use of quantum computing protocols on encrypted data is crucial for the permanent implementation of virtual pathology in hospitals and universities. Quantum computing may well represent the technological singularity to create new classifications and taxonomic rules in medicine.

Keywords: Digital pathology, Medicine, Singularity, Quantum, Artificial Intelligence, Bioinformatics

1. Introduction

In the past two decades, we experienced some new inventions in technology with the development of quad-core processors (four independent units called cores able to read and execute central processing unit instructions) and 5G networks. This environment in information technology (IT) allows us a more efficient, stable, and faster communication than ever. Currently, the 5G network is considered the milestone that will open the conversation to the next level. There is crescent popularity, widespread use and increasing dependency on wireless technologies in our societies, both Western and Eastern civilizations. This demand has produced an unimaginable industrial revolution that may show some spectra of Orwellian nature [1]. There is increasing public exposure to broader and higher frequencies of the electromagnetic spectrum and data are transmitted as fast as never before [2]. The evolution from current 2G, 3G, and 4G to 5G wireless technologies is increasing worldwide. However, the promise of a convenient and comfortable lifestyle with a massive 5G interconnected telecommunications network has raised not only the expansion of broadband with shorter wavelength radiofrequency radiation but also highlighted the concern that health and safety issues may remain unknown [2]. Currently and in the future, the effects of radiofrequency electromagnetic radiation are and will be challenging if not impossible to identify epidemiologically. This challenge relies on the lack of an unexposed control group. Nevertheless, it is inconceivable to carry out some steps in our daily life without using the telecommunication network. In this chapter, some of the new exciting aspects of the evolution of digital pathology in diagnostics and teaching are discussed.

2. Digital pathology

Digital pathology (DP) can be shortly demarcated and, probably, clearly defined as the digitalization of gross and microscopic tissue specimens subject to electronic capture of the photons as well as the management, analysis, and distribution of images. DP has been considered a terrific technology that is transforming the benchmark and protocols of work of pathologists after the impressive revolution operated in imaging radiology a decade earlier. Telemetric measurement of body temperatures in experimental animals implanted with commercially available transmitters has been automated using the Commodore C-64 microcomputer since the 1980s [3]. Also, in the 1980s, digitalization of 2D gels started, and high-performance liquid chromatographic system based on the Commodore 64 personal computer were common [4, 5]. The routine work of pathologists involves the identification of data and patterns in gross and microscopic tissue sections to deliver a diagnosis that can be rendered to the clinician and to the patient for further investigation or for starting therapy. The work of the pathologist is not quite different from the radiologist's job focusing on images, although most of the radiologic images are on black and white, while the pathologists use some dyes to facilitate the discrimination of morphologic structures on the tissue. The work of the pathologist is crucial in closing the loop, and reaching the diagnosis. The pathologist is also focusing on teaching. In the past, cases valuable for teaching were cut and mounted on glass slides that have been used to be projected using a film-based camera mounted on light microscopes and archival slides used for clinical rounds or multidisciplinary clinical team meetings as well as educational seminar presentations. This analog presentation was also used for forensic (medico-legal) purposes being broadly accepted in court proceedings for both civil and criminal law systems. Currently, archival tissue collections and new teaching cases are scanned and converted to static digital images. The images of gross and microscopic pathology specimens are continuously captured by digital cameras, tablets, iPads, phablets, and smartphones and the images downloaded via media card, universal serial bus (USB) interphase or wireless connections into personal computers or university servers for storage ready for teaching or discussion in the setting of multidisciplinary team clinical meetings. The digitized images may have different extensions such as tiff, jpg, and gif and the quality of the image increases proportionally with the number of pixels of the image or a digitized static image. The term "virtual microscopy" has been used to describe the acquisition, management, and storage of digitalized microscopic images [6]. Virtual microscopy systems are capable of complete digitization of the histology and cytology slides. This process is also known as whole-slide digitation or whole-slide imaging (WSI). In 1997, the first virtual microscopy system was described by the Computer Science Department at the University of Maryland and the Pathology Department at Johns Hopkins Hospital, Baltimore, Maryland [7, 8]. Fifteen years ago, in 2003, the European Organization for Research and Treatment of Cancer (EORTC) printed the results of a poll on virtual microscopy systems to that date [9]. Rojo et al. [10] provided a comparative description of 31 potential solutions available on the market as early as 2006 that can perform a whole slide imaging (WSI) or assistance in complete slide review for anatomic pathology applications. Digital imaging can be subdivided into two classes according to the aim, including the digital microscope and virtual microscopy-aided systems. The digital microscopes aim to create a digital image from an analogic image detected with a light microscope. Conversely, diagnosis-aided systems can detect the region of interest (ROI) and give data arising from the analysis of biomedical signals. There are two different devices including the motorized microscopes and scanners. In the motorized microscopes, there are two classes of components. The first class includes pieces of proper light microscopy (e.g., eyepieces, multiple lenses, motorized revolver, position control, and spotlight control), while the second component deals with the capture of the images using a camera joined up to the microscope. The virtual microscopy devices include an optical microscope system, an acquisition system (photography/camera), a software program that controls the scan process, and a digital slide viewer. Optional components of the virtual microscopy include the slide feeder or image-processing programs. The most critical components are the light microscope and the acquisition camera. Good microscopy needs to have an optical quality of high level. The optical quality is largely determined by the quality of the lenses (objective) and by the class of the eyepieces. Good, quality objective lenses have a standard, which are achromatic lenses. Since diverse colors refract through a curved lens at different angles, an achromatic lens produces an enhanced, "flatter" specimen image of the specimen than it would otherwise be obtained. However, achromatic lenses are of less quality than semi-plan or plan objectives, which are "perfect lenses" and are typically required for sophisticated biological research with double the price of achromatic objectives. Also, it is useful to confirm that the objectives are DIN (Deutsch Industry Norm) compatible. DIN objectives are convenient since they are interchangeable. They are transposable from one DIN compatible microscope to another. The wider the eyepieces are, the easier the viewing. Thus, "widefield" (WF) or "super wide field" (SWF) eyepieces are crucial, although the wider the lens, the smaller eye ports, which means there is a decrease of the size of the magnification power. There are four primary categories of illumination: tungsten, fluorescent, halogen, and light-emitting diode (LED). Tungsten is the basic illumination for entry-level microscopes, but halogen and LED microscopes are of higher quality. Halogen produces strong, white light and usually, includes a variable rheostat with adjustable light intensity, while LED, especially if used with rechargeable batteries, makes the microscope fully portable with the opportunity to use it in environments with limited electrical outlets. Fluorescent lighting or epi-fluorescent microscopes are for biological research and similar applications. Moreover, the microscope should have an iris diaphragm and good quality condenser—preferably, an Abbe condenser which allows for greater adjustments and most good quality microscopes include iris diaphragms and Abbe condensers as standard. Finally, a mechanical stage is also valuable for compound microscopes. This situation is critical particularly when viewing specimens at high magnifications. A good camera is also a crucial component and a charged coupled device (CCD) sensor in the camera provides an analog signal. Digital cameras convert the analog signal into digital. It is important to choose the right image resolution or CCD size, i.e., the number of pixels the sensor can detect. The connection of the camera with the personal computer is through a FireWire port, and card adapters may be needed. In virtual microscopy, the high resolution can move at different speeds. There is about 32 mm/s (Zeiss Mirax Scan), or more at 38 mm/s (Aperio ScanScope T2), 41.22 mm/s (LifeSpan Alias), or even 180 mm/s (Olympus SIS.slide). The stage accuracy is about 1–3 μm, although some types can get accuracy or minimum distance of 2 nm (0.002 μm) to 15 nm (0.015 μm) for the z-axis and 250 nm (0.25 μm) for the x-axis and y-axis. About the computer hardware, most DP solutions should be based on workstations with at least two microprocessors, 2.8–3.6 GHz or higher, and at least 4 GB of random-access memory (RAM). The operating system used by the control devices and the workstations is usually Windows XP Professional, Vista, 7, 8 or 10 (Microsoft Redmond, Wash.). The endorsed way for handling the storage is using centralized (enterprise) storage servers of the hospital or healthcare institution. This solution may not be an option if IT personnel or healthcare administrators raise security issues. Thus, alternatives would use intranet servers or with storage up to 100 terabytes (TB). Recently, the Nimbus Data company unveiled a new 100 TB solid-state drive (SSD) making it the world's largest SSD currently available. Different from the hard-disk drive (HDD), an SSD is like a memory stick. There are no moving parts and information is stored in microchips. Nimbus Data developed advanced flash memory solutions that power data-driven innovation and one of these solutions include ExaFlash® All-Flash Arrays and ExaDrive® Solid State Drives. This solution is accelerating data storage, simplifying data management, and improving data protection for cloud infrastructure, data analytics, AI-rich content, high scientific computing, and numerous other applications that may be considered unconceivable currently. However, the minimum recommended configuration should include six disks, each of 300 GB (0.3 TB); 10 k rpm hot swap for a total of 3.8 TB. All virtual microscopy solutions comprise a flat thin film transistor (TFT) monitor (20–23 inches). These screens must be high resolution with a TFT screen of 2560 × 1600 pixels, with 200-ppm resolution. This screen size allows a visual field four times larger than the standard microscope field of view. Different aspects should be considered during the digitalization process, such as the digitization speed, the maximum size of the sample, the focus quality, the digitization at diverse planes, the procedures for slide scanning and image assembling (with or without correction), and the formats used to store the scanned samples. The digitization speed, also known as total scanning time, is probably one of the most important aspects to consider before choosing among these systems. The evaluation should be based on specific factors. It is wise to list the area size to be scanned and the objective lens used (e.g., ×20 or ×40 as objective). Further, we list the charge-coupled device (CCD) camera size, the model of motorized stage, the required time on the previsualization stage, the time for a panoramic view, the selection of the area of interest, the choice of focusing method, as well as the number of points (focusing) needed. It is crucial to remember that slides with irregular surface require a higher number of points, which reduces the scanning speed. Moreover, it is important to consider the number of planes at the z-axis to be digitized, the speediness to obtain data from the CCD camera to the personal computer (PC), and the transfer from the PC to the storage device. Devices with a slide feeder have time to upload and download a slide in about 6–8 seconds, which is a good time for many laboratories. The total time, including the code bar reading, maybe around 15 seconds. The total scanning surface is forced to the motorized stage used and to the histologic slide type. The number of focusing points, also known as "focusing map" may be manual or automatically set. Multiple planes digitization through the z-axis may be a requirement for visualizing thick tissue slides or cytology slides with 3D clusters. Thus, the scanning system should work similar to the microscope fine focus control of the light microscopy on conventional histologic slides. Different systems can provide the digitization through the z-axis, at least in one area of the slide. For diagnostic purposes, scanning only a region of interest is not an option, because the pathologist may need to scan on the whole slide. Thus, WS Scanning method and stitching may be an option in some cases. Typically, the acquisition of microscopic fields is square-by-square, from the slide's upper left corner to the lower right one and the final image is a mosaic composed of multiple files. The assembling procedure of the slide squares may be performed in two different ways. We can use a mechanical adjustment tiling the borders of each fragment. Alternatively, we can use some software adjustment, which stitches the images. The final result may be considered as multiple files (typically thousands of Joint Photographic Experts Group or JPEG files)—in one or several folders, several files with one or multiple resolutions with the method used by Zeiss Mirax Scan and Zoomify viewer, and/or a single compressed file (JPEG2000, JPEG, TIFF). Flashpix (MicroBrightField Virtual Slide), or other formats (VSI extension in Olympus SIS.slide, .svs) may be encountered. SVS files are used by some medical/microscope scanners such as Aperio, scan scope (AxioVision), and others. They are essentially based upon the TIFF format and utilize the tiled image capabilities. Digital Slide Visualization and processing include x-axis and y-axis movements (lateral and vertical) displacement through the screen, objective shifting or zooming, displacement of the z-axis, and the x-axis and y-axis movements. One of the original problems was the low screen refreshment during the horizontal and vertical displacements. This disadvantage was due to the large amount of data that needed to be transferred between the different parts of the computer (central processing unit, hard disk, graphic card, and memory) or through the communication network. The fragmentation of the images may be quite disturbing for the pathologist who needs to review several files for diagnostic purposes. A solution is partitioning large images into small pieces according to the required magnification and buffering adjacent pieces (prefetching) in the viewer. However, quad-core processor based computer and 5G networks may be part of the solution as well. Histological slides, and especially cytopathology slides, may require the capture of multiple z-planes to get a perfectly focused image. Simultaneous and synchronized displacement on multiple windows is also useful options. Moreover, it is possible to include bookmarks on digital slides, facilitating the retrieval of interesting positions in subsequent case reviews. Virtual slides can be visualized and interpreted simultaneously by several consultants in pathology creating the virtual "multi-headed microscope" allowing innumerable users to review the same areas considering that not only one takes control of the session. Thus, different pathologists can review different parts of the same slide at the same time. Most of the systems can scan a digital slide using the highest image quality available (objective ×40) in about 1 hour. This time may be a limiting factor and shortening to 10–15 minutes should be a choice in the future. Future systems should improve the technical aspects, such as the scanning speed, the necessary bandwidth on networks, requirements for storage, user interfaces, improvement of focusing, and detection of tissue or cytology areas. The intellectual process of analyzing and interpreting pathology images to provide a final diagnostic is one of the central aspects of the pathologist's work. Therefore, both image and report must always include the name of the consultant pathologist and department where that intellectual work has been performed. The enterprise-centralized and electronic storage is the best option and should be based on what is labeled the

Picture Archiving and Communication System (PACS), which will permit an efficient way of seeking pathology images. This aspect will be possible, thanks to the Digital Imaging and Communications in Medicine (DICOM) image format, which is being used for radiology images and adapted to be also used for pathology images.

3. Whole slide imaging/virtual microscopy

The introduction of whole slide imaging (WSI) has created some wonderful opportunities for the pathologist or generally speaking for the morphologist or biologist. It allowed capturing images of the entire pathology slide without the need to select only a few regions of interest. The new platforms with 64 bit and quad-core processors and the development of high-resolution cameras allowed the manufacturing of digital slides at high resolution harboring uniquely multiple magnifications and focal planes. This set of data processed in a computer allows a full simulation of light microscopy. The operator (e.g., pathologist or technologist) can scan the slides rapidly and focus zooming in and out in the monitor using the keyboard, mouse, or his/her finger determining the quality of the image and gathering information to make the diagnosis. The robotic microscopic scanner mechanically scans histologic glass slides containing the tissue already processed and stained. A software combines individual scanned fields into a composite digital image [11–14]. The acquisition time has been reduced since a scanner was commercialized and time, which has been a limiting factor, will shorten even further in the future. The operator may be able to open the final file using several viewing software with optional user-friendly interfaces. This procedure makes it possible for the operator to navigate to various areas of the virtual slide or zoom in/out changing the magnifications without operating a revolver. The new technology applied with the WSI can be used for primary diagnosis by the pathologist, for publication of scientific data in peer-reviewed biomedical journals, to capture static images for reporting, archiving or computer-aided analysis, and educational activities in the setting of new concepts for universities and hospitals. A few decades ago the introduction of multi-headed microscopy allowed multiple viewers to follow the operator navigating a light microscope connected with few guest binoculars. This simple step was multiplied using a camera connecting the microscope with a big screen able to open the participation of guests from dozens to hundreds. However, the virtual microscopy has opened the scenario to unrestricted access to viewing, no need to recut slides for teaching and overcome the quality deterioration of staining. The WSI slides are obviously more interactive than static images. They are easier to share with multiple users on several platforms, they can work on diverse operating systems, anywhere and at any time. Training materials can be standardized. Moreover, files can be made available by hyperlinks using restricted codes to access specific file servers [11–14]. Since the introduction of virtual microscopy, we have faced numerous and virtually unlimited educational activities, including graduate schools, training in different medical specialties, E-learning, and tele-education for remote communities that are not easily accessible. Education has not been limited to medical only but involved dental, biological, and veterinary schools worldwide [15]. There are e-learning and virtual workshops with virtual atlases on the web that have been able to be a primary source for hundreds or thousands of new doctors. The virtual microscopy has started a revolution promoting knowledge, which is web-based learning and made available by several societies including the United States and Canadian Academy of Pathology (USCAP), the International Academy of Pathology, and the International Academy of Cytopathology (IAC) [16]. In the United Kingdom (UK), the National Health Service (NHS) promotes Clinical Governance and clinical excellence with a specific institute nationwide labeled National Institute for Health and Care Excellence (NICE) [17]. Clinical governance describes a systematic approach to maintain and improve the quality of patient care. In similarity to the plan-do-check-act cycle, which is also known as Deming or Shewhart cycle, the clinical governance constitutes an official and unique framework through which the NHS is accountable for the ongoing improvement of quality of the clinical service with the aim safeguarding high standards of clinical care and creating a crucial environment focused on clinical excellence. Although communication failure is the most likely cause for medical errors, a substantial number of errors may be linked to a decrease of professional skills contributing to fatalities in healthcare. In 1999, Quality System Essentials were promoted to laboratory practices by the National Committee specifically for Clinical Laboratory Standards (now Clinical Laboratory Standards Institute [CLSI]). The essentials identify 10 or more major laboratory activities that are important components of a laboratory quality program [2, 3]. The updated and modernized quality system essentials that should be provided to each operator (e.g., pathologist) include updated equipment, smooth improvement of the diagnostic process, regular assessment and measurement of safety, and professional and personal development among others. All of these essentials were established to guarantee that data reported from the diagnostic laboratory unit are as accurate as possible. They should serve the requirements of both patients and clinicians. An imperative component in the control of any laboratory procedure is the constant and diligent participation of the operator in an external quality assurance (EQA) or proficiency testing program to validate that the operator is updated with the diagnostic criteria and skills are maintained. An EQA plan in place allows the healthcare to provide (University or hospital) to be certain that quality indicators are in place. There are numerous EQA programs worldwide, and they constitute a fundamental part of continuing professional development (CPD) of health care professionals [4]. The purpose of EQA in pathology is both to maintain good running standard operating procedures and to improve the performance of all sub-specialties. It will ensure that patients have access to a high-quality service wherever they live without constraints of physical barriers. Previously, we compared four slide survey programs from four geographical regions (United Kingdom, Germany, USA-Canada, and Australasia) concerning the EQA in pathology for pediatric pathologists in the setting of continuing professional development [17]. We found that the United Kingdom scheme, which has specific time frames (2 circulations/year, 30 slides), partial confidentiality, and numerous sources of data and assessors, can be used as an archetypal for revalidation. The US-Canadian and Australasian schemes only partially seem to fulfill the revalidation requirements. The German IAP scheme appears to be essentially an educational program and may be unsuitable for revalidation. WSI is widely implemented in the Australasian QA programs of the Royal College of Australia. The diagnostic scores of the pathologists undergoing the College promoted Performance Improvement Program (PIP) in Surgical Pathology online only without using histological glass slides do not appear compromised by the converting to WSI [18]. Pathology is in the center of a radical transformation in medicine, which is driven by many factors. Foremost, there is the advancement of precision medicine, an imbalance of pathology jobs across regions, and a need for more efficiency and effectiveness in the diagnostic workflow. In healthcare, technological innovation and its implementation at several sites are growing at an increasingly fast pace across specialties. Pathologists spend 30–40% of their work with administrative duties, and the frustration may exasperate with an increasing rate of burnout colleagues in several countries. The number of duties may be simplified, and technological innovation may help the pathologist to decrease the burden of the diagnostic procedures, but also install a system to red flags situations that may be borderlines. The introduction of AI in WSI will be the next step and will help to increase the accuracy of pathology diagnosis and reporting. The introduction of algorithms that allow the machine to follow the diagnostic procedure operated by the pathologist using an eye tracking system and algorithms able to identify the discrepancies of pathology reports before signing out will help in the aim to reach extreme accuracy in medicine. The breakdown of geographical barriers operated by WSI will be implemented by the next step of a new healthcare system where AI will support the diagnostic procedure. There will be an enhanced collaboration allowing pathologists to seek second opinions more quickly, collaborating with multidisciplinary care teams more effectively, and distribute workloads across sites more evenly. Data from patient's history and unique risk factors will be studied by a background algorithm allowing the pathologist to have a companion for suggested differential diagnoses. The integration of data across clinical systems, lab examinations, and radiology with pathology images applying artificial intelligence to derive understandings is called computational pathology, which is far more convoluted than a file with stacked images of a glass slide. This revolution will implement the highest levels of accuracy and can be implemented to any specialty. This scenario is happening now as evidenced by the most recent congress of European urologists. Prof. Guo from Nanjing, China, claimed that smart software could diagnose prostate cancer as well as a pathologist (https://eau18.uroweb.org/smart-software-can-diagnose-prostate-cancer-as-well-as-a-pathologist/). All these algorithms seem to reconnect to the Bayes' theorem, which benefits us finding the probability of an event A given event B, written P(A|B), in terms of the probability of B given A, written P(B|A), and the single probabilities of A and B. Consequently, P(A|B) = P(A) * P(B|A)/P(B). Thus, in this scenario, event A is the event the patient has a specific disease, and event B is the event that the patient's test is positive. Thus, P(B|notA) represents the probability of a "false positive" rate, i.e., the patient's test is positive even though the patient does not have the disease. If the specific disease has an incidence of one in 10,000 people and a specific test has an accuracy of 99%, P(B|A) = 0.99, P(A) = 0.0001, and P(B) may be consequent by conditioning on whether event A does or does not occur, i.e., P(B) = P(B|A) * P(A) + P(B|notA) * P(notA) or 0.99 * 0.0001 + 0.01 * 0.9999. Thus, the ratio the pathologist gets from Bayes' theorem is less than 1%. This result relies on the disease, which is very rare. The number of false positives significantly surpasses the people who truly have the disease.

4. Gross pathology imaging and 3D printing

Three-dimensional (3D) printing uses 3D data to produce 3D physical models has been a powerful discovery and engine in science and medicine. Starting with computer-aided design (CAD) models for industry, 3D manufacturing is entering at the full title in medicine for undergraduate and postgraduate education [19]. Computer software can build up the model from a series of photographs on cross-sections that resemble to realistic sections from the original model. 3D printing is attained by placing down consecutive layers of powdered material or liquid plastic resins which are used to build 3D models at high temperature and sliced with laser technology. In the setting of 3D printing, the most critical techniques include ink-jetting, deposition modeling, laminated object manufacturing (LOM), and laser sintering. The ink-jet technique uses a method similar to two-dimensional (2D) inkjet printers whereby it deposits liquid plastic resins in striated lines. Infused deposition modeling a technique is applied to extruding and layering filaments of thermoplastic materials, which are melted. LOM uses a laser cutter technique of shaping and sticking (gluing) layers of plastic films or paper. Finally, laser sintering includes stereolithography and selective laser sintering with curing photopolymers by a UV laser (stereolithography) and fusing small particles such as thermoplastic metal, ceramic, or glass by high-power laser (selective laser sintering) [20]. 2D digital photographs, sequential X-rays, and images of computed tomography (CT)/magnetic resonance imaging (MRI) are useful to create 3D CAD models by software reconstruction and laser scanning of objects. MRI was used in the past in guiding dissection of specimens for teaching purposes [21]. 3D printing has been used in orthopedic surgery and vascular surgery to guide surgeons during procedures [22–24]. The 3D reconstruction may revive anatomic pathology museums with the possibility to create several 3D models for undergraduate and postgraduate teaching. These specimens can be scanned by CT or MRI and the information provided be used to develop singular 3D models that may be produced for hundreds of learners. The advantages are that the learners do not need to be exposed to toxic solutions, such as formaldehyde, that students do not need to overcrowd a classroom or a museum hall, but they have no hassle in examining each specimen with time and investigate details. It may be very encouraging and reassuring when learners discover and participate in the inspection of the sample at the same time. There is the advantage to go back to the sample at any time. These specimens are durable, not infectious, and not fragile like the original ones. The robustness of these specimens will also allow the reproducibility of teaching in classes of the future. There is also the opportunity to utilize precious digital photographic collections in building 3D models of specimens that are not available anymore. 3D printing can create realistic models of almost any complex profile or geometric feature with extreme accuracy and opportunities are invaluable at this time. Some 3D printers with price ranging from hundreds of dollars to several thousands of dollars are commercially available. 3D printed models can then be used to demonstrate very complex lesions such as congenital heart defects of different age, including the transposition of the great arteries and hypoplastic ventricles. There will be enormous resources for learning using 3D printed models for undergraduate and postgraduate students, anatomic pathology residents, radiology residents, and other medical practitioners such as surgeons for educational and training purposes. Teaching curricula can be implemented with 3D models. While we expect the cost of living increases over time, in the next couple of decades the rate at which the price of a college education has gone up is utterly alarming. A 3D model may cost approximately $ 500, but the price may increase to several thousand in case of extreme accuracy. Production costs of 3D models do not need to spike up the admission fees to college and universities enormously. With increased demand, 3D computing and modeling will potentially become more affordable on mass production. At rounds or multidisciplinary clinical team meetings, 3D models can be used to teach topography of pathological lesions and adopt the best therapy possible. Current 3D printing of human anatomic pathology specimens is a reality but merits further investigations for application in teaching college and university students. The increase in complexity of CAD software will allow reaching that level of accuracy for the complete satisfaction of the learning process.

5. Telepathology

The introduction of microscope-integrated telepathology systems enables geographically remote stakeholders to view the live tissue histology slide as seen by the study pathologist within the local microscope. Telepathology is the practice of pathology at a distance using technologies. Although the concept and first telepathology devices are now more than 20 years old [25–27], the introduction of quad-core processors and 5G technologies is renovating this nearby field of virtual microscopy. Simultaneous online viewing and dialog between study pathologist and remote operators in high-speed intranet or internet platform is becoming a reality in many countries. Telepathology is an efficient and cost-effective means for inter-professional histopathology consultation, pathology working groups, and peer review, facilitating collaboration and sound science and economic benefits by enabling more timely and informed clinical decisions. In 1986, the mane of telepathology was coined by Dr. Ron Weinstein. Differently, from the meta- or diachronous virtual microscopy, telepathology is a singular specifically synchronous two-way communication between the host and recipient. Telepathology has also been variously named: teleconsultation, telemicroscopy, teleconferencing, remote robotic microscopy, and web conferencing. In 1987, Weinstein first reported telepathology and the network of pathology diagnostic services on breast tissues by remote workstation-controlled light microscope attached to a high-resolution video camera and a telecommunication linkage [28]. Since the 1990s, similar analog technologies have been used for remote intraoperative frozen section services in northern Norway of Scandinavia [29, 30]. Telepathology is currently used for several fields of pathology, including cytopathology and ultrastructural pathology [31–36]. The approval of the Food and Drug Administration of the United States (US FDA) of these different methodologies has broadened a field in laboratory services, which was not known before [37, 38]. The three major telepathology supported systems currently used are static, real-time, and, of course, virtual microscopy. In the static system, pre-captured still digital images are deposited on a secure server with encryption. The disadvantages of static telepathology are that the operator controls everything including acquiring the images, while the audience is passive participants. In teleconsultation, the consultant histopathologist has no remote control of the physical microscopic glass slide and has limited fields of view to examine. Static TP systems are, nevertheless, welcome in some parts of the world with limited resources, shortages of particularly trained personnel, and lack of continuing professional education programs [39]. Tele-oncology has been proved to facilitate access to care and decrease health care costs with teleconsultations may take place in a syn-, asynchronous, or blended format. There are a few examples of successful applications that include cancer telegenetics, bundling of cancer-related telepathology-supported applications, remote chemotherapy supervision, symptom management, survivorship care, palliative care, and multidisciplinary approaches to increase access to cancer clinical trials [40]. It is careful to be a simple, cost-effective, reliable and efficient means to provide diagnostic and educational support to pathologists in the developing world improving pathology and laboratory medicine in low-income and middle-income countries. New technologies, including point-of-care testing and telepathology, can partake a substantial role in service delivery of laboratory medicine and pathology if used appropriately [41]. The physical geography of Canada is extensively varied with boreal forests prevailing throughout the country and ice areas prominently in northern Arctic regions and through the Rocky Mountains, and the flat Canadian Prairies in the southwest of the country. There is the vast distance between some parts of the country and telepathology is playing a significant role in some areas [42–44]. In the University Health Network (UHN), is a multi-site academic institution in Toronto. The UHN comprises several downtown hospitals and remote hospitals in Northern Ontario, WSI has been effectively utilized for telepathology in primary intraoperative frozen section diagnosis and secondary/tertiary teleconsultation [43, 45]. Likewise, in the Province of Quebec, the implementation of the telepathology project (Eastern Quebec) provides uniform frozen section diagnosis and teleconsultation services across a vast geographic region comprising up to 21 sites [44]. Real-time and WSI/virtual microscopy in telepathology systems may be implemented in the Prairies as well as in Northern Western territories. The future may be brighter because of faster networks and fast digitalization.

6. Social media and mobile device use

There is a terrific increase of time pathologists spend on the internet to search for pathologies, criteria or images that may help them in narrowing the differential diagnosis of challenging cases. The advances in computing power, cheaper prices for single device, and the exponential growth of web search for online learning resources have permitted the launch of platforms that are internet-based that are helping for publication and digital education. There are numerous digital atlases online, and there is a proliferation of multiple web-based technologies for continuing professional development of human and veterinary pathologist at a pace that we were not thinking before [46–57]. Telepathology using smartphones and tablets with Skype and its alternatives, including FaceTime, Viber, Talky, WeChat, and WhatsApp, among others, for live, synchronous online communication are feasible for clinical and educational uses [58]. The purpose of an iPad tablet or similar android device to download digitalized images of gross and microscopic pathology from a Web server for E-learning has been found to provide a satisfactory solution in low-resource countries as well as in the middle- and high-resource countries, because the pathologist can directly access the information at fingertip [59]. In a review of social media use in medical education, the incorporation of social media tools boosted the engagement of the learners, feedback from the audience and tighter collaboration and professional development [60–64]. Although probably up to a few years ago, the most commonly cited challenges were technical issues, variable learner motivation, and privacy/security concerns, currently, the high-speed internet, the increased competition among learners in a highly competitive world, and the use of https protocols with 2-key authentication seem to have demolished the above-raised challenges.

7. Artificial intelligence as the "third revolution in pathology"

In the 1980s the introduction of immunohistochemistry or the application of immunologic methods using antibodies against specific epitopes in situ directly on the tissue allowed a complete change of various diagnoses based exclusively on morphologic criteria. The identification of cell of origin and differentiation pathways allowed the re-classification of numerous pathologies, e.g., malignant Non-Hodgkin's lymphomas with the acquisition of knowledge that will shape the advancements in hematology and hematopathology for decades [65, 66]. The introduction of genomic and proteomic platforms may also represent an important revolution, probably, the second one after the immunohistochemistry. The genomic and proteomic medicine identified a new niche in medicine that has been focused for years from investigators of public health issues, i.e., precision medicine [67–71]. The "Third Revolution" in pathology is probably represented by the artificial intelligence (AI) [72]. AI is defined as intelligence demonstrated by machines, differently from the natural intelligence displayed by humans and specific animals. Thus, any device that perceives its surroundings and takes actions that maximize its chance of successfully achieving its goals may be considered showing an AI behavior. The correct acquisition and interpretation of external data and the integration of such data and results with the surrounding is the principle of the adoption by the machine of flexible adaptation.

8. Artificial intelligence and classroom

AI may be able teachers to identify students that may need some additional help or individuals with special needs that may struggle in a typical classroom. AI algorithms have been designated to increase the production of learning and the efficiency and effectiveness in learning. There are some paramount roles of AI in education. They include automation of grading with an approach tailored explicitly to short answered question other than multiple choice questions, teacher's support using chatbot able to communicate directly with students, student's aid with future students having an AI lifelong learning companion starting from high-school to university and postgraduate education adopting a new model of AI-controlled continuing professional development. Moreover, AI may be able to identify each student's strengths and weaknesses in a way that may be more standard than conventional teaching, which may be linked to the current motivation of the teacher. There is a personalized learning curriculum with an AI machine able to help students with special needs by adapting teaching material to lead them to success without being downscaled for mental r physical barriers. AI will allow teachers to Act as learning motivators and help to mentor undergraduate and postgraduate students to the best suitable path for them. As AI takes on more of an education role by providing students with the necessary information, this procedure will change the position of teachers in the classroom. Educators will move into the role of classroom supervisor, facilitator or learning motivator and adopt a previously unimaginable relationship with the students. Some examples of classroom-based AI include Thinkster Math, brain, and Content Technologies Inc. Thinkster Math (http://get.hellothinkster.com/why-tabtor-is-now-thinkster/), which is a math tutor able to identify the level of each student allowing each student to improve the logic process by providing video assistance for stuck students and immediate, personalized feedback. Brainly (https://brainly.com/) is the social media site for classroom questions allowing users to ask questions and receive verified answers from fellow students. Content Technologies, Inc. (http://contenttechnologiesinc.com/) is an AI company using Deep Learning to create customized textbooks. Teachers carefully import curricula (syllabi) into a CTI engine. The CTI equipment then masters the content and uses specific algorithms to create tailored books and coursework based on core concepts. Mika (https://www.carnegielearning.com/products/software-platform/mika-learning-software/) is another AI based on math, and like Thinkster Math, Carnegie Learning's Mika harbors AI-based tutoring tools for learners, who may be too busy for after-school tutors. This solution has also been promoted for students who require personalized attention. Finally, Netex Learning (http://www.netexlearning.com/en/) teachers design curriculum across a variety of digital platforms and devices (iPad, android or surface devices). The use of Netex allows teachers to create customized materials to be published on any digital platform while providing tools for video sessions, adapted assignments, and learning analytics (https://www.thetechedvocate.org/5-examples-artificial-intelligence-classroom/). There will be plenty of apps in the future able to target pathology residents in their curriculum preparation and the proposed limitation of the pathology education to core-competencies only is a tragic evolution. The identification and implementation of these technologies should form the basis for venture companies able to shape the transforming platform of work of pathologists. An application to improve pathology teaching is the use of eye-tracking technology [73, 74]. During the teaching of histopathology skills to medical students and postgraduates, the use of eye tracking allowed a better performance at the final score in learners that took advantage of this technique compared to learners that did not utilize it.

9. Challenges of digital pathology education

DP is far from the niche described a few years ago. DP is a stable platform in many universities and colleges. Radiology images are chiefly acquired as digital data and saved in robust picture archiving systems [75]. Hartman et al. [75] describe the challenges using digital pathology for second opinion intraoperative consultations for over 10 years implementing an incremental rollout for digitalization in pathology on subspecialty benches. They began with cases that contained small amounts of tissue (biopsy specimens). The authors successfully scanned over 40,000 slides through their digital pathology system and emphasized that a successful conversion to digitalization in pathology requires pre-imaging adjustments, integrated software, and post-imaging evaluations. The limitations in the implementation of digital pathology include: (1) Infrastructure and resources support, although the cost of acquisition and maintenance of DP equipment, networking equipment, and staffs expenses are cheaper than a few years ago. (2) Integration into an existing laboratory information system (LIS) or Provincial Health Network (PHN) portals such as the upcoming Epic software implementation in several regions (e.g., Alberta, Canada) [76–79] rather than a stand-alone DP education system may attract investments from the government or the private sector or creating public-private partnerships. (3) Acceptance of digital pathology images in the diagnosis (4) Engagement of all pathologists in practice or training.

10. Artificial neural networks in medicine

Artificial neural networks (ANN) are increasingly a desirable technique for solving machine learning and AI issues. The variety of neural network type and their use of diagnosis and therapy in medicine requires skilled knowledge to choose the most appropriate approach. ANN may be considered as simplified models of the human brain neuronal networks. In both natural and artificial, the essential requirement for a system is that it should attempt to capture the necessary information for further processing. The simplest ANN that may be listed here is the threshold logic unit or TLU. A processing unit for numbers with n inputs $x_1, x_2,..., x_n$ and one output y constitute the TLU. In the TLU, there is a threshold θ, and each input x_i is associated with a weight w_i. A TLU computes the function and then output a "1" if this sum exceeds a threshold, and a "0" otherwise. TLUs mimic the thresholding comportment of biological neurons *in vivo*. This simple logical unit may become more complicated and apply to various areas of medicine, such as diagnostic systems, biochemical analysis, image analysis, and drug development. ANNs are very useful in medicine and applications to have been described in the literature dealing with problems in cardiology and oncology. ANNs are an AI technique that uses a set of nonlinear equations to mimic the neuronal connections of biological systems. ANNs are useful for pattern recognition and outcome prediction applications and have the potential to bring AI techniques to the personal computers of practicing pathologist, assisting them with a variety of diagnostic procedure, such as hepatocellular carcinoma [80–83]. The benefits to utilize ANNs is that they are not affected by external factors such as fatigue, working conditions and emotional or mood state. ANNs may represent a useful AI companion in the routine diagnostic pathology as it has been used in several other fields in medicine, such as to analyze blood and urine samples, track glucose levels in diabetics, and determine ion levels in body fluids. There are numerous applications including tumor detection in ultra-sonograms, classification of chest X-rays, blood vessel classification in MRI, determination of skeletal age from X-ray images, and determination of brain maturation, among others. ANNs are also useful in the development of drugs for treating cancer and AIDS and in the process of modeling biomolecules. There is also the ability of ANNs to provide sensor fusion which is the combining of values from several different sensors. Sensor fusion empowers the ANNs to acquire complex relationships among the individual sensor values, which would otherwise be lost if the values were independently analyzed. Pathology is an imaging-based discipline in medicine which deals with the nature of disease like radiology. Pattern recognition starts with the idea of classifying input data into identifiable classes by use of significant feature attributes of the data, where the feature attributes are extracted from a background of irrelevant detail. This pattern recognition has been used primarily in radiology [84–92]. ANNs are used in pattern recognition because of their ability to learn and to store knowledge, and they can achieve very high computation rates which are vital in an application like telemedicine. Another approach for applications of image-driven machine learning is a "deep learning" architecture labeled as convolutional neural networks (CNNs). CNNs are a deep learning architecture procedure constituted by a set of layers of individual modules able to extract progressively and sequentially higher levels of abstraction from input images. This procedure is far more sophisticated than the human eye and can discern immediately features that are important for a classification task. AlexNet [93–98] and GoogLeNet [95, 97–107] became quite popular most recently. Their uptake has been speeding up by the availability of open source software such as Caffe, Theano, and Tensorflow. These frameworks of deep learning interface efficiently with Graphical Processing Units (GPUs) to provide speed improvements at which models can be developed and tested. Neural networks together with random forests (RF), and support vector machines (SVMs) are machine learning algorithms. Esteva et al. were able to create and train a CNN to differentiate between benign and malignant skin lesions obtaining an accuracy pretty similar as dermatologists on a test set of cases verified by follow-up biopsies [108]. In **Table 1**, some relevant terms of machine learning in pathology are grouped.

Artificial intelligence (AI)	A context where a machine executes the execution of cognitive tasks
Artificial neural networks (ANNs)	Computing structure with several stacked layers that analyze information from the input to the desired output, with mathematical optimization that is at the basis for a process driving knowledge extraction and learning from the data (input) concerning the production (output).
Convolutional neural networks (CNNs)	An ANN-like architecture, but devoid of the constraint of every stacked layer and applicable for image recognition tasks.
Machine learning (ML)	An AI field, which stresses the use of algorithmic approaches to train machines in performing tasks such as classification, prediction, and pattern recognition.
Deep learning (DL)	An AI and ML subfield that controls large-scale datasets and consecutively complex mathematical architecture to fulfill a machine learning task.
ImageNet	A dataset of large-scale (10 million) images annotated by nouns in the photos with several degrees of granularity.
Technological singularity	An event showing a singular technological advance or sum of innumerable technological advances that in aggregate could lead to a break in the psychologic and somatic evolution of humans with entirely unpredictable results.

Table 1.
The most useful definitions of frameworks of machine learning and beyond.

Image recognition in pathology has used a discrete number of hand-crafted features, which are time-consuming and are limited in scope, while deep learning identifies its elements from a large number of training examples able to identify patterns that may be unrecognized by humans. There are three tasks in "deep learning" that need to be differentiated, including detection, segmentation, and classification. Litjens et al. trained a CNN for prostate and breast biopsies to improve the objectivity and efficiency of histologic (microscopic) slide analysis. All slides containing prostate cancer and micro- and macro-metastases of breast cancer could be recognized automatically. Moreover, 30–40% of the slides containing benign and normal tissue could be excepted without the use of any additional immunohistochemical marker or human intervention [109]. Murthy et al. investigated the automated classification of the nuclear shapes and visual attributes of cells of glioma, a tumor of the central nervous system, using CNNs on pathology images of automatically segmented nuclei, proposing three methods that improve the performance of a previously-developed semi-supervised CNN. On a dataset of 2078 models, the combination of the proposed approaches was able to cut the error rate and shape classification by 21.54% and 15.07%, respectively [110]. It is not inconceivable that computers in the future will exceed human decision making demonstrating their superiority over humans in identifying new categories [60, 111].

11. Artificial intelligence and basic research

Image-based recognition of developmental pathways has been a pillar in identifying several milestones in developmental biology [112–119]. In systems biology, networks and network-based methods are starting a new analysis of the functional organization of gene networks [120]. In translational bioinformatics, there is the union of translational medicine and bioinformatics. In this setting, translational medicine moves fundamental discoveries of biology from the research bench into the patient-care setting and iteratively uses clinical observations to inform basic biologists. Translational medicine is focusing on patient care, including the creation of new diagnostic procedures, prognostic markers, prevention strategies, and therapeutic protocols based on biological discoveries with an explicit goal of affecting profoundly clinical care [121]. AI is helping to decipher non-coding genes after that 17 years ago the sequencing of the human genome was reached. Currently, one in eight of the 22,210 coding genes listed by the Ensembl/GENCODE, RefSeq and UniProtKB reference databases are differently marked across the three sets [122]. Mappings of tumor-infiltrating lymphocytes (TILs) based on histological images through computational staining using a convolutional neural network trained to classify patches of images will be important in identifying the interaction of cancer with the surrounding environment [123]. The fabrication of functional DNA nanostructures operating at a cellular level could be crucial in determining the pathways to check how more natural-like orchestration is present at cellular level comparing to the rigid and restrictive conventional approaches adopted so far [124]. Currently, we are witnessing a renewed interest in adapting ANN for pharmaceutical research and computer-assisted drug discovery, and design will be a daily task in the future [125]. We specially emphasize deep neural networks, restricted Boltzmann machine networks, and convolutional networks. The Virtual Physiological Human and research studies into nanotechnology will confidently produce yet more unpredictable opportunities, leading to substantial changes in biomedical research and practice [126].

12. Quantum computing and pathology imaging

The language called "R" is a free open source programming language, which is mainly used for data analytics and statistical analysis. Compared with commercial software, open source software allows the operator to become a programmer and change the code. R is enabling users to develop custom AI apps to arrange within their organization with applications for predictive modeling, deep learning, extracting mission-critical information from reams of text, and several other applications. A revolutionary concept in digital data processing is quantum computing, which is based on the fundamental principles by which nature operates, i.e., quantum mechanics [127]. In a classic computer, the process works with bits, which at any given time can be in one of two states, i.e., 0 or 1. Conversely, quantum computers use qubits. These units can exist in any superposition of states 0 and 1 and are represented by a complex number, which is a number that can be expressed in the form a + bi, where a and b are real numbers, while i is a solution of the equation $x^2 = -1$, and it is called imaginary number, because no real number satisfies this equation. When N qubits are in superposition, a combination of 2^N states are created. While a traditional computer can only hold one of these states at a time, quantum computers can perform significant operations on superpositions of states. The most basic operations performed on qubits are defined by quantum gates, which are pretty similar to logical gates used in standard computers using bits. The state of a quantum computer, a set of qubits called quantum register, can be visualized in some ways, typically as a 2D or 3D graph, on which points or bars represent superpositions of qubits, while their color or bar height represent amplitude and phase of a given superposition. Instituted in 1999, D-Wave Systems is considered as the world's first quantum computing company. D-Wave is the leader in the progress and distribution of quantum computing systems and software, and a few applications have been recently reported [128–131]. Quantum computing users have already developed over 100 early applications in areas including image analysis, optimization, machine learning, pattern recognition, anomaly detection, cybersecurity, financial analysis, software/hardware verification, and validation, bioinformatics/cancer research, traffic flow, manufacturing processes, and internet advertising. However, quantum computing is a work in progress, because D-Wave quantum computers do not currently perform arbitrary quantum gate operations on sequences of qubits. Quantum Computing Playground (http://www.quantum-playground.net/#/home) is a browser-based WebGL Chrome platform. It features a graphics processing unit (GPU)-accelerated quantum computer with a simple integrated development environment (IDE) interface and its scripting language with debugging and 3D quantum state visualization features. Quantum Computing Playground can resourcefully simulate quantum registers up to 22 qubits, run some algorithms (e.g., Grover's and Shor's algorithms), and has a variety of quantum gates built into the scripting language itself. All currently known and useful quantum algorithms that can run on quantum computers are based on the ability of the quantum system, upon specific rearrangement, to behave in unison. Large chunks of data can be processed at once, operating primarily on only a few particles, that is, in a massively parallel manner. This aspect will allow tasks that would require centuries of computing on a standard computer to require only a few minutes on a quantum computer. A key challenge for quantum computers is to provide and maintain isolation of individual qubits involved in the computation. Extreme and stable cooling is required to make wire circuits behave in a quantum fashion. Operated by an electrical signal from a classical computer, these systems must be maintained at these extremely low temperatures by a vast refrigeration apparatus involving a rare helium-3 isotope. Standard encryption methods rely on a code for the operator to access encrypted data. However, the key must be shared and can be decoded by unauthorized persons seeking to 'hack' a system using several software programs (most of them open-source) available in internet. With quantum computing, the core and the data can be secured indefinitely with guaranteed unbreakable encryption. Such strong security is possible because quantum encryption relies on the laws of nature (quantum mechanics) to furnish it. Thus, cryptography is expected to be the first application of quantum computing to enter medical practice to secure medical records and communication. "Big data" research and machine learning are likely to be one of the fields to advance quickly with the advent of real-world functional quantum computers. A statistical model requires rational decisions about variable definitions and their inter-relationships. In machine learning, there are few assumptions and algorithms are derived from computer programs that evaluate millions of data elements and all their potential directions of effect and interactions. The more an algorithm is derived from raw data and with less human input, the more it fits into machine learning. Machine learning that informs clinical practice in real time depends on growing databases containing regularly updating medical record information and linked to other sources of data (e.g., wearable technology). To deal with this complexity future machine learning programs will require computational power of quantum computing to deliver results in real time. It is expected that a quantum MRI machine will generate extremely precise imaging allowing even the visualization of single molecules. Using artificial intelligence, quantum computing can be applied to interpreting diagnostic images, histology images other than radiology images. Not only will image detail be exponentially improved but the physician can be aided in understanding results because active machine learning can train a quantum computer to identify abnormal findings with a precision better than the human eye. Combining "big data" (i.e., data that are too complicated to work on using traditional data processing application software) with quantum computing will provide access to the current evidence and enable meaningful use of the electronic data continuously generated in the delivery of care. Realization of personalized medicine will need to draw on analysis of mega-data and bring together measures of physiology, imaging, genomics, wearable technology, screening measures, patient records, environmental measures and more. Currently, we realize that we may be at the dawn of a revolution in computing. We have numerous examples of machine learning algorithms and artificial intelligence that may leverage the power of quantum computing to deliver real time results.

13. Technological singularity

The technological singularity may be considered an event that shows a single technological advance or may represent a sum of many technological advances that in aggregate could lead to a break in the psychologic and physical evolution of humans with entirely unpredictable and unfathomable results [60]. In this hypothesis, there is the concept that artificial superintelligence will abruptly prompt blockbusting technological growth, resulting in impenetrable changes to human civilization. Currently, it is not inconceivable that AI may generate software-based AI learning with "deep learning" on "big data" to enter a phase of self-improvement cycles, with each new and more intelligent generation appearing algorithms will be installed becoming operative. It may swiftly create an intelligence burst resulting in a powerful superintelligence that would, qualitatively, far surpass the human intelligence. Such time is already started and may coincide with the progress of quantum computing (**Figure 1**).

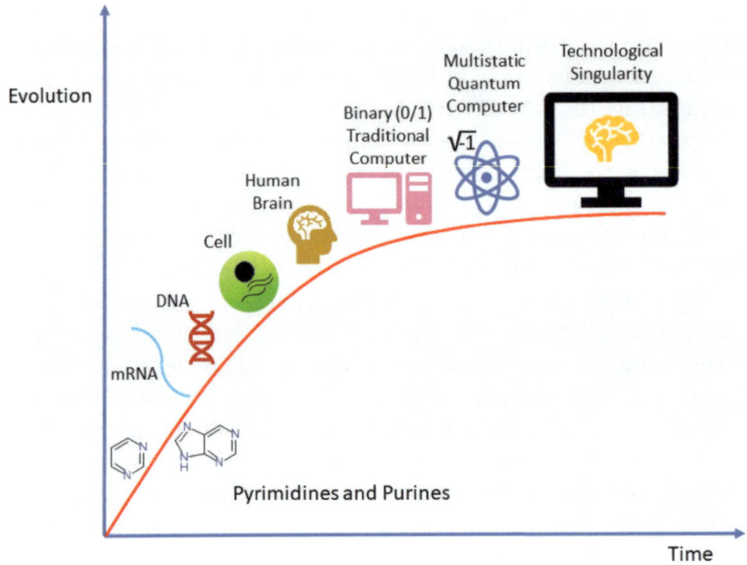

Figure 1.
Evolutionary framework.

In the last few decades, there has been accelerating progress of technology and changes in the mode of human life. These states may give the appearance of approaching some essential singularity in the human history signalizing fears and concerns that the new superintelligence would continue to upgrade itself and annihilate humans considered ineffective and inefficient. Apart of science fiction, there is substantial ground that technological singularity started already with some applications of D-wave and processes of hidden Markov model (HMM) that run most of our daily and professional life [132]. HMM are useful in everyday life in many activities, such as speech recognition (e.g., Siri or Cortana), speech synthesis, speech tagging, machine translation, partial discharge, handwriting recognition, activity recognition, transportation forecasting. HMM is also useful in our professional life in activities, including single-molecule kinetic analysis, gene prediction, alignment of bio-sequences, deoxyribonucleic acid (DNA) motif discovery, time-series analysis, protein folding, chromatin state discovery, document separation in scanning solutions, sequence classification, metamorphic virus detection, solar irradiance variability, and computational finance. Although most individuals may suggest that the artificial superintelligence may be fully functional around 2050, there is no certainty that this may really happen. Multifractality and HMM-based integrated framework may represent two of the pathways to discover it in the nearest future.

14. Conclusions

In conclusion, the rapid advancement of information technology has allowed the gradual acceptance of DP in diagnostic routine and education. The use of digital pathology in clinical services may go back to the early steps using personal computers, such as Commodore 64, but is now well recognized in multi-site medical centers with more than one location as well as in geographically very diverse health sites. The use of quad-core processing, 5G technologies, and quantum biocomputing will change the image of colleges and universities in the 3rd decade of this century. It is up to us to use these new technologies to build students at the highest level of teaching. The initial limitation of funding should be overcome using private donations from charities or benefactors or instituting public-private partnerships.

Acknowledgements

This chapter is dedicated to the 73rd birthday of Professor Kim Solez, who is an American pathologist and co-founder of the Banff Classification, the first standardized international classification for renal allograft biopsies. In 2011, he pioneered a unique graduate-level medical course Technology and the Future of Medicine at the University of Alberta. I am honored to work with Professor Solez, whose contributions to digital pathology and artificial intelligence have been inspiring to me.

Author details

Consolato M. Sergi
Department of Laboratory Medicine and Pathology, University of Alberta, Edmonton, AB, Canada

*Address all correspondence to: sergi@ualberta.ca

References

[1] Orwell G. Nineteen Eighty-Four. A Novel. United Kingdom: Secker & Warburg; 1949

[2] Russell CL. 5G wireless telecommunications expansion: Public health and environmental implications. Environmental Research. 2018;**165**:484-495. DOI: 10.1016/j.envres.2018.01.016

[3] Ruf T, Heldmaier G. Computerized body temperature telemetry in small animals: Use of simple equipment and advanced noise suppression. Computers in Biology and Medicine. 1987;**17**(5):331-340. Available from: https://www.ncbi.nlm.nih.gov/pubmed/3677620

[4] Grisham CM, Marquard F, Jorgensen PL. Versatile high-performance liquid chromatographic computer system for solvent delivery, gradient control and data acquisition using the commodore 64 personal computer. Journal of Chromatography. 1985;**333**(2):301-307. Available from: https://www.ncbi.nlm.nih.gov/pubmed/3840490

[5] Levenson RM, Maytin EV, Young DA. Low-cost two-dimensional gel densitometry. Analytical Biochemistry. 1986;**158**(2):294-301. Available from: https://www.ncbi.nlm.nih.gov/pubmed/3812974

[6] Felten CL, Strauss JS, Okada DH, Marchevsky AM. Virtual microscopy: High resolution digital photomicrography as a tool for light microscopy simulation. Human Pathology. 1999;**30**(4):477-483. Available from: https://www.ncbi.nlm.nih.gov/pubmed/10208472

[7] Afework A, Beynon MD, Bustamante F, Cho S, Demarzo A, Ferreira R, et al. Digital dynamic telepathology—The virtual microscope. In: Proceedings of the AMIA Symposium. 1998. Available from: https://www.ncbi.nlm.nih.gov/pubmed/9929351:912-6

[8] Ferreira R, Moon B, Humphries J, Sussman A, Saltz J, Miller R, et al. The virtual microscope. In: Proceedings of the AMIA Annual Fall Symposium. 1997. Available from: https://www.ncbi.nlm.nih.gov/pubmed/9357666:449-53

[9] Teodorovic I, Therasse P, Spatz A, Isabelle M, Oosterhuis W. Human tissue research: EORTC recommendations on its practical consequences. European Journal of Cancer. 2003;**39**(16):2256-2263. Available from: https://www.ncbi.nlm.nih.gov/pubmed/14556915

[10] Rojo MG, Garcia GB, Mateos CP, Garcia JG, Vicente MC. Critical comparison of 31 commercially available digital slide systems in pathology. International Journal of Surgical Pathology. 2006;**14**(4):285-305. DOI: 10.1177/1066896906292274

[11] Pantanowitz L, Szymas J, Yagi Y, Wilbur D. Whole slide imaging for educational purposes. Journal of Pathology Informatics. 2012;**3**:46. DOI: 10.4103/2153-3539.104908

[12] Pantanowitz L, Wiley CA, Demetris A, Lesniak A, Ahmed I, Cable W, et al. Experience with multimodality telepathology at the University of Pittsburgh Medical Center. Journal of Pathology Informatics. 2012;**3**:45. DOI: 10.4103/2153-3539.104907

[13] Park S, Pantanowitz L, Parwani AV. Digital imaging in pathology. Clinics in Laboratory Medicine. 2012;**32**(4):557-584. DOI: 10.1016/j.cll.2012.07.006

[14] Amin M, Sharma G, Parwani AV, Anderson R, Kolowitz BJ, Piccoli A, et al. Integration of digital gross pathology images for enterprise-wide access. Journal of Pathology Informatics. 2012;**3**:10. DOI: 10.4103/2153-3539.93892

[15] Doyle S, Monaco J, Feldman M, Tomaszewski J, Madabhushi A.

An active learning based classification strategy for the minority class problem: Application to histopathology annotation. BMC Bioinformatics. 2011;**12**:424. DOI: 10.1186/1471-2105-12-424

[16] Khalbuss WE, Pantanowitz L, Parwani AV. Digital imaging in cytopathology. Pathology Research International. 2011;**2011**:264683. DOI: 10.4061/2011/264683

[17] Sergi C, Mikuz G. External quality assurance as a revalidation method for pathologists in pediatric histopathology: Comparison of four international programs. BMC Clinical Pathology. 2008;**8**:11. DOI: 10.1186/1472-6890-8-11

[18] Pantanowitz L, Sinard JH, Henricks WH, Fatheree LA, Carter AB, Contis L, et al. Validating whole slide imaging for diagnostic purposes in pathology: Guideline from the College of American Pathologists Pathology and Laboratory Quality Center. Archives of Pathology & Laboratory Medicine. 2013;**137**(12):1710-1722. DOI: 10.5858/arpa.2013-0093-CP

[19] Mahmoud A, Bennett M. Introducing 3-dimensional printing of a human anatomic pathology specimen: Potential benefits for undergraduate and postgraduate education and anatomic pathology practice. Archives of Pathology & Laboratory Medicine. 2015;**139**(8):1048-1051. DOI: 10.5858/arpa.2014-0408-OA

[20] Gross BC, Erkal JL, Lockwood SY, Chen C, Spence DM. Evaluation of 3D printing and its potential impact on biotechnology and the chemical sciences. Analytical Chemistry. 2014;**86**(7):3240-3253. DOI: 10.1021/ac403397r

[21] Sergi C, Dorfler A, Albrecht F, Klapp J, Jansen O, Sartor K, et al. Utilization of magnetic resonance imaging in autopsy planning with specimen preservation for thoraco-omphalopagus symmetricus conjoined twins. Teratology. 1998;**58**(3-4):71-75. DOI: 10.1002/(SICI)1096-9926(199809/10)58:3/4<71::AID-TERA1>3.0.CO;2-C

[22] Inzana JA, Olvera D, Fuller SM, Kelly JP, Graeve OA, Schwarz EM, et al. 3D printing of composite calcium phosphate and collagen scaffolds for bone regeneration. Biomaterials. 2014;**35**(13):4026-4034. DOI: 10.1016/j.biomaterials.2014.01.064

[23] Li L, Jiang Q. Editorial on the original article entitled "3D printing of composite calcium phosphate and collagen scaffolds for bone regeneration" published in the Biomaterials on February 14, 2014. Annals of Translational Medicine. 2015;**3**(Suppl 1):S2. DOI: 10.3978/j.issn.2305-5839.2015.04.03

[24] Zhao X, Liu L, Wang J, Xu Y, Zhang W, Khang G, et al. In vitro vascularization of a combined system based on a 3D printing technique. Journal of Tissue Engineering and Regenerative Medicine. 2016;**10**(10):833-842. DOI: 10.1002/term.1863

[25] Weinstein RS, Graham AR, Lian F, Braunhut BL, Barker GR, Krupinski EA, et al. Reconciliation of diverse telepathology system designs. Historic issues and implications for emerging markets and new applications. Acta Pathologica, Microbiologica, et Immunologica Scandinavica. 2012;**120**(4):256-275. DOI: 10.1111/j.1600-0463.2011.02866.x

[26] Weinstein RS, Graham AR, Richter LC, Barker GP, Krupinski EA, Lopez AM, et al. Overview of telepathology, virtual microscopy, and whole slide imaging: Prospects for the future. Human Pathology. 2009;**40**(8):1057-1069. DOI: 10.1016/j.humpath.2009.04.006

[27] Weinstein RS. Prospects for telepathology. Human Pathology. 1986;**17**(5):433-434. Available from: https://www.ncbi.nlm.nih.gov/pubmed/3516858

[28] Weinstein RS, Bloom KJ, Rozek LS. Telepathology and the networking of pathology diagnostic services. Archives of Pathology & Laboratory Medicine. 1987;**111**(7):646-652. Available from: https://www.ncbi.nlm.nih.gov/pubmed/3606341

[29] Eide TJ, Nordrum I. Current status of telepathology. Acta Pathologica, Microbiologica, et Immunologica Scandinavica. 1994;**102**(12):881-890. Available from: https://www.ncbi.nlm.nih.gov/pubmed/7888156

[30] Elford DR. Telemedicine in northern Norway. Journal of Telemedicine and Telecare. 1997;**3**(1): 1-22. DOI: 10.1258/1357633971930139

[31] Dietz RL, Hartman DJ, Zheng L, Wiley C, Pantanowitz L. Review of the use of telepathology for intraoperative consultation. Expert Review of Medical Devices. Nov 2018;**18**:1-8. DOI: 10.1080/17434440.2018.1549987. PubMed PMID: 30451027. [Epub ahead of print]

[32] Eccher A, Brunelli M, Pantanowitz L, Parwani A, Girolami I, Scarpa A. Innovation in transplantation: The digital era. Journal of Pathology Informatics. 2018;**9**:33. DOI: 10.4103/jpi.jpi_55_18

[33] Chantziantoniou N, Mukherjee M, Donnelly AD, Pantanowitz L, Austin RM. Digital applications in cytopathology: Problems, rationalizations, and alternative approaches. Acta Cytologica. 2018;**62**(1):68-76. DOI: 10.1159/000484434

[34] Farahani N, Pantanowitz L. Overview of Telepathology. Clinics in Laboratory Medicine. 2016;**36**(1):101-112. DOI: 10.1016/j.cll.2015.09.010

[35] Zhao C, Wu T, Ding X, Parwani AV, Chen H, McHugh J, et al. International telepathology consultation: Three years of experience between the University of Pittsburgh Medical Center and KingMed Diagnostics in China. Journal of Pathology Informatics. 2015;**6**:63. DOI: 10.4103/2153-3539.170650

[36] Farahani N, Pantanowitz L. Overview of Telepathology. Surgical Pathology Clinics. 2015;**8**(2):223-231. DOI: 10.1016/j.path.2015.02.018

[37] Abels E, Pantanowitz L. Current state of the regulatory trajectory for whole slide imaging devices in the USA. Journal of Pathology Informatics. 2017;**8**:23. DOI: 10.4103/jpi.jpi_11_17

[38] Evans AJ, Bauer TW, Bui MM, Cornish TC, Duncan H, Glassy EF, et al. US Food and Drug Administration approval of whole slide imaging for primary diagnosis: A key milestone is reached and new questions are raised. Archives of Pathology & Laboratory Medicine. 2018;**142**(11):1383-1387. DOI: 10.5858/arpa.2017-0496-CP

[39] Sohani AR, Sohani MA. Static digital telepathology: A model for diagnostic and educational support to pathologists in the developing world. Analytical Cellular Pathology (Amsterdam). 2012;**35**(1). DOI: 25-30. DOI 10.3233/ACP-2011-0032

[40] Sirintrapun SJ, Lopez AM. Telemedicine in cancer care. American Society of Clinical Oncology Educational Book. 2018;**38**:540-545. DOI: 10.1200/EDBK_200141

[41] Sayed S, Cherniak W, Lawler M, Tan SY, El Sadr W, Wolf N, et al. Improving pathology and laborastory medicine in low-income and middle-income countries: Roadmap to solutions. Lancet. 2018;**391**(10133):1939-1952. DOI: 10.1016/S0140-6736(18)30459-8

[42] Hanna MG, Pantanowitz L, Evans AJ. Overview of contemporary guidelines in digital pathology: What is available in 2015 and what still needs to be addressed? Journal of Clinical Pathology. 2015;**68**(7):499-505. DOI: 10.1136/jclinpath-2015-202914

[43] Evans AJ, Chetty R, Clarke BA, Croul S, Ghazarian DM, Kiehl TR, et al. Primary frozen section diagnosis by robotic microscopy and virtual slide telepathology: The university health network experience. Seminars in Diagnostic Pathology. 2009;**26**(4):165-176. DOI: https://www.ncbi.nlm.nih.gov/pubmed/20069778

[44] Tetu B, Boulanger J, Houde C, Fortin JP, Gagnon MP, Roch G, et al. The Eastern Quebec telepathology network: A real collective project. Medical Sciences (Paris). 2012;**28**(11):993-999. DOI: 10.1051/medsci/20122811021

[45] Pantanowitz L, Valenstein PN, Evans AJ, Kaplan KJ, Pfeifer JD, Wilbur DC, et al. Review of the current state of whole slide imaging in pathology. Journal of Pathology Informatics. 2011;**2**:36. DOI: 10.4103/2153-3539.83746

[46] Cheng J, Mo X, Wang X, Parwani A, Feng Q, Huang K. Identification of topological features in renal tumor microenvironment associated with patient survival. Bioinformatics. 2018;**34**(6):1024-1030. DOI: 10.1093/bioinformatics/btx723

[47] Crawford LW, Foley JF, Elmore SA. Histologsy atlas of the developing mouse hepatobiliary system with emphasis on embryonic days 9.5-18.5. Toxicologic Pathology. 2010;**38**(6):872-906. DOI: 10.1177/0192623310374329

[48] Savolainen SM, Foley JF, Elmore SA. Histology atlas of the developing mouse heart with emphasis on E11.5 to E18.5. Toxicologic Pathology. 2009;**37**(4):395-414. DOI: 10.1177/0192623309335060

[49] Bian J, Zhao Y, Salloum RG, Guo Y, Wang M, Prosperi M, et al. Using social media data to understand the impact of promotional information on laypeople's discussions: A case study of lynch syndrome. Journal of Medical Internet Research. 2017;**19**(12):e414. DOI: 10.2196/jmir.9266

[50] Bois MC, Maleszewski JJ. Virtual journal club: An example of the growing importance of social media in pathology. Cardiovascular Pathology. 2018;**32**:30-31. DOI: 10.1016/j.carpath.2017.10.004

[51] Madke B, Gardner JM. Enhanced worldwide dermatology-pathology interaction via Facebook, twitter, and other social media platforms. The American Journal of Dermatopathology. 2018;**40**(3):168-172. DOI: 10.1097/DAD.0000000000000963

[52] Isom J, Walsh M, Gardner JM. Social media and pathology: Where are we now and why does it matter? Advances in Anatomic Pathology. 2017;**24**(5):294-303. DOI: 10.1097/PAP.0000000000000159

[53] Madrigal E, Jiang XS, Roy-Chowdhuri S. The professional twitter account: Creation, proper maintenance, and continuous successful operation. Diagnostic Cytopathology. 2017;**45**(7):621-628. DOI: 10.1002/dc.23710

[54] Jiang XS, Madrigal E, Roy-Chowdhuri S. A twitter primer: Dos and don'ts for cytopathologists. Diagnostic Cytopathology. 2017;**45**(7):577-579. DOI: 10.1002/dc.23722

[55] Lepe M, Gardner JM. Fine social aspiration: Twitter as a voice for cytopathology. Diagnostic Cytopathology. 2017;**45**(8):705-713. DOI: 10.1002/dc.23713

[56] Perales MA, Drake EK, Pemmaraju N, Wood WA. Social media and the adolescent and young adult

(AYA) patient with cancer. Current Hematologic Malignancy Reports. 2016;**11**(6):449-455. DOI: 10.1007/s11899-016-0313-6

[57] Evans P, Krauthammer M. Exploring the use of social media to measure journal article impact. AMIA Annual Symposium Proceedings. 2011;**2011**: 374-381. Available from: https://www.ncbi.nlm.nih.gov/pubmed/22195090

[58] Sahin D, Hacisalihoglu UP, Kirimlioglu SH. Telecytology: Is it possible with smartphone images? Diagnostic Cytopathology. 2018;**46**(1):40-46. DOI: 10.1002/dc.23851

[59] Ghosh A, Brown GT, Fontelo P. Telepathology at the armed forces Institute of Pathology: A retrospective review of consultations from 1996 to 1997. Archives of Pathology & Laboratory Medicine. 2018;**142**(2):248-252. DOI: 10.5858/arpa.2017-0055-OA

[60] Solez K, Bernier A, Crichton J, Graves H, Kuttikat P, Lockwood R, et al. Bridging the gap between the technological singularity and mainstream medicine: Highlighting a course on technology and the future of medicine. Global Journal of Health Science. 2013;**5**(6):112-125. DOI: 10.5539/gjhs.v5n6p112

[61] Cheston CC, Flickinger TE, Chisolm MS. Social media use in medical education: A systematic review. Academic Medicine. 2013;**88**(6):893-901. DOI: 10.1097/ACM.0b013e31828ffc23

[62] Chretien KC, Kind T. Climbing social media in medicine's hierarchy of needs. Academic Medicine. 2014;**89**(10):1318-1320. DOI: 10.1097/ACM.0000000000000430

[63] Kind T. Social media milestones: Entrusting trainees to conduct themselves responsibly and professionally. Journal of Graduate Medical Education. 2014;**6**(1):170-171. DOI: 10.4300/JGME-D-13-00439.1

[64] Kind T, Patel PD, Lie D, Chretien KC. Twelve tips for using social media as a medical educator. Medical Teacher. 2014;**36**(4):284-290. DOI: 10.3109/0142159X.2013.852167

[65] Callea F, Sergi C, Medicina D, Pizzorni S, Brisigotti M, Fabbretti G, et al. From immunohistochemistry to in situ hybridization. Liver. 1992;**12**(4 Pt 2):290-295. Available from: https://www.ncbi.nlm.nih.gov/pubmed/1447961

[66] Sergi C, Consalez GG, Fabbretti G, Brisigotti M, Faa G, Costa V, et al. Immunohistochemical and genetic characterization of the M Cagliari alpha-1-antitrypsin molecule (M-like alpha-1-antitrypsin deficiency). Laboratory Investigation. 1994;**70**(1):130-133. Available from: https://www.ncbi.nlm.nih.gov/pubmed/8302013

[67] Lippi G, Cadamuro J, von Meyer A, Simundic AM, European Federation of Clinical C, Laboratory Medicine Working Group for Preanalytical P. Practical recommendations for managing hemolyzed samples in clinical chemistry testing. Clinical Chemistry and Laboratory Medicine. 2018;**56**(5):718-727. DOI: 10.1515/cclm-2017-1104

[68] Perkins BA, Caskey CT, Brar P, Dec E, Karow DS, Kahn AM, et al. Precision medicine screening using whole-genome sequencing and advanced imaging to identify disease risk in adults. Proceedings of the National Academy of Sciences of the United States of America. 2018;**115**(14):3686-3691. DOI: 10.1073/pnas.1706096114

[69] Caskey T. Precision medicine: Functional advancements. Annual Review of Medicine. 2018;**69**:1-18. DOI: 10.1146/annurev-med-041316-090905

[70] Senft D, Leiserson MDM, Ruppin E, Ronai ZA. Precision oncology: The road ahead. Trends in Molecular Medicine. 2017;**23**(10):874-898. DOI: 10.1016/j.molmed.2017.08.003

[71] Pintus R, Bassareo PP, Dessi A, Deidda M, Mercuro G, Fanos V. Metabolomics and cardiology: Toward the path of perinatal programming and personalized medicine. BioMed Research International. 2017;**2017**:6970631. DOI: 10.1155/2017/6970631

[72] Salto-Tellez M, Maxwell P, Hamilton P. Artificial intelligence—The third revolution in pathology. Histopathology. 2018;**74**(3):372-376. DOI: 10.1111/his.13760

[73] Hamilton PW, Wang Y, McCullough SJ. Virtual microscopy and digital pathology in training and education. Acta Pathologica, Microbiologica, et Immunologica Scandinavica. 2012;**120**(4):305-315. DOI: 10.1111/j.1600-0463.2011.02869.x

[74] Krupinski EA, Tillack AA, Richter L, Henderson JT, Bhattacharyya AK, Scott KM, et al. Eye-movement study and human performance using telepathology virtual slides: Implications for medical education and differences with experience. Human Pathology. 2006;**37**(12):1543-1556. DOI: 10.1016/j.humpath.2006.08.024

[75] Hartman DJ, Pantanowitz L, McHugh JS, Piccoli AL, OLeary MJ, Lauro GR. Enterprise implementation of digital pathology: Feasibility, challenges, and opportunities. Journal of Digital Imaging. 2017;**30**(5):555-560. DOI: 10.1007/s10278-017-9946-9

[76] Scott GD, Schrandt C, Ho CC, Chung MC, Zhou D, Shi RZ. Interfacing complex laboratory instruments during a change to epic beaker. Journal of Pathology Informatics. 2018;**9**:24. DOI: 10.4103/jpi.jpi_21_18

[77] Blau JL, Wilford JD, Dane SK, Karandikar NJ, Fuller ES, Jacobsmeier DJ, et al. Implementation of epic beaker anatomic pathology at an academic medical center. Journal of Pathology Informatics. 2017;**8**:47. DOI: 10.4103/jpi.jpi_31_17

[78] Chung MC, Gombar S, Shi RZ. Implementation of automated calculation of free and bioavailable testosterone in epic beaker laboratory information system. Journal of Pathology Informatics. 2017;**8**:28. DOI: 10.4103/jpi.jpi_28_17

[79] Krasowski MD, Wilford JD, Howard W, Dane SK, Davis SR, Karandikar NJ, et al. Implementation of epic beaker clinical pathology at an academic medical center. Journal of Pathology Informatics. 2016;**7**:7. DOI: 10.4103/2153-3539.175798

[80] Faust K, Xie Q, Han D, Goyle K, Volynskaya Z, Djuric U, et al. Visualizing histopathologic deep learning classification and anomaly detection using nonlinear feature space dimensionality reduction. BMC Bioinformatics. 2018;**19**(1):173. DOI: 10.1186/s12859-018-2184-4

[81] Mobadersany P, Yousefi S, Amgad M, Gutman DA, Barnholtz-Sloan JS, Velazquez Vega JE, et al. Predicting cancer outcomes from histology and genomics using convolutional networks. Proceedings of the National Academy of Sciences of the United States of America. 2018;**115**(13):E2970-E29E9. DOI: 10.1073/pnas.1717139115

[82] Kyrgiou M, Pouliakis A, Panayiotides JG, Margari N, Bountris P, Valasoulis G, et al. Personalised management of women with cervical abnormalities using a clinical decision support scoring system. Gynecologic Oncology. 2016;**141**(1):29-35. DOI: 10.1016/j.ygyno.2015.12.032

[83] Gheonea DI, Streba CT, Vere CC, Serbanescu M, Pirici D, Comanescu M, et al. Diagnosis system for hepatocellular carcinoma based on fractal dimension of morphometric elements integrated in an artificial neural network. BioMed Research International. 2014;**2014**:239706. DOI: 10.1155/2014/239706

[84] Miller DD, Brown EW. How cognitive machines can augment medical imaging. American Journal of Roentgenology. 2019;**212**(1):9-14. DOI: 10.2214/AJR.18.19914

[85] Pesapane F, Codari M, Sardanelli F. Artificial intelligence in medical imaging: Threat or opportunity? Radiologists again at the forefront of innovation in medicine. European Radiology Experimental. 2018;**2**(1):35. DOI: 10.1186/s41747-018-0061-6

[86] Fazal MI, Patel ME, Tye J, Gupta Y. The past, present and future role of artificial intelligence in imaging. European Journal of Radiology. 2018;**105**:246-250. DOI: 10.1016/j.ejrad.2018.06.020

[87] Yamashita R, Nishio M, Do RKG, Togashi K. Convolutional neural networks: An overview and application in radiology. Insights Imaging. 2018;9(4):611-629. DOI: 10.1007/s13244-018-0639-9

[88] Miller DD, Brown EW. Artificial intelligence in medical practice: The question to the answer? The American Journal of Medicine. 2018;**131**(2):129-133. DOI: 10.1016/j.amjmed.2017.10.035

[89] Fooladi M, Sharini H, Masjoodi S, Khodamoradi A. A novel classification method using effective neural network and quantitative magnetization transfer imaging of brain white matter in relapsing remitting multiple sclerosis. Journal of Biomedical Physics and Engineering. 2018;**8**(4):409-422. Available from: https://www.ncbi.nlm.nih.gov/pubmed/30568931

[90] Halabi SS, Prevedello LM, Kalpathy-Cramer J, Mamonov AB, Bilbily A, Cicero M, et al. The RSNA pediatric bone age machine learning challenge. Radiology. 2018;**290**(2):498-503. DOI: 10.1148/radiol.2018180736

[91] Mendelson EB. Artificial intelligence in breast imaging: Potentials and limitations. American Journal of Roentgenology. 2018;**212**:293-299. DOI: 10.2214/AJR.18.20532

[92] Chartrand G, Cheng PM, Vorontsov E, Drozdzal M, Turcotte S, Pal CJ, et al. Deep learning: A primer for radiologists. Radiographics. 2017;**37**(7):2113-2131. DOI: 10.1148/rg.2017170077

[93] Ito N, Kawahira H, Nakashima H, Uesato M, Miyauchi H, Matsubara H. Endoscopic diagnostic support system for cT1b colorectal cancer using deep learning. Oncology. 2019;**96**(1):44-50. DOI: 10.1159/000491636

[94] Yu Y, Wang J, Ng CW, Ma Y, Mo S, Fong ELS, et al. Deep learning enables automated scoring of liver fibrosis stages. Scientific Reports. 2018;**8**(1):16016. DOI: 10.1038/s41598-018-34300-2

[95] Noguchi T, Higa D, Asada T, Kawata Y, Machitori A, Shida Y, et al. Artificial intelligence using neural network architecture for radiology (AINNAR): Classification of MR imaging sequences. Japanese Journal of Radiology. 2018;**36**(12):691-697. DOI: 10.1007/s11604-018-0779-3

[96] Kajikawa T, Kadoya N, Ito K, Takayama Y, Chiba T, Tomori S, et al. Automated prediction of dosimetric eligibility of patients with prostate cancer undergoing intensity-modulated radiation therapy using a convolutional neural network. Radiological Physics and Technology. 2018;**11**(3):320-327. DOI: 10.1007/s12194-018-0472-3

[97] Lam C, Yi D, Guo M, Lindsey T. Automated detection of diabetic

retinopathy using deep learning. AMIA Joint Summits on Translational Science Proceedings. 2018;**2017**:147-155. Available from: https://www.ncbi.nlm.nih.gov/pubmed/29888061

[98] Lee H, Hong H, Kim J, Jung DC. Deep feature classification of angiomyolipoma without visible fat and renal cell carcinoma in abdominal contrast-enhanced CT images with texture image patches and hand-crafted feature concatenation. Medical Physics. 2018;**45**(4):1550-1561. DOI: 10.1002/mp.12828

[99] Kumagai Y, Takubo K, Kawada K, Aoyama K, Endo Y, Ozawa T, et al. Diagnosis using deep-learning artificial intelligence based on the endocytoscopic observation of the esophagus. Esophagus. 13 Dec 2018. DOI: 10.1007/s10388-018-0651-7. PubMed PMID: 30547352. [Epub ahead of print]

[100] Lee JH, Kim DH, Jeong SN, Choi SH. Detection and diagnosis of dental caries using a deep learning-based convolutional neural network algorithm. Journal of Dentistry. 2018;**77**:106-111. DOI: 10.1016/j.jdent.2018.07.015

[101] Du Y, Zhang R, Zargari A, Thai TC, Gunderson CC, Moxley KM, et al. Classification of tumor epithelium and stroma by exploiting image features learned by deep convolutional neural networks. Annals of Biomedical Engineering. 2018;**46**(12):1988-1999. DOI: 10.1007/s10439-018-2095-6

[102] Ahn JM, Kim S, Ahn KS, Cho SH, Lee KB, Kim US. A deep learning model for the detection of both advanced and early glaucoma using fundus photography. PLoS One. 2018;**13**(11):e0207982. DOI: 10.1371/journal.pone.0207982

[103] Chi J, Walia E, Babyn P, Wang J, Groot G, Eramian M. Thyroid nodule classification in ultrasound images by fine-tuning deep convolutional neural network. Journal of Digital Imaging. 2017;**30**(4):477-486. DOI: 10.1007/s10278-017-9997-y

[104] Takahashi H, Tampo H, Arai Y, Inoue Y, Kawashima H. Applying artificial intelligence to disease staging: Deep learning for improved staging of diabetic retinopathy. PLoS One. 2017;**12**(6):e0179790. DOI: 10.1371/journal.pone.0179790

[105] Cicero M, Bilbily A, Colak E, Dowdell T, Gray B, Perampaladas K, et al. Training and validating a deep convolutional neural network for computer-aided detection and classification of abnormalities on frontal chest radiographs. Investigative Radiology. 2017;**52**(5):281-287. DOI: 10.1097/RLI.0000000000000341

[106] Cerentini A, Welfer D, Cordeiro d'Ornellas M, Pereira Haygert CJ, Dotto GN. Automatic identification of glaucoma using deep learning methods. Studies in Health Technology and Informatics. 2017;**245**:318-321. Available from: https://www.ncbi.nlm.nih.gov/pubmed/29295107

[107] Zhou T, Han G, Li BN, Lin Z, Ciaccio EJ, Green PH, et al. Quantitative analysis of patients with celiac disease by video capsule endoscopy: A deep learning method. Computers in Biology and Medicine. 2017;**85**:1-6. DOI: 10.1016/j.compbiomed.2017.03.031

[108] Esteva A, Kuprel B, Novoa RA, Ko J, Swetter SM, Blau HM, et al. Dermatologist-level classification of skin cancer with deep neural networks. Nature. 2017;**542**(7639):115-118. DOI: 10.1038/nature21056

[109] Litjens G, Sanchez CI, Timofeeva N, Hermsen M, Nagtegaal I, Kovacs I, et al. Deep learning as a tool for increased accuracy and efficiency of

histopathological diagnosis. Scientific Reports. 2016;**6**:26286. DOI: 10.1038/srep26286

[110] Murthy V, Hou L, Samaras D, Kurc TM, Saltz JH. Center-focusing multi-task CNN with injected features for classification of Glioma nuclear images. IEEE Winter Conference on Applications of Computer Vision. 2017;**2017**:834-841. DOI: 10.1109/WACV.2017.98

[111] Levine AB, Grewal JK, Jones SJM, Yip S. Machine learning in pathology: A primer on techniques and applications. Canadian Journal of Pathology. 2018;**10**(3):52-59

[112] Parajuli N, Valtuille L, Basu R, Famulski KS, Halloran PF, Sergi C, et al. Determinants of ventricular arrhythmias in human explanted hearts with dilated cardiomyopathy. European Journal of Clinical Investigation. 2015;**45**(12):1286-1296. DOI: 10.1111/eci.12549

[113] Corfield A, Meyer P, Kassam S, Mikuz G, Sergi C. SNPs: At the origins of the databases of an innovative biotechnology tool. Frontiers in Bioscience (Schol Ed). 2010;**2**:1-4. Available from: https://www.ncbi.nlm.nih.gov/pubmed/20036923

[114] Fish JH 3rd, Schwentner I, Schmutzhard J, Abraham I, Ciorba A, Martini A, et al. Morphology studies of the human fetal cochlea in turner syndrome. Ear and Hearing. 2009;**30**(1):143-146. DOI: 10.1097/AUD.0b013e3181906c30

[115] Amella C, Cappello F, Kahl P, Fritsch H, Lozanoff S, Sergi C. Spatial and temporal dynamics of innervation during the development of fetal human pancreas. Neuroscience. 2008;**154**(4):1477-1487. DOI: 10.1016/j.neuroscience.2008.04.050

[116] Sergi C, Benstz J, Feist D, Nutzenadel W, Otto HF, Hofmann WJ. Bile duct to portal space ratio and ductal plate remnants in liver disease of infants aged less than 1 year. Pathology. 2008;**40**(3):260-267. DOI: 10.1080/00313020801911538

[117] Goodman PH, Buntha S, Zou Q, Dascalu SM. Virtual Neurorobotics (VNR) to accelerate development of plausible neuromorphic brain architectures. Frontiers in Neurorobotics. 2007;**1**:1. DOI: 10.3389/neuro.12.001.2007

[118] Hargitai B, Szabo V, Cziniel M, Hajdu J, Papp Z, Szende B, et al. Human brain of preterm infants after hypoxic-ischaemic injuries: No evidence of a substantial role for apoptosis by using a fine-tuned ultrasound-guided neuropathological analysis. Brain and Development. 2004;**26**(1):30-36. Available from: https://www.ncbi.nlm.nih.gov/pubmed/14729412

[119] Sergi C, Adam S, Kahl P, Otto HF. The remodeling of the primitive human biliary system. Early Human Development. 2000;**58**(3):167-178. Available from: https://www.ncbi.nlm.nih.gov/pubmed/10936437

[120] Emmert-Streib F, Dehmer M. Networks for systems biology: Conceptual connection of data and function. IET Systems Biology. 2011;**5**(3):185-207. DOI: 10.1049/iet-syb.2010.0025

[121] Altman RB. Translational bioinformatics: Linking the molecular world to the clinical world. Clinical Pharmacology and Therapeutics. 2012;**91**(6):994-1000. DOI: 10.1038/clpt.2012.49

[122] Abascal F, Juan D, Jungreis I, Martinez L, Rigau M, Rodriguez JM, et al. Loose ends: Almost one in five human genes still have unresolved coding status. Nucleic Acids Research. 2018;**46**(14):7070-7084. DOI: 10.1093/nar/gky587

[123] Saltz J, Gupta R, Hou L, Kurc T, Singh P, Nguyen V, et al. Spatial organization and molecular correlation of tumor-infiltrating lymphocytes using deep learning on pathology images. Cell Reports. 2018;**23**(1):181-193, e7. DOI: 10.1016/j.celrep.2018.03.086

[124] Ong HS, Syafiq-Rahim M, Kasim NH, Firdaus-Raih M, Ramlan EI. Self-assembly programming of DNA polyominoes. Journal of Biotechnology. 2016;**236**:141-151. DOI: 10.1016/j.jbiotec.2016.08.017

[125] Gawehn E, Hiss JA, Schneider G. Deep learning in drug discovery. Molecular Informatics. 2016;35(1):3-14. DOI: 10.1002/minf.201501008

[126] Maojo V, Kulikowski CA. Reflections on biomedical informatics: From cybernetics to genomic medicine and nanomedicine. Studies in Health Technology and Informatics. 2006;**124**:19-24. Available from: https://www.ncbi.nlm.nih.gov/pubmed/17108499

[127] Solenov D, Brieler J, Scherrer JF. The potential of quantum computing and machine learning to advance clinical research and change the practice of medicine. Missouri Medicine. 2018;**115**(5):463-467. Available from: https://www.ncbi.nlm.nih.gov/pubmed/30385997

[128] Jiang S, Britt KA, McCaskey AJ, Humble TS, Kais S. Quantum annealing for prime factorization. Scientific Reports. 2018;**8**(1):17667. DOI: 10.1038/s41598-018-36058-z

[129] O'Malley D. An approach to quantum-computational hydrologic inverse analysis. Scientific Reports. 2018;**8**(1):6919. DOI: 10.1038/s41598-018-25206-0

[130] Gardas B, Dziarmaga J, Zurek WH, Zwolak M. Defects in quantum computers. Scientific Reports. 2018;**8**(1):4539. DOI: 10.1038/s41598-018-22763-2

[131] Chamon C, Mucciolo ER, Ruckenstein AE, Yang ZC. Quantum vertex model for reversible classical computing. Nature Communications. 2017;**8**:15303. DOI: 10.1038/ncomms15303

[132] Mukhopadhyay S, Das NK, Kurmi I, Pradhan A, Ghosh N, Panigrahi PK. Tissue multifractality and hidden Markov model based integrated framework for optimum precancer detection. Journal of Biomedical Optics. 2017;**22**(10):1-8. DOI: 10.1117/1.JBO.22.10.105005

Chapter 10

Calmness in Virtual Environments Enhance User's Spatial Presence Experience

Nadia Diyana Mohd Muhaiyuddin and Dayang Rohaya Awang Rambli

Abstract

Presence has been described to be crucial in several virtual reality (VR) applications. Among the factors influencing presence, realistic virtual environment has been examined extensively from the angle of geometry-based virtual reality (GBVR) application. The visual of the applications has been manipulated by altering numerous technological characteristics or by adding more sensory information (such as touch and smell). However, realistic virtual environment in GBVR application often required complex programming and takes longer time to develop. As such GBVR application is not acceptable for the application that needs to have a collection of realistic panoramic virtual environments. An alternative solution for above statement is image-based virtual reality (IBVR) application. IBVR refers to photo-based images, stitched together to develop a realistic panoramic virtual environment. Based on this method, many realistic virtual environments can be created in much less time but with limited interaction function. Despite this limitation, realistic virtual environment in image-based virtual reality is expected to enhance user's spatial presence experience, which is supported by spatial presence theoretical model. There a few levels in this theoretical model before the formation of spatial presence, and the most important part in this theoretical model is primary egocentric reference frames (PERF), adapting calmness to produce spatial presence experience. Thus, this chapter describes the summary on adapting calmness as PERF.

Keywords: presence, spatial presence, virtual reality, image-based virtual reality, interactivity

1. Introduction

Virtual reality (VR) is one of the technologies that can produce artificial virtual environment or medium which user can attach and communicate whether in low or high interactivity [1, 2]. VR is grouped with image-based virtual reality (IBVR) and geometry-based virtual reality (GBVR). The most popular is GBVR that has fascinated the most presence researcher because GBVR application can deliver high interactivity and high immersion toward user's presence experience [3, 4]. However, developing high realistic artificial environment in GBVR is time-consuming [4]. As an alternative, a promising type of VR that can produce high realistic artificial environment in much less time is IBVR.

IBVR is defined as simulated artificial environments from a collection of stitch photographs which users can interact and navigate in a 3D realistic artificial environment despite the absence of geometric programming. IBVR can produce more than one realistic virtual environment with a low performance processor. The main navigation functions of IBVR are zooming in/out the margin in artificial environment, hotspot hopping from between a few artificial environments and pan the artificial environment in 360 degrees.

Interactivity in IBVR is limited for navigation compared to GBVR which provides high interactivity to navigate and manipulate. Despite the limited navigation function in IBVR, users can experience presence. The formation is that, however, according to [5–7], despite high interactivity, the degree of user's mind of acceptance of artificial environment more than the real surrounding is essential to experience user's presence. Thus, in [6], a spatial presence theory is proposed which does not focus on interactivity; however, the most important aspect to produce user's spatial presence experience is because of the user acceptance on the visual or the spatial of the artificial environment. This theory convinces that IBVR with high realistic artificial environment and limited functions is still capable of producing and enhancing user's spatial presence experience.

2. Problem statement

Realistic panoramic artificial environment provided by IBVR application, to date, lack of research has been found investigating spatial presence in it due to its low and limited navigation capability that primes researchers and anecdotes believe that it offers low sense of presence [2]. Most important is users can relax when watching the virtual environment or mediated environment to enhance spatial presence experience. Examples of mediated environment are videos, movies, documentaries, pictures, and books. A few researches specify that the collection of realistic plot in mediated environments could elicit and enhance user's spatial presence experience [6]. Thus, it is expected that IBVR which compresses stitched images to produce artificial environments could induce spatial presence experience among users.

There is a researcher who conducts a study of the model parts, namely components and user actions [16]. Based on previous researches, none of them discusses the media characteristics that are involved in order to reach the PERF hypothesis first before a user starts experiencing spatial presence experience. Even though in spatial presence theory by [11], the researches concentrates on the fact that media characteristics can increase user's spatial presence experience via the PERF hypothesis. In addition, no research is conducted on the specific criteria of PERF hypothesis.

3. Literature review

Wirth [11] defined spatial presence as "a feeling of being bodily present in a mediated environment (self-location) and a feeling of being able to act in synthetic environment (possible action)." A spatial presence theoretical model that integrates media factors and human factors are presented in [11], and the formation of a user's spatial presence experience is shown in **Figure 1**.

The formation of spatial presence theoretical model as shown in **Figure 1** is from components in the bottom to produce first level and components to produce second level. Components consist of four parts which are media factors, process components, user actions, and user factors. The formation started from the "empty slot" to adapt mind to the visual in the media. Empty slot is user's mind giving attention

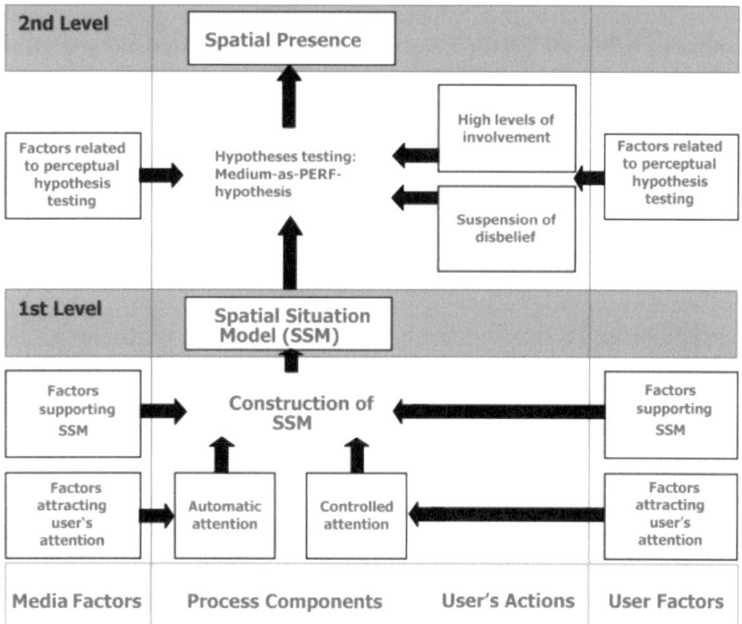

Figure 1.
Spatial presence theoretical model from [11].

to the media. Then, the user's mind will keep receiving input from the media until the percent of adapting media is higher than real surrounding. From this theory, the primary egocentric reference frame is important in bridging the user's mind to spatial presence.

In the second step, a user's spatial situational model allows the user to accept the primary egocentric reference frame (PERF). PERF can be defined as the process where a user's mental model accepts the existence of the mediated environment and unconsciously leaves behind the user's mental model of the real environment.

Based on the diagram of the spatial presence theory in **Figure 1**, primary egocentric reference frame (PERF) is intermediate between three important relationships. The first correlation is between spatial situational feeling and spatial presence experience. The second correlation is between media factors and spatial presence experience. The third correlation is between the user's action and spatial presence experience. These correlations conclude that PERF is an important role in creating a user's spatial presence experience.

The existence of PERF is due to the hypothesis which is constructed by an individual. This hypothesis is developed based on the first individual's perception about what he/she watches. For example, when an individual sees pictures of food, he/she assumes that the food in the picture is delicious. So, PERF hypothesis is that the food is delicious. Once this hypothesis is received by an individual, then the spatial presence experience exists.

Basically from the literature review, a persuasive media factor is agreed by the researchers to produce a user's spatial presence experience. However, lacks of specific characteristics are produced by the researchers about the media factors that can produce a user's spatial presence experience. In fact, this theory informs the reader that spatial presence experience exists if a user feels it as situational. Based on the explanation of the previous subsections, it has been noted that there are a few steps that the user's mind have to experience before experiencing a user's spatial presence experience. Spatial presence theory mentions that if the user is consciously watching the virtual environment, he will unconsciously forget about what is happening around him/her which means that the user is experiencing spatial presence experience.

As mentioned in the previous section, the spatial presence theoretical model from [6] is suitable for the development of the spatial presence model for IBVR. This section reviews the related work that applies spatial presence theory from [6]. Even though the selected theory is introduced in 2003, the enhancement and validation of the theory is continuously interested by the researcher until 2015. The related works on the selected spatial presence theory are presented in **Table 1** and the descriptions are the following paragraphs.

Wirth [6] presented a spatial presence theory. Again, the author highlights that spatial presence is about the feeling of the synthetic environment that the user has after the PERF stage [6]. Spatial presence is caused by an unconscious spatial cognition. The author indicates that the user responds to the possible actions in the synthetic environment [14]. In the author's words, "the experience of this feeling in virtual environments, mediated real (remote) environments, or real environments is referred to as spatial presence" [14, p. 163]. What is more from author, "a perceptual emotion consciously experienced as the feeling of being there in virtual environments, mediated real (remote) environments, or real environments is referred to as spatial presence" [15, p. 899].

Sacau et al. [9] also proposed a few individual factors that measured user's spatial presence experience. The authors start with proposing two individual factors that can provoke user's spatial situational model; domain specific interest and spatial visual imagery; while absorption is proposed as the individual factor that can provoke user's spatial presence experience. Moreover, the authors also highlight that PERF is about a condition that can construct spatial presence experience.

Lukowska [10] describes that a research is also needed to give attention for presence experience. The author's research is about the formation of spatial presence from physical environment to virtual environment. Attention to the VR application makes him/her feel presence. If there is an auditory signal in the physical environment, the user feels distracted. The attention shifts from the virtual environment to physical environment. However, when the user neglects the auditory signal, then the user can shift the attention back to virtual environment. There are two important descriptions related to this model: efficacy of shifting and absorption level. Efficacy of shifting is about the influence of the process in the mediated environment such as VR application in feeling presence. Absorption level is about the impact on a detection process by affecting the perception threshold level.

Enhancement on the model follows with [8]; the role of emotional involvement and trait absorption are proposed to enhance spatial presence theoretical model. Their research indicates that these factors provide a formation process in developing

Author	Timeline	Theory
[6]	Theoretical model	Illustrated diagram
[9]	Theory enhancement	Propose individual factors
[10]	Theory confirmation	Formation on spatial presence
[12]	Theory confirmation	Validating users factors
[8]	Theory enhancement	Proposed emotion
[13]	Theory confirmation	2 factor in spatial presence

Table 1.
Related work on selected spatial presence theory.

user's presence experience. However, a further investigation has to be considered before these factors are applied in spatial presence theoretical model.

Besides enhancing the spatial presence model, Hofer et al. [12] validated the model by using structural equation modeling. There are some items for a variable that is received and discarded. Once again the addition is carried out on part of the user experience factor of spatial presence. These factors are the emotional involvement and absorption trait can make the user experience spatial presence. These additions were validated and show that emotional involvement plays an important role in creating spatial presence but through this validation, it is evident that there also exist two parts, spatial situational model and spatial presence.

4. Research methodology

After the three locations in IBVR applications are developed, testing is conducted. Three steps are involved in this study: familiarization session, constructing elicitation, and understanding the personal construct of the respondents.

4.1 Familiarization session

During this phase, the objective of the study was explained to the users to enable them to list the features in IBVR application that can create a spatial presence. Users were also allowed to explore the virtual environment and this environment is not be used in the following experiment. Before the study starts, respondent is shown with location of flower farm but this location will not be shown in the study. The purpose to show the flower farm is to teach the respondents on a few functions in this application such as hotspot and panning.

Users are allowed to try the IBVR application because of the mental model theory. Mental model for familiar and unfamiliar users with the IBVR application is different [11]. If users are not accustomed to using the application, they may feel bad or lose their willingness to use the application. In contrast, users who are familiar with computer applications already know how to use the IBVR application even though they are unfamiliar with the system. These users should not have a problem exploring the system during an experiment when they are alone in the room.

4.2 Construct elicitation/grid completion

A description of how to develop the personal construct in the repertory grid form is provided below.

- First, a respondent writes the IBVR characteristics that they believe can enhance their spatial presence experience in the "positive" column of the form.

- Second, in the "negative" column, a respondent writes the opposite feature of the IBVR characteristics that they wrote in the "positive" column.

- Third, a respondent rates the three locations in the "rate the type of locations" column. All users are asked to rate each construct in a scale of 1 to 10 (1 = least desired to feel presence and 10 = most desired to feel presence). As a reminder, the respondents are not given examples of IBVR characteristics so that their mental models are not disturbed. The characteristic of such personal constructs is that they are based on individual mental models.

Finally, after respondents were satisfied with their answer, they rated the locations in the repertory grid form. The respondents rated each construct in a scale of 1 to 10 (1 = least desired to feel presence and 10 = most desired to feel presence).

Upon completion of the listing, a short unstructured interview was conducted to understand the meaning of each feature listed by the users. During this session, the user was able to provide additional ideas regarding the IBVR application that they viewed during the construct elicitation session.

4.3 Understanding personal construct from respondents

The repertory grid approach lists IBVR characteristics in the form of quantitative and qualitative data so as to gain a deeper understanding of the IBVR characteristics listed by the respondents. Gathering information from respondents using the unstructured interview technique is important to gain consistent results from them. The interview began by asking participants which IBVR characteristics can provide high impact for their spatial presence. Users then have to justify their answers.

Even though the respondent listed four or six IBVR characteristics, not all IBVR characteristics were considered acceptable. This is because during the interview it became clear that some IBVR characteristics noted down actually refer to the similar IBVR characteristics. As such, instead of four items, only three items were used for analysis. Furthermore, there was a respondent that was not confident with the IBVR characteristic that s/he wrote on the repertory grid form. In that case, the IBVR characteristic was rejected or deleted.

Besides removing any irrelevant IBVR characteristics, grouping is also important before analyzing the data. Every time, after the data from the repertory grid is collected, the data were grouped based on the results of the interviews since there are 100 respondents to avoid confusion.

Furthermore, based on this categorization, it is much easier to group the IBVR characteristics manually. Even though researchers suggested inserting all the data to NVivo, which will give us the result of grouping by using the Word Cloud technique [16], for this study, the data is grouped manually. This is because a different respondent may have given the same IBVR characteristic but the description of that IBVR characteristic is different from the one given by another respondent. In such cases, this IBVR characteristic is not suitable to be part of the same group.

5. Result and analysis

In this study, three locations were used in IBVR application. Five basic features were developed in all locations in IBVR application. These are hotspot, panning, storyline, recorded natural sound, and animation. These features were listed by the respondents in the repertory grid form. These features were also further discussed by the users in the repertory grid form.

Some respondents indicated that the calmness features in the IBVR application helped them feel presence. There are three features of calmness: calm panoramic view, calm color, and calm sound. These features are described in the following subsections. The calmness group in cluster grid for calm panoramic view (a), calm panoramic view (b), calm color (a), calm color (b), calm sound (a), and calm sound (b) is 81.5%, 88.5%, 85.2%, 81.5%, 81.5%, and 81.5%, respectively.

5.1 Calm panoramic view

Respondents argue that a calm panoramic view is one factor that could enhance spatial presence experience. An example of negative and positive statement is

"Scenery uncomfortable/unpleasant/visual displays a collection of scenery - Scenery comfort/pleasant/visual displays a collection of calm scenery." The respondents liked the panorama virtual environment if they had a preference for that location in the real environment. Therefore, the virtual environment in the IBVR application must have more than one location so that the respondents could choose their favorite place.

Calm panoramic view is realistic panoramic virtual environments that make user feel calm. Based on the interviews, putting additional distracting object should be avoided in a panoramic virtual environment. User will only appreciate the beauty of the environment if there is no [17] distracting object in the virtual environment.

5.2 Calm color

The respondents also described calm colors in a panoramic view as one factor that could enhance their spatial presence experience. An example of negative and positive statement is "Bright color/hot weather/low temperature - Soothing/cool color/comfortable weather/high temperature/refreshment colour." The reason they chose this location was because they liked the panoramic view. The calm colors that were indicated by the respondents were defined as the light parameters of the panoramic view.

Calm color is about the level of light for panoramic virtual environment which is shown as scenery in a sunny day when the weather is nice and warm. The color of the visual is not too bright to make the user feel calm [17].

5.3 Calm sound

The respondents noted that natural sounds in the field made them feel calm. Hence, they felt as being located within the virtual environment. Examples of negative and positive statement is "Natural sound that distracts my feeling, non-calm sound, I heard the natural sound and I feel distracted, natural sound, the sound make me not calm - Natural sound makes me calm, calming sound, I heard the natural sound and felt calm, meditation natural sound, the sound makes me calm." In further examination of the interview output, it was concluded that the respondents preferred a natural sound if they liked the virtual environment. Thus a respondent's belief of a sound being calm is subjective. Nevertheless, the most important aspect about sounds is that the sound makes them calm.

Calm sound is defined as meditation sound that is usually used by therapists to make a patient feel calm. The recorded natural sounds make the user feel calm [18].

Respondents also indicate that calmness in the IBVR application have helped them feel spatial presence. When the respondents feel calm when exploring the panoramic virtual environments in IBVR application, they eventually feel spatial presence experience. There are three features of calmness: calm panoramic view, calm color, and calm sound.

6. Discussion

Soothing music can make the user feel calm [28]. As expected, the results of this study are similar to the finding of the aforementioned. A recorded natural sound is required to make users feel calm. Calmness is created if the user prefers the location which is accompanied by the recorded natural sound. As mentioned in [22], users do not feel distracted in a noisy environment if they hear their favorite music. The findings of this research are similar with [23]. The natural sound in a user's favorite virtual environment can make the user feel calm. If they do not like the natural sound, then they will feel distracted. Consequently, they will lose their attention to the virtual environment and spatial presence experience will not be achieved.

The finding also indicates that the existence of objects in a virtual environment is important in creating calmness. What is more, objects that do not infuriate the respondent are necessary to make him/her feel comfortable and calm. These findings support that a beautiful and clean environment which is in line with the user's favorite places can produce calmness for the user.

Besides a calm environment, this research also identified that the color of the virtual environment is not accepted as the factor in user's calmness. This finding does not support the report of [19–21] which mention the user's emotion when the user watches a dull, gloomy, and attractive virtual environment with the different color of the bench. In Baños et al.'s [19] research, there are colors for each virtual environment. But for this research, there are no specific colors in the virtual environment. Besides that, when the IBVR application is developed, the level of the brightness is same. The user might overlook that the color of visual is an element that produces perceptual realism.

7. Conclusions

This research identified that calmness can produce user's presence experience. Furthermore, the psychology researchers also stated that realistic panoramic virtual environments can produce spatial presence. Furthermore, factors in IBVR such as calm sound and calm scenery make users experience spatial presence when they interact with IBVR application. From calmness, users can experience spatial presence.

Author Notes

This article is adapted from PhD thesis entitled Spatial Presence Model for Image-based Virtual Reality (SPM4IBVR).

Author details

Nadia Diyana Mohd Muhaiyuddin[1*] and Dayang Rohaya Awang Rambli[2]

1 School of Multimedia Technology and Communication (SMMTC), Universiti Utara Malaysia (UUM), Kedah, Malaysia

2 Department of Computer, Information, and System (CIS), Universiti Teknologi PETRONAS (UTP), Perak, Malaysia

*Address all correspondence to: nadia.diyana@uum.edu.my

References

[1] Williams P. Virtual reality and tourism: Fact or fantasy? Tourism Management. 1995;**16**(6):423-427

[2] Guttentag DA. Virtual reality: Applications and implications for tourism. Tourism Management. 2010;**31**(5):637-651

[3] Luciani A, Urma D, Marlière S, Chevrier J. PRESENCE: The sense of believability of inaccessible worlds. Computers and Graphics. 2004;**28**(4):509-517

[4] Casati R, Pasquinelli E. Is the subjective feel of 'presence' an uninteresting goal? Journal of Visual Languages and Computing. 2005;**16**(5):428-441

[5] Jeong EJ, Biocca FA, Bohil CJ. Sensory realism and mediated aggression in video games. Computers in Human Behavior. 2012;**28**(5):1840-1848

[6] Wirth W et al. A process model of the formation of spatial presence experiences. Media Psychology. 2007;**9**(3):493-525

[7] Vorderer P et al. MEC Spatial Presence Questionnaire. 2004

[8] Wirth W, Hofer M, Schramm H. The role of emotional involvement and trait absorption in the formation of spatial presence. Media Psychology. 2012;**15**(1):19-43

[9] Sacau A, Laarni J, Hartmann T. Influence of individual factors on presence. Computers in Human Behavior. 2008;**24**(5):2255-2273

[10] Lukowska M. "Influence of shifting attention and absorption on spatial presence formation." In: The International Society for Presence Research Annual Conference (ISPR); 2011. pp. 26-28

[11] Wirth W et al. A Process Model of the Formation of Spatial Presence Experiences. 2003

[12] Hofer M, Wirth W, Kuehne R, Schramm H, Sacau A. Structural equation modeling of spatial presence: The influence of cognitive processes and traits. Media Psychology. 2012;**15**(4):373-395

[13] Hartmann T et al. The spatial presence experience scale (SPES): A short self-report measure for diverse media settings. Journal of Media Psychology. 2015

[14] Schubert TW. A new conception of spatial presence: Once again, with feeling. Communication Theory. 2009;**19**:161-187. ISSN: 1050-3293

[15] Willans T. Spatial presence in virtual worlds as a perceptual emotion: An expansion on cognitive feeling? In: 2012 Sixth International Conference on Complex, Intelligent, and Software Intensive Systems; 2012. pp. 899-904

[16] Tomico O, Karapanos E, Lévy P, Mizutani N. The repertory grid technique as a method for the study of cultural differences. International Journal of Design. 2009;**3**(3)

[17] de Kort YAW, Meijnders AL, Sponselee AAG, IJsselsteijn WA. What's wrong with virtual trees? Restoring from stress in a mediated environment. Journal of Environmental Psychology. 2006;**26**(4):309-320

[18] Serafin S. Sound design to enhance presence in photorealistic virtual reality. In: Proceedings of the 2004 International Conference on Auditory Display; 2004. pp. 4-7

[19] Baños R, Botella C, Liaño V, Guerrero B, Rey B, Alcañiz M. "Sense of Presence in Emotional Virtual Environments," No. 12004. pp. 156-159

[20] Freeman J, Lessiter J, Keogh E, Bond FW, Chapman K. Relaxation Island: Virtual, and Really Relaxing. 2004. pp. 67-72

[21] Nordahl R, Serafin S, Nilsson NC, Turchet L. Enhancing realism in virtual environments by simulating the audio-haptic sensation of walking on ground surfaces. IEEE Virtual Reality. 2012;**2012**:73-74

[22] Kallinen K. The Effects of Background Music on Using a Pocket Computer in a Cafeteria: Immersion, Emotional Responses, and Social Richness of Medium. 2004. pp. 1227-1230

[23] Kallinen K, Kallenbach J, Ravaja N. The effects of content type and presentation style on user experiences of multimedia content on a tablet PC. Lecture Notes in Computer Science (Including Subseries Lecture Notes in Artificial Intelligence Lecture Notes in Bioinformatics). 2011;**6764 LNCS**(PART 4):466-475

Chapter 11

BloodHero: The Power of Gamification in Social Habit

Daniela Domingos, Luis Felipe Lima, Thiago Messias, José Feijó, Anthony Diniz and Heliana Soares

Abstract

The lack of blood in hemocenters is an intermittent problem in the Brazilian health system; due to the difficulty of attracting blood donors, according to the World Health Organization (WHO), each country must maintain 3–5% of its population as regular blood donors. However, the number of regular donors in Brazil, in recent years, has not reached 3% of the population. In order to attract periodic volunteer blood donors, the objective of this study was to develop a mobile application, called BloodHero, to work as a social network, with a game methodology, known as gamification, to encourage blood donation. Initiatives and interactions favorable to blood donation, within the application, will generate points that will be used for in-game competitiveness. Another contribution given to those that use this software is the interaction between users who can donate blood and patient users, where these second ones can share their stories or use this software as a tool to find someone compatible with their blood type for donation.

Keywords: social habits, blood donation, app, social network, gamification

1. Introduction

Blood transfusion is one of the fundamental pillars for large elective surgeries, for urgent care, and for the treatment of oncological or chronic diseases. In Brazil, in 2014, according to the Health Portal of the Unified Health System, only a number of elective surgeries increased by 11.7%, in relation to the previous 2 years, representing about 2.4 million procedures performed with the need for blood transfusion [1].

Blood is an important tissue for the survival of other tissues and, so far, cannot be replaced by any other liquid or be artificially produced [2], what makes blood donation a fundamental practice for the performance of transfusions.

However, the collection of blood bags in Brazil is insufficient, caused by the lack of voluntary donors. According to the World Health Organization (WHO), for a population to maintain stocks of blood bags, at a satisfactory level, 3–5% of the population has to donor, at least once a year, but Brazil's annual average is 1.8% [3]. Translating in numbers, Brazil, with its population of about 210 million people, would need 6.3 million people to donate blood, at least once a year, but the average donation recorded, in previous years, was about 3.7 million.

The difficulties in attracting new blood donors are evidenced mainly by five reasons that repel the individual from the cause [4]:

- Misinformation—People do not understand the process, what is its purpose, and its importance.
- The fear of donating blood—Some myths created about the donation process and reactions prevent the attraction of new donors.
- Medical disqualification—Here there are two points: The first one is related to hematopoietic diseases, sexually transmitted diseases, and other diseases, which can be transmitted through donation, and the second, people who are momentarily unable to donate blood, often do not donate anymore.
- Apathy—People who do not care about the cause.
- Convenience—People who understand the need for donation, support the cause, but are not drawn to moving to practice.

On the other hand, when analyzing the reasons that lead to the practice of blood donation, we find [4]:

- Altruism—Donors who understand the need for donation and propose to help the cause.
- The replacement—When, for a surgical procedure of a close person, requires the donation.
- Social pressure—When an entire community engages in a cause, the individual feels motivated to participate as well.
- Advertising—The individual is pushed by the advertising appeal.
- Reward—When the donor materially and/or spiritually benefits from the process.

Some different strategies, such as demythologization and clarification and awareness about the process [5, 6], tax incentives, benefits, transport to donation site, and campaigns [7, 8], are used in several countries for attracting new donors, but it is still necessary to mobilize large capital and personal investments.

With this problem of the lack of blood donations, we developed some strategies to try to engage more people with the cause. The first step was to identify the best channel for propagation of the tool to be developed. From this need, the creation of an app was chosen, added to the social network, aimed at encouraging blood donation. Social networks reach about 1.5 billion people. In Brazil, social networks reach about 80% of the population [9].

However, the elaboration of this work, by this way, would be just another social network application focused on blood donation. In order to contribute positively to this development, the concept of gamification, for project implementation, was applied. Therefore, the objective of this work was to develop a mobile application, called BloodHero, whose main purpose is to attract and retain new blood donors, arousing empathy through virtual social networks, encouraging, and educating through gamification methodology. This application will promote interaction between users (donors, people able to donor, and patients who need donors) in publications and chats through bonus points, achievements—rewards—and levels of experience.

2. Theoretical aspects

2.1 Blood donation

Blood is responsible for the entire distribution of molecules to tissues. Its functions include gas exchange through the red blood cells, defense against foreign bodies by leukocytes, transport of nutrients and hormones by plasma, and coagulation through platelets. It is produced by the red bone marrow or hemocytopoietic tissue, found in long bones [10].

The blood type is conditioned by multiple alleles, the main ones being the ABO system and the Rh factor (+ and −). It causes the possibility of existing eight main possibilities: A+, A−, B+, B−, O+, O−, AB+, and AB−. Each one of these types is characterized by the presence of agglutinogens (A, B, and Rh) and agglutinins (anti-A, anti-B, and anti-Rh). They are directly linked to the compatibility used when blood transfusion is required, observed in **Table 1** [11].

Blood donation is the process of collecting blood from a volunteer to, after a series of treatments and examinations, be stored in a blood bank and, when needed, used in a transfusion [12–15].

According to the WHO, blood donation should be voluntary and unpaid, to avoid risk [3]. Before the donation, the candidate undergoes two previous stages, called screening: an interview/questionnaire, where questions are asked to check blood-related diseases, in order to improve the safety of the donor and patient, and a clinical examination, aiming at ascertaining the health conditions of the donor and if there is something that will harm him at the time of donation [2]. Any identified risks will lead to the donor's temporary or final rejection.

Being fit, the donor passes to the collection stage, where 400–450 ml of the blood tissue is withdrawn. The average collection time is 10 minutes, and reactions rarely occur. The blood volume of an adult is 62.4 ml per kg, that is, a normal adult male, weighing 75 kg, has the total volume of 4680 ml of blood.

Replacement of the blood volume by the organism occurs within 24 hours, for the blood plasma, and 4 weeks, for the red blood cells; however, the recovery of iron can take 8 weeks for the man and 12 weeks for the woman. Because of this, the maximum frequency of donation of blood for men is four times a year, with a minimum interval of 2 months between donations. For women, the maximum frequency is three times a year, with a 3-month interval between donations. Donors must be between 16 and 69 years old and weigh, at least, 50 kg [1].

In Brazil, Ministerial Order No. 158, of February 4, 2016, regulates the entire chemotherapy process, emphasizing that blood donation should be voluntary,

Blood type	Agglutinogene	Agglutinins	Receives from	Donates for
A+	A	Anti-B	O−, O+, A− e A+	A+, AB+
A−	A	Anti-B e anti-Rh	A−, AB−	A−, A+, AB− e AB+
B+	B	Anti-A	O−, O+, B− e B+	B+, AB+
B−	B	Anti-A e anti-Rh	O− e B-	B−, B+, AB− e AB+
AB+	A e B	None	All	AB+
AB−	A e B	None	All the −	AB+ e AB−
O+	None	Anti-A e anti-B	O+ e O−	All the +
O−	None	Anti-A, anti-B e, anti-RH	O−	All

Table 1.
Blood characteristics and compatibility.

anonymous, and altruistic and the donor should not, directly or indirectly, receive any remuneration or benefit by his donation.

2.2 Blood donation incentive methods

Several strategies are used to attract and retain new blood donors; [7] divide these strategies into three categories: host, campaigns, and educational strategies.

"Reception" refers to the donors' care, removal of barriers that hampers donation, to the easy access to donation, training of vein puncture technicians, to minimize needle fear, and donor awareness to encourage family and friends, which have brought great results [7].

Campaigns are contingent strategies that occur for a particular purpose. Results are very expressive, as the campaign of the soccer clubs of the Minas Gerais, a Brazilian State, which disputed a championship of blood donation. Their campaign attracted 22 thousand donors in the first quarter of 2014. Solidary hazing, promoted by several universities, has also brought positive results. Some strategies seek to raise awareness among companies and institutions to promote campaigns and improve the donor recruitment system [7].

Educational strategies seek to raise awareness in new donors, based on information about the need for donation. As in South Africa, the creation of Club 25 seeks the motivation of young donors with education about donation [3]. According to [7], educational strategies are more effective, based on the encouragement of future donors and should participate in the youth's habit as a social responsibility.

Other strategies are based on psychology, sociology, and anthropology, in order to understand the values, beliefs, and attitudes of the donor, in the formation of awareness about the donation, since child. There are incentive strategies with health workers, with partnerships in various sectors to favor the cause [7].

In Europe, the population is well aware of blood donation. Therefore, many countries include benefits to donors, such as tax incentives, donation days, transport to donation centers, and meals, what is reflected in numbers: 37% of Europeans are blood donors [8].

A study by Johns Hopkins University, in the United States, suggests that reward strategies such as gift cards and gifts can contribute to the growth of donation numbers, without compromising the quality of the collected blood.

2.3 Mobile devices

Mobile devices, more precisely the smartphones, according to [16] are defined as a "mobile phone that offers advanced features similar to those of a notebook." In 2007, its arrival, along with the onset of Internet accessibility, was the beginning of a new era, driven by significant changes in interpersonal relationships, market, and in the use of services. Brazil has a continuous growth in the number of active smartphones, what made it the fourth country, in the world, in number of smartphones, with around 198 million handsets [17], and according to data from the National Telecommunications Agency, it accounts with almost 300 million active lines, about 1.4 lines per inhabitant.

The technological evolution has made smartphones become real portable computers and already occupies the first position as a personal tool. Smartphones are used in several areas, such as communication, entertainment, information, medicine, education, security, transportation, commerce, and services [18].

Data from Nielsen [19] show that smartphones are well distributed across classes, with 35% of users in class C, 50% in class B, and 12% in class A. Its main uses are for news applications, music, videos, social networks, communicators, and e-mail.

2.3.1 Native development

According to Silva [20], applications with native development are those that are intended for a specific platform. Platforms differ in the following aspects: operating system (OS), programming languages, and integrated development environment (IDE). Although native implementation takes longer, native applications are recommended for more demanding audiences, who are looking for agility and reliability.

2.3.2 Operating system mobile: Android

According to Sobell [21], the operating system (OS) is defined as a program that manages the capabilities of the computer. The OS manages the hardware resources and schedules tasks, as well as provides the user with a pleasant interface.

In Brazil, the mobile operating systems that have a considerable part of the market are Android (developed by Google), iOS (Apple), and Windows Phone (Microsoft). According to Conceição [22], by the abundance of devices with its OS, Android leads sales with 93.5% of the slice, followed by iOS, with 4.8%, and Windows Phone, with 1.6%.

Android is a Linux-based OS, with a direct-manipulation interface, designed primarily for devices with touch screens, but it also has interfaces for television, car, and watches. Google makes the Android OS code available under the open-source license [23], what reflects worldwide usage, and makes it a sales leader since 2013, and, according to Google, it has more than 2 billion active users, which consume more than 1.4 million applications.

Android has a wide guide for the development of the virtual environment of the application, the Material Design. According to Google, the guide is beyond a visual standardization of applications in Android, because it is also a varied library of common objects, tested to promote a better user experience [24]. The Material Design provides the guide to color palette, flow of screens, themes, fonts, object style, scaling, animations, and any other features related to the application design.

Google offers the free IDE for Android application development, Android Studio, the environment, as well as a code editor, which offers features to optimize the developer's implementation for Android applications such as Gradle—the compilation system flexible; emulator; unified environment for all versions; Instant Run monitoring; integration with GitHub, test tools, and frameworks; code verification tools; and compatibility with other programming languages and with Google development services [25].

2.4 Social networks

One of the main exponents for the use of smartphones is social networks. They are defined as the environment where personal relationships are developed and maintained by individuals with the same interests, which exchange experiences [26]. These environments are not necessarily virtual, i.e., most of them are still face-to-face. Therefore, what we call social networks are actually virtual social networks (VSN).

According to Marteleto [27], social networks are spaces that represent "[...] a set of autonomous participants, uniting ideas and resources around shared values and interests." The author complements that over the years, networks are taking a role as organizational tools. According to Tomaél [26], social network is a place where each individual has its function and its cultural identity, which encourages coexistence with other individuals and promotes a coherence of the network environment. It is a dynamic, nonlinear, flexible, self-organized, and decentralized environment, established by egalitarian cooperative relationships.

Given their characteristics, social networks are environments where the sharing of information and knowledge works consistently.

2.4.1 Elements of a VSN platform

The survey of the most popular VSNs, such as Facebook, Instagram, LinkedIn, YouTube, and Pinterest, intuitively shows several common elements that are related both to social dynamics and to the theme proposed for each VSN. Among these elements, it stands out:

- The profile—It is the space destined to identify a user for the virtual community, usually contains the relevant information of the user to the interested public, where the most common are name, photograph, date of birth, e-mail, and city, but also, according to the topic covered and the consent by the user, there may be more personal, professional, and educational information.

- Publication—This is the element where some subject will be presented on the subject of VSN. It is one of the main activities for user interaction. They can use various media or even the set of them in their display. Generally, they are produced by VSN users and have common characteristics, such as subject text, date and time of publication, media (image or video), and interaction buttons.

- Tags—They are keywords that produce a common connection between publications or a reference to the user. Typically, publications are included to identify a relevant subject or a notable person on the subject.

- Interaction buttons—These are the key points for dissemination and thermometer of relevance of the subject of the publication. The buttons are used mainly for evaluation, discursion, and propagation of publications in the VSN or in other virtual environments.

- Chat—It is the place where two or more users can exchange instant messages, simultaneously, which can be public or private to the participants.

- Groups—They are user group formations that have a common interest, even this one disagreeing with the main theme of a VSN.

- Notifications—It is the registration system about activities involving the user. They are usually invitations for new friends/followers, interaction with user publications, invitation to any event, direct messages, and updates in the chat, being usually informed to the user by the user application.

2.4.2 VSN in support to social causes

It is noteworthy requests to support social causes, campaigns (September yellow, October pink, November blue, vaccination), blood donation [37], financial support to charities, animal adoption campaign, and others, in VSN publications [38]. Publications have a remarkable power to raise awareness, as they are a platform for the use of appealing strategies, and awaken the emotional side of many users, especially cause activists.

According to Navarro [39], the use of VSN for the support of entities on community issues is growing, because the young public is largely connected to VSN and a significant proportion, 54% according to Lynx [40], believe that the responsibility to solve social problems belongs to everyone who owns the networks. Linked to this, some companies take advantage from the VSN, according to [38], founder of Curtida. Social—start-up that unites companies to community issues in RSV, entities that support social campaigns obtain immediate results, besides having the brand linked for a long time to the supported actions.

2.4.3 VSN in support to blood donation

Empathy on the subject makes many individuals, who are part of VSN, especially those with a broader subject and usually with a large user base, such as Facebook, Instagram, and WhatsApp, use their resources to promote the cause. It is common to see, in these networks, shared messages requesting donation, supporting publicity pages, and profiles for blood donation.

Not very evidenced, there are VSNs, or services for VSNs, which explore more directly this issue. Among them, “Salve Mais Um” [41] is a VSN that was born from the observation of a patient’s difficulty in finding blood donors and the reach of VSNs in social issues. “Salve Mais Um” interfaces people who are in need of donation and social networks, so donors are encouraged to donate by getting to know the patients.

2.5 Gamification

One of the methodologies that has been gaining notoriety is gamification. It is defined as the use of game dynamics to motivate actions that are often difficult to achieve, such as learning, engaging people, and problem solving [42]. As the basic principle of gamification is having fun, the method allows a remarkable experience, and its playful form turns, what was not attractive to the most, in a single moment. All this implies a greater participation of users and collaborators [43].

Gambling can be implemented in a variety of ways; according to Webster and Watson [44], games can be based on points, classifications, achievements/icons, levels, history, goals, feedback, rewards, progress, and/or challenges. These rewards make users of the platform, to which gamification has been implemented, re-interact again. Hamari et al.’s review [42], about the efficiency of gamification, shows that this methodology yields positive results both in behavior and in the psychology of individuals.

According to Almeida [43], the success of gamification is due to the experience that the user has beyond the acquisition of the product. Strategy turns gaming into a strong brand-customer relationship strong enough to keep them loyal.

2.5.1 Types of players

According to Zichermann [45], the more you get to know your players, the easier is to model an experience that will guide their behaviors along the path you want. Bartle [46] classifies players into four main types, such as socializers, explorers, achievers, and killers:

- Socializers are players interested in relating to others, characterized by having the goals of prestige only by interaction between players.

- Explorers are interested in unraveling the game environment, and they are characterized by the knowledge of the mechanics of the game, even if they distance themselves from interacting with other players or have not completed the game's challenges.

- Achievers are motivated by the challenges of the game, and they aim to complete all the activities of the game, especially those of greater difficulty and those of greater rewards.

- Killers are the most overrated players in games, as their goals are focused on being more skilled than other players, focused on winning the best scorecards and/or powers disputes. The killer tends to publicly display his glories, not momentarily satisfied.

2.5.2 Elements of gamification

Games, despite their distinctions in relation to the gaming experience, have in common the very remarkable characteristics. Among these elements, it stands outs [45]:

- Points: These are the main rewards for the player's performance, as it is a numerical reward multiplied by their difficulty in relation to other tasks. They are widely used in sports games but also in point-of-use mechanics and role-playing experiences (RPGs).

- Feedback: It is the statistical and quantitative disposition of the performance of the player; the efficiency in the goal achieved is passed on to the player for his incentive and consequently is converted into engagement.

- Levels: They show experience, indicate progress, effort, engagement, and wisdom of the player with the game. Levels give status to the player, referring to his disposition to the proposal of the game; in this way, many platforms prioritize the players of higher levels, making this become the main objective of the beginners.

- Achievements: They are the collectable rewards of the game, usually with some visual characteristic identity and achieved when certain specific activities are performed in the game. According to Zichermann [45], this type of reward is one of the best options for social incentive, because it is done as the goal of players who do not crave competition and cherish the social appeal of strategy.

- Rankings: The forms of competition where the points or other quantifiable element of the game are classified in an order that indicates success.

- Quiz: The question-and-answer game, as they are known, is used with an interesting method to support education. The technique of learning from error is widely used in this type of game. In addition, the quiz has the ability to incorporate other elements of play and become a memorable experience.

The gamification, in the context of health, has been beneficial in several areas, being one of them its use in the development of new treatment tools for both children and adults [47].

The gamification, in the BloodHero, is the core of the differential that it presents. Every action taken on the application results in points to the user, that is, from each donation of blood, each acquired point becomes the currency of exchange for benefits and products presented within the application.

3. The BloodHero application

At BloodHero, the concept of social networking and gamification comes together to produce a new tool linked to blood donation. The social network applied to BloodHero serves as a channel for publicizing the project, the history of patients who need donors, brands that link themselves to social causes, such as blood donation, and various other pieces of information related to this topic.

Gambling brings a new range of benefits to the user, among them the exchange of points for products. The adoption of rewarding the user with points for the actions taken throughout the application brings engagement and fidelity to the use of the app.

The application was proposed in order to guarantee a great commitment of the users. The bibliographic research, data observed in visits to blood centers, statistical analyzes of sites of some institutions, and mobile applications that use gamification, were the pieces of information taken into account for the production of the proposed app.

3.1 Data acquisition

The visits to blood centers aimed at understanding the profile of new and veteran donors and strategies for donor acquisition. Psychologists responsible for the donor acquisition sectors in "Hemominas," the public blood center of Minas Gerais, Ana Carolina Ferreira, and the "Hemoservice," the private blood center of Belo Horizonte, Cinara Sá de Araújo, were prepared to answer doubts about the motivation of the donors, about donation incentive programs, recurrent campaigns and costs involved, and the entire process from donation to transfusion.

In the analysis of institutions, it was researched sites of 20 institutions, which include target audiences, between 16 and 30 years old, in different segments: McDonalds, Chiquinho, Hemonorte, Hemominas, Hemoservice, Hering, Lacoste, Adidas, Nike, CVC, Blue, Gamestation, Amazing Pixel, Netflix, TelecineNow, Cinemark, UCI Cinemas, Rastapé, Pink Elephant, Samsung, and Apple. The model of interaction with users and information about the corporation were transcribed.

Additionally, the analysis of web and mobile applications was carried out with eight mobile applications, related to the theme "blood donation," "Hemoliga," "DoeSempre," Blood 24/7, blood donor, "Partiu Doar Sangue," "Eu curto doar," Hemogram, and Doe Blood Mobile, with the aim of quantifying systems and verifying methods and philosophies in common.

It also analyzed 12 web and mobile game applications and some other apps that use gamification: Asked [28]; FlappyBird [29]; Fruit Ninja [30]; HayDay [31]; Pokemon GO [32]; Angry Birds [33]; PasseiDireto; Skoob [34]; Icatu Insurances, "vivendoeAprendendo" [35]; Nike [48], NikePlus [48]; Google Maps [25]; and Cartola FC [36]. It analyzed the characteristics in common of games and how they are arranged to the players.

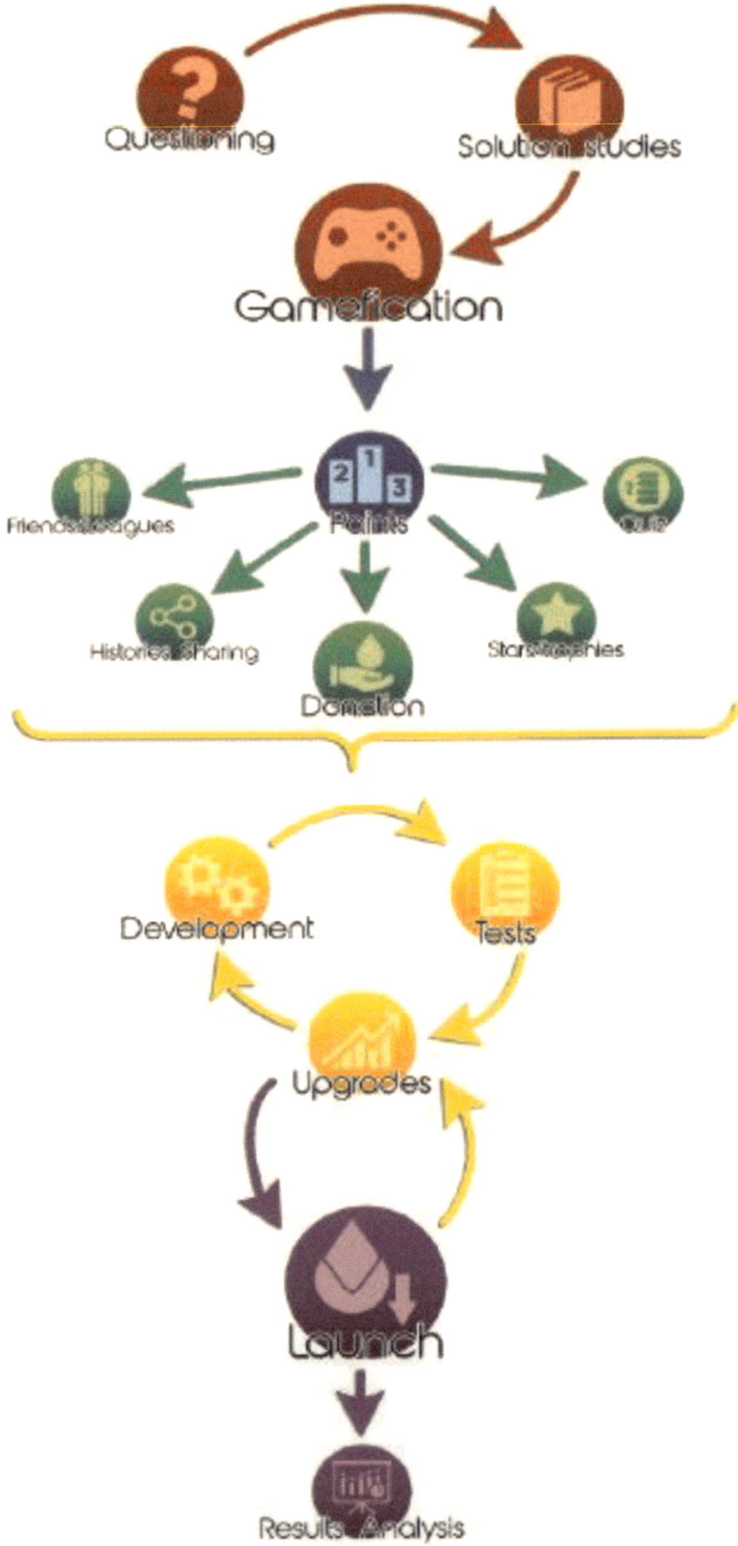

Figure 1.
Descriptive block diagram of the app.

Android OS was chosen as the target platform, for the ease of content for supporting development, as well as for the broader reach of users on the platform. Therefore, application dynamics and visual identity were designed to be developed in the Android Studio IDE, using Java and XML programming languages, following material design standards.

3.2 Application flowchart

Results from the data acquisition were relevant to the application design, although they did not escape from the expected bibliographic review; the information was taken into account in the construction of the modules and the interactive environment. Those results were applied to define the public, to model the social network, the information system for blood donation, and to the gamification system. For the design, it was based on the observation of the systems, the material design, and the tools made available for development.

For improving the application, an initial Portuguese version was designed, called version 1 (**Figure 1**), illustrated by the block diagram, which contains the

Figure 2.
BloodHero login screen.

fundamental activities of the complete idealization of the application. Once the whole project is finished, the intention is translating the app to other languages.

Based on the interviews in the blood centers, and the forms of public research, obtained from the bibliographical references, the answers showed that the ideal target audience (those who are interested both in social causes, VSNs, and games) are young people of the Z and Y generation, specifically people between the ages of 16 and 30, regardless of their ability to perform blood donation. To do this, the application should promote direct interaction between users.

The user's first contact with BloodHero will be through the Log in task, shown in **Figure 2**. From that screen, the registered user will include log in information and password to access the application, for those who are not registered yet, the screen will offer the option of registering himself (herself).

For registering and joining the application, the user will have to provide the following information: name and surname, genre, city, blood type, date of birth,

Figure 3.
Profile on BloodHero.

date of the last donation, picture/photo of the user, e-mail/telephone, nickname/login, and password. Once the registration is performed, the user is taken to the screen where he (she) can invite/request friends to have access to all the activities of BloodHero. The application will identify the user as a "Hero."

In the profile screen (**Figure 3**), the information with the authorization of the Hero, relevant to the VSN dynamics, will be made available to the users who access it. He (she) will see the photo, name and surname, whether he is logged in, city, blood type, points, level, past achievements, leagues, and friends. The profile will be the main screen, from where the user will be taken to other activities, update his (her) personal information, and access credentials. When viewing another user's profile, the option to request friendship will be available.

As the interaction between "Heroes" and publications (called "Stories," by the app) receive points, which will be explained in the following topics, it was necessary modeling a mechanism to fit the content, in a way that publications should only contain subjects related to blood donation. From this, the production of a story can be done as follows: A story requesting a donation—Here the user can insert text and media (image and video) for personal support, the information of the user will be made available to other users who have interest in helping (**Figure 4**).

This publishing form (**Figure 4**) has interaction buttons. The "Assist"—by checking this option, the user may have access to more information about the patient and the activity of connecting donors; the "Comment," this option leads to an interaction activity with the subject of the publication; and "Share," which causes the user to include the story in the list of his (her) friends' posts and/or to spread it in external VSNs. Additionally, when the user selects the "Assist" option, in a publication, the user is sent to the Assist activity, where the information of the patient that needs donation is made available to the Hero, as well as the button "connect donor," where he (she) can send the Hero to an activity where he (she) can indicate friends with a blood type compatible to the interested patient.

Publications will have a list of comments related to the stories, but each hero may comment only once in each story. Comments will have the "Like" button, which indicates approval of the message by other users.

The groups, named by the app as "Leagues" (**Figure 5**), will bring Heroes with similar interests together. The goal is to get users to interact using their common interests for blood donation. The Hero can join in many Leagues, as he (she) wants; however, it will be allowed to be created only one League per Hero. The user who creates the league will be the Leader of the group. In the league registration activity, the following information should be provided: league title, description, representative image/photo, and classification—closed (when the Hero participation in the league requires the leader's invitation), open (when any hero can participate the

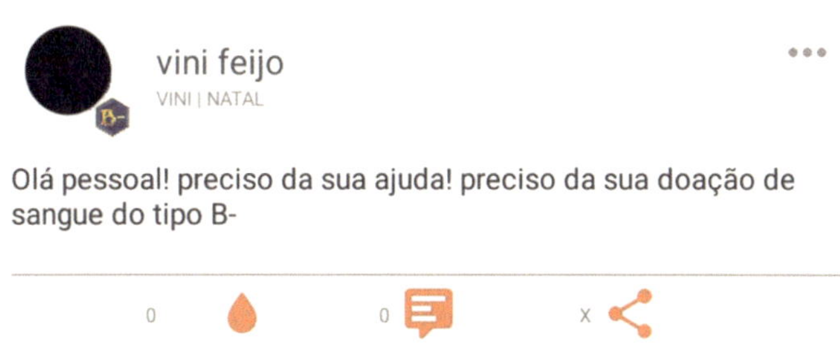

Figure 4.
A story for requesting blood donation in BloodHero.

Figure 5.
Representation of a "League" in BloodHero.

league), and open to requests (when league participation can be requested from the leader). Once created, the user is requested to send participation invitation to other Heroes, in a way that any registered user can be invited.

3.3 BloodHero in donation support

The application will also keep information about blood donation. The purpose is to facilitate the Hero's access to the cause. The application will show maps, all the information, and rules necessary for the practice of the blood donation.

In the map screen (**Figure 6**), markers will indicate all the blood centers in the city and possible campaigns for donation, present and future. Clicking on each of the markers, individual information of each blood center or event will be shown.

Figure 6.
Maps and information about blood centers and blood collection sites.

In the case of blood centers, the click will show the name, address, contact information, e-mail, and telephone number.

The information reached by the "I Want to Donate" activity, made available in the application, will guide the donor to the donation preparation. Information about how the donation process is carried out will be provided, how important it is, what care the donor should take before donating, what situations will impede the donation, the physiological process of blood replacement, blood types, the ABO system and the RH factor, and the Ministry of Health regulations related to the donation.

3.4 BloodHero gamification

The mechanics behind the game, at BloodHero, were based on the statistical analyses of mobile electronic games and sites of institutions using gamification. Mechanics were modeled for points, levels, feedback and achievements, and quiz and competitions, among Leagues.

Action	Rule	Points	Frequency
Registration	Record all the information required by the application	+400	Unique
To assist	Check the "Assist" option on a story	+5	By history
Comment	Comments on stories, since that they are well evaluated by other Heroes	+1	By "like"
Indicate a Donor	Indicate compatible donor to a publication (request)	+100	By compatible donor indicated
Quiz	Hit the right alternative	+200	For each correct alternative
	Participate in the game of questions	+10	By participation

Table 2.
Table of quotation and rules of points.

3.4.1 Rules for points

The rules for accumulating points are based on the Hero's interactions with the application, on promotions to attract new users, and attitudes in favor of blood donation. The rules for punctuation are divided into the tables: quotation of points and publication rules.

The basic quotation of the points follows the rules described in **Table 2**.

3.4.2 Rules and mechanics for quiz

The game of questions and answers aims at maintaining a frequency of access of the hero to the application, but also promoting learning about blood donation, and is named "Quiz."

BloodHero will provide at least one question per week. Questions will be about the process, importance, curiosities, and facts about blood donation. Each question will be objective and will have four alternatives, from where only one will be true. If the hero hits the question, he (she) will receive the correct points, and more information about the question will be provided in case of errors, although the points will not be counted. The correct alternative will be evidenced, and the information about the subject will be made available.

3.4.3 Calculation and title for levels

The levels will be calculated by the application and each one of them will have a title, shown in **Table 3**. The profile will be made available for viewing and will show the Hero's experience and involvement with blood donation. They will have a limit of 20, where the points needed to reach each the level are expressed by Eq. (1), adapted from the game strategy equation [49].

$$\text{Required Points} = \left(20 * (\text{level} - 1)^3\right) - \left(10 * (\text{level} - 1)^2\right) + \left(1 * (\text{level} - 1)\right) \tag{1}$$

where the coefficient "20" represents the maximum level reached by each player, the coefficient "10" describes half of the maximum possible level reached by each player, and the coefficient "1" characterizes the player's initial level. The term (level 1) was used to make the initial score equals to zero, when starting the game.

Level	Title	Points required
1	Newbie Hero/Newbie Heroin	0
2	Unknown Hero/Unknown Heroin	11
3	Started Hero/Started Heroin	122
4	Adept Hero/Adept Heroin	453
5	Benevolent Hero/Benevolent Heroin	1124
6	Courageous Hero/Courageous Heroin	2255
7	Brave Hero/Brave Heroin	3966
8	Fearless Hero/Fearless Heroin	6377
9	Strong Hero/Strong Heroin	9608
10	Super Strong Hero/Super Strong Heroin	13,779
11	Incredible Hero/Incredible Heroin	19,010
12	Super Incredible Hero/Super Incredible Heroin	25,421
13	Bright Hero/Bright Heroin	33,132
14	Scintillating Hero/Scintillating Heroin	42,263
15	Great Hero/Great Heroin	52,934
16	Excellent Hero/Excellent Heroin	65,265
17	Super Excellent Hero/Super Excellent Heroin	79,376
18	Majestic Hero/Majestic Heroin	95,387
19	Powerful Hero/Powerful Heroin	113,418
20	Super Powerful Hero/Super Powerful Heroin	133,589

Table 3.
Table of level titles.

3.4.4 Rules for league competition

Leagues will have points that will be calculated from the sum of points of each player, given by Eq. (2). The app uses the calculation to get the overall score of users belonging to the Leagues and uses that score to show the competition of the best among them.

$$\text{League Points} = \sum_{N=0}^{\text{Number of league users}} \text{Player points N} \tag{2}$$

where the overall score of the league is given by the sum of the scores of all the players who joined it. For example, if League A has 10 players, each one with 100 points, the league will have 1000 points.

The League ranking (**Figure** 7) will be available on BloodHero, which can be filtered by location (neighborhood, city, state, country, and continent) or by keywords in each League.

3.4.5 Rules for achievements

To satisfy the conquering players, BloodHero will feature several collectibles [49]. Achievements will be the rewards for activity in supporting the application dynamics. They will be gradually delivered, while the user increases his (her) interaction indicatives by depicting the individual effort. The goals for achieving them are predefined by the application (**Figure 8**).

Figure 7.
League ranking.

Figure 8.
BloodHero application achievement examples.

Once the required codes are reached, achievements are added to the user's list of collectibles. They have a representative image, a title, and a brief description.

4. Conclusions and expectations

Brazil has a deficit of 2.5 million donations a year, that is, people who are able to donate, because of the lack of information, lack of custom, fear, or other factors, do not donate. Adding the value and benefits of gamification to blood donation, the increasing amount of blood donations and, consequently, increase blood stocks is expected.

About 50% of the Brazilian population is able to donate blood; however, there is a lack of connection between people who can donate and the act of donating blood. Bringing new technologies to stimulate new donations and reduce this lack of donor connection is essential to modify the current Brazilian scenario.

This application will not totally change this reality, but it can increase donor/donor numbers, saving more lives and proving that the health area is always open to receive new technologies and developments, aimed at improving the quality of life of the population.

The expectations with this project are to increase blood donations, to engage the population with this social cause, and show that new technologies can be applied in the health area [47].

Another expectation is concluding the development to launch the BloodHero application, which is in the prototype stage.

Acknowledgements

The authors thank LabSIM and LabSIS labs, at the Federal University of Rio Grande do Norte, for their support in this research.

Author details

Daniela Domingos[1], Luis Felipe Lima[1], Thiago Messias[1], José Feijó[1], Anthony Diniz[2] and Heliana Soares[1*]

1 Federal University of Rio Grande do Norte, Natal, Brazil

2 Federal University of Sao Paulo, Sao Paulo, Brazil

*Address all correspondence to: helianabs@gmail.com

References

[1] Ministério da Saúde, Brasil. Redefine o Regulamento Técnico de Procedimentos Hemoterápicos. Portaria 158 de 04 de Fevereiro de; 2016

[2] Kauffman P, Helito AS. Saúde: Entendendo as Doenças, a Enciclopédia Médica da Família. São Paulo: Nobel; 2007

[3] WHO. Global Consultation on Universal Access to Safe Blood Transfusion [Online]. 2007. Available from: http://www.who.int/bloodsafety/sbt_global_consultation/en [Accessed: December 12, 2017]

[4] Oswalt RM. A review of blood donor motivation and recruitment. Transfusion. 1977;**17**:123-135

[5] Rodrigues RN et al. Aspectos sócio demográficos e culturais da doação de sangue em Belo Horizonte. In: Seminário Sobre a Economia Mineira, Diamantina. Vol. 2. 2005. pp. 513-531

[6] Zou S, Musavi F, Notari EP, Fang CT. Changing age distribution of the blood donor population in the United States. Transfusion. 2008;**48**:251-257

[7] Rodrigues RSM, Reibnitz KS. Estratégias de captação de doadores de sangue: Uma revisão integrativa da literatura. Texto and Contexto Enfermagem. 2011;**20**:384-391

[8] Parlamento Europeu. 2nd Report on Voluntary and Unpaid Donation of Blood and Blood Components [Online]. 2011. Available from: http://ec.europa.eu/health/sites/health/files/blood_tissues_organs/docs/blood_reportdonation_en.pdf [Accessed: December 8, 2015]

[9] Logica Digital. 2018. Available from: https://www.logicadigital.com.br/ [Accessed: November 2, 2018]

[10] Araguaia M. Sangue; Brasil Escola [Online]. 2017. Available from: http://brasilescola.uol.com.br/biologia/sangue.htm [Accessed: December 10, 2017]

[11] Moraes, Paula Louredo. Sistema ABO e fator Rh; Brasil Escola [Online]. 2017. Available from: http://brasilescola.uol.com.br/biologia/genetica-problema.htm [Accessed: December 11, 2017]

[12] Araguaia M. Doação de Sangue; Brasil Escola [Online]. 2017. Available from: http://brasilescola.uol.com.br/saude/doacao-sangue.htm [Accessed: August 17, 2017]

[13] Fundação Hemominas. Hemominas Registra 22 mil Torcedores em Campanha para Doação de Sangue [Online]. 2014. Available from: http://www.hemominas.mg.gov.br/banco-de-noticias/27-parcerias/181-hemominas-registra-22-mil-torcedores-em-campanha [Accessed: May 31, 2017]

[14] Tison GH, Liu C, Ren F, Nelson K, Shan H. Influences of general and traditional Chinese beliefs on the decision to donate blood among employer organized and volunteer donors in Beijing, China. Transfusion. 2007;**47**(10):1871-1879

[15] Marcis M. Economic Rewards to Motivate Blood Donations. Jhons Hopkins University; 2013

[16] Torres C. A Bíblia do Marketing Digital. São Paulo: Novatec editora Ltda; 2009

[17] Capelas B. Até o fim de 201, Brasil terá um Smartphone por Habitante, diz FGV. Estadão [Online]. 2017. Available from: http://link.estadao.com.br/noticias/gadget,ate-o-fim-de-2017-brasil-tera-um-smartphone-por-habitante-diz-pesquisa-da-fgv [Accessed: July 26, 2017]

[18] Coutinho GL. A Era dos Smartphones: Um Estudo exploratório

Sobre o uso do Smartphones no Brasil; UnB; 2014

[19] Nielsen Holding NV (NLSN). 68 Milhões Usam a Internet pelo Smartphone. Mobile Report [Online]. 2015. Available from: http://www.nielsen.com/br/pt/press-room/2015/68-milhoes-usam-a-internet-pelo-smartphone-no-Brasil.html [Accessed: July 21, 2017]

[20] Silva MM, Santos MTPO. Paradigmas de Desenvolvimento de Aplicativos para Aparelhos Celulares. Vol. 3. São Carlos: TIS; 2014. pp. 162-170

[21] Sobell MG. Practical Guide to Ubuntu Linux; Cananda. 4th ed. 2014

[22] Conceição U. Kantar: No Brasil, Android Lidera com 93.5% das Vendas de Smartphones. Meu Smartphone [Online]. 2017. Available from: https://www.meu-smartphone.com/kantar-no-brasil-android-lidera-com-935-das-vendas-de-smartphones/ [Accessed: July 20, 2017]

[23] Developers Android Studio [Online]. 2017. Available from: https://developer.android.com/studio [Accessed: July 20, 2017]

[24] Developers Android Studio. Material Design [Online]. 2017. Available from: https://developer.android.com/design/material/index.html [Accessed: July 20, 2017]

[25] Rasmussen L, Rasmussen JE. Google Maps [Online]. 2017. Available from: https://www.google.com.br/maps [Accessed: October 27, 2017]

[26] Tomaél MI, Alcará AR, Chiara IG. Das redes sociais à inovação. Ciencia da Informacao. 2005;**34**(2):93-104

[27] Marteleto RM. Análise de redes sociais: aplicação nos estudos de transferência da informação. Ciência da Informação. 2001;**30**(1):71-81

[28] Etermax Mobile Games. Perguntados [Online]. 2013. Available from: http://www.triviacrack.com/ [Accessed: October 21, 2017]

[29] Dotgears ND. FlappyBird [Online]. 2013. Available from: http://flappybird.io/ [Accessed: October 27, 2017]

[30] Deo S. Halfbrick Studios Pty Ltda. Fruit Ninja [Online]. 2017. Available from: https://fruitninja.com/ [Accessed: October 27, 2017]

[31] Paananen I. Supercell Games. Hay Day [Online]. 2016. Available from: http://haydaygame.com/ [Accessed: October 27, 2017]

[32] Hanke J. Niantic, Inc. Pokemon Go [Online]. 2017. Available from: https://www.pokemongo.com/pt-pt/ [Accessed: October 27, 2017]

[33] Rovio LK. Angry Birds [Online]. 2017. Available from: [Accessed: October 27, 2017]

[34] Moreira L. Skoob [Online]. 2010. Available from: https://www.skoob.com.br/ [Accessed: October 27, 2017].

[35] ICATU. Vivendoe Aprendendo [Online]. 2013. Available from: http://vivendoeaprendendo.com.br/game [Accessed: October 27, 2017]

[36] Globo Comunicações e Participações S/A. Cartola FC [Online]. 2010. Available from: http://globoesporte.globo.com/cartola-fc/ [Accessed: October 27, 2017]

[37] Ministério da Saúde, Brasil. Pagina Oficial No Facebook @minsaude. 2017. Available from: https://www.facebook.com/minsaude/ [Accessed: December 9, 2017]

[38] Velloso N. Como Divulgar a Sua Empresa? Curtida. Social [Online]. 2017. Available from: http://blog.curtida.social/

divulgar-empresa/ [Accessed: July 23, 2017]

[39] Navarro V. Causas Sociais Sob a Ótica da Empresa e do Público. Meio & Mensagem [Online]. 2016. Available from: http://www.meioemensagem.com.br/home/comunicacao/2016/11/29/causas-sociais-sob-a-otica-das-empresas-e-do-publico.html [Accessed: July 23, 2017]

[40] Flor W. Causa Social Contribui Para uma Marca Vender Mais? Causas e Marcas. Estadão [Online]. 2017. Available from: http://economia.estadao.com.br/blogs/causas-e-marcas/causa-social-contribui-para-uma-marca-vender-mais [Accessed: July 23, 2017]

[41] Ferreira G. Salve Mais Um. 2010. Available from: http://salvemaisum.com.br/web/iniciativa [Accessed: August 22, 2017]

[42] Hamari J, Koivisto J, Sarsa H. Does Gamification Work? — A Literature Review of Empirical Studies on Gamification. In: International Conference on System Science. Vol. 47. 2014

[43] Almeida D. Empresas Que Usam A Gamificação Para Engajar Clientes. MindMiners [Online]. 2017. Available from: https://mindminers.com/inovacao/veja-9-empresas-que-usam-gamificacao-para-engajar-clientes [Accessed: August 2, 2017]

[44] Webster J, Watson RT. Analyzing the past to prepare for the future: Writing a literature review. MIS Quarterly. 2002;**26**:xiii-xxiii

[45] Zichermann G, Cunningham C. Gamification by Design: Implementing Game Mechanics in Web and Mobile Apps. Canadá: O'Reilly Media Inc.; 2011

[46] Bartle RA. Heart, Clubs, Diamonds, Spades: Players who suit MUDs. Colchester, Essex, Reino Unido: MUSE Ltd; 1996

[47] Kim J. MHealth Apps can Drive Patient Engagement for Physicians [Online]. 2013. Available from: http://searchhealthit.techtarget.com/opinion/MHealthapps-can-drive-patient-engagement-for-physicians [Accessed: May 9, 2016]

[48] Nike. Nike+ [Online]. 2017. Available from: https://www.nike.com.br/corrida/app-nike-plus [Accessed: October 27, 2017]

[49] Kleper LC. A Enciclopédia Tibiana Brasileira. 2017. Available from: https://www.tibiawiki.com.br/ [Accessed: October 10, 2017]